2009

INTERNATIONAL BUSINESS TRANSACTIONS
IN A NUTSHELL

Eighth Edition

By

RALPH H. FOLSOM

Professor of Law
University of San Diego

MICHAEL WALLACE GORDON

John H. & Mary Lou Dasburg Professor of Law
University of Florida

JOHN A. SPANOGLE

William Wallace Kirkpatrick Professor of Law
The George Washington University

A Thomson Reuters business

Mat #40757013

COPYRIGHT © 1981, 1984, 1988, 1992, 1996 WEST PUBLISHING CO.
COPYRIGHT © West, a Thomson business, 2000, 2004
© 2009 Thomson/Reuters

    610 Opperman Drive
    St. Paul, MN 55123
    1–800–313–9378

Printed in the United States of America

ISBN: 978-0-314-19521-0

TEXT IS PRINTED ON 10% POST
CONSUMER RECYCLED PAPER

We dedicate this book:

> to Paris and the University of San Diego Institute of International and Comparative Law

> to the Escuela Libre de Derecho (Mexico) and The University of Florida exchange program

> And to all those who work to promote the harmonization of international commercial law

*

PREFACE TO THE EIGHTH EDITION

This eighth edition of **International Business Transactions in a Nutshell** is the sixth written by the three co-authors. The first two editions were authored by the late Professor Donald T. Wilson and published in 1981 and 1984. Because of the size of our fourth edition, further expansion to cover developments between 1991 and 1995 could be accomplished only if we split the Nutshell in two. The most recent editions represent such a division, and the *International Business Transactions* Nutshell (8th edition) is published concurrently with the *International Trade and Economic Relations* Nutshell (4th edition).

This edition of the *International Business Transactions* Nutshell focuses on documentary international sales and use of letters of credit, E-commerce, technology transfers, foreign investment transactions, expropriations and remedies, EU business competition law, extraterritorial antitrust, international business litigation and international commercial arbitration. The *International Trade and Economic Relations* Nutshell covers government imposed restrictions on imports and exports, the GATT/WTO, free trade agreements and customs unions, and economic integration with an emphasis on the European Union and the North American Free Trade Agreement.

The two Nutshells are intended to provide our readers with a broad introduction to the people and institutions who practice international business law, and the government and multilateral organizations which both encourage and restrict trade and economic relations. The divisions between them reflect our value judgments as to what ought to be included in introductory volumes on a very broad subject which is constantly affected by change. These judgments will be familiar to those who have read or adopted our *International Business Transactions: A Problem–Oriented Coursebook*, originally published in 1986, with many editions since then. For detailed, footnoted professional coverage of the area, please see our *Hornbook on International Business Transactions* or its concise student version, *Principles of International Business Transactions*.

We have been aided by colleagues at our own law schools and others both in this country and abroad, by student research assistants and by persons in the practice. We welcome continued suggestions for the next edition.

RALPH H. FOLSOM
rfolsom@sandiego.edu
MICHAEL W. GORDON
gordon@law.ufl.edu
JOHN A. SPANOGLE
aspanogle@law.gwu.edu

October, 2008

OUTLINE

OUTLINE

Page

*

TABLE OF CASES

References are to Pages

D

F

H

J

K

M

TABLE OF CASES

*

INTERNATIONAL BUSINESS TRANSACTIONS
IN A NUTSHELL

Eighth Edition

*

INTRODUCTION

FROM BROCKTON AND BUR-
BANK TO BANGKOK AND
BEIJING

Representing a Boston client who sells goods to a
buyer in Burbank, California, creates relatively few
issues which are not similarly present if the buyer
is in Brockton (i.e., the same state as the seller,
Massachusetts). Both sales are likely to constitute
a standard, domestic documentary sale transaction.
Unlike a face-to-face transaction, the seller will not
meet the buyer and hand over the goods simultaneously as the buyer hands over the money. Payment is likely to be required upon presentation of
the *documents* by the seller to the buyer, not upon
an inspection of the goods by the buyer after the
goods have arrived. A letter of credit may be used
to reduce risks and avoid a situation where either
the seller or the buyer has possession of both the
goods and the money at the same time. Use of a
letter of credit adds to the transaction an issuing
bank, and perhaps a second confirming bank. The
Boston seller may be willing to accept the letter of
credit issued by a Brockton or Burbank bank, without confirmation by a bank in, or closer to, Boston.
The sale to Brockton will be in dollars, just as will

be the sale to Burbank. The parties will correspond in English.

Perhaps the most significant features unique to the Burbank purchase involve which state's law will apply and which state's courts will be the appropriate forum if there is a conflict. But the rules of commercial law of Massachusetts and California are nearly identical. Both states have adopted the Uniform Commercial Code. The California lawyer representing the Burbank buyer passed a different bar exam than the Boston lawyer. But nearly all of the substantive law on each exam was the same, rooted in the common law tradition and expressed in state legal systems containing many common features. The two lawyers studied the common law in their respective law schools, and they may even have gone to the same law school. Although a continent apart, the Massachusetts and California lawyers for the buyer and seller could exchange practices, and quickly function with little loss of efficiency and skill.

But what if the sale from Boston is not to either a buyer in Brockton or in Burbank, but to a buyer in Bangkok? This international transaction will involve two different business and social cultures, and two different legal systems. The economy of Thailand is less developed than the economy of the United States and may present some problems unique to developing nations, such as a less efficient infrastructure at the port of entry for unloading the goods. Risk of damage thus is greater, and insurance rates will be higher. Customs officials might demand "unofficial" payments to admit the goods. As in the case of the sale to Brockton or Burbank, the sale to Bangkok probably will involve the use of a documentary sale and almost certainly involve a letter of credit. But the usage of documentary sales and letters of credit may differ in each nation. Commonly used commercial terms, such as c.i.f. or f.o.b., may have different meanings and place different risks on the parties in each nation. The parties may help resolve this by specifying the use of the Paris based International Chamber of Commerce Incoterms, which provide interpretations of commercial terms usually accepted by courts. Wanting assurance that the goods received are the same as the goods ordered, the Bangkok buyer may wish to have a third party inspect the shipment and certify that the goods shipped are the same as the goods ordered. Such certification would be required before the buyer would be obligated to pay the seller.

The letter of credit in an international transaction is also more complex. If the Bangkok buyer uses a Bangkok bank as the issuing bank of the letter of credit, the Boston seller is almost certain to require that a United States bank, very likely with an office in Boston, confirm the letter of credit. The Boston seller does not wish to have to go to Bangkok to challenge the Bangkok bank if a conflict over the letter of credit arises. The Boston seller will prefer to go to a Boston bank to present the documents for payment, thus avoiding having to send the documents to an agent in Bangkok for presentation to a Bangkok bank. Additionally, letters of credit may be irrevocable or revocable. The Boston seller will insist on the irrevocable form, but practice in Bangkok might be to issue revocable letters. As in the case of rules applicable to the documentary sale, the parties may choose international rules generally accepted to govern letters of credit. They will almost certainly be the Uniform Customs and Practice for Documentary Credits (UCP). They are also a product of the International Chamber of Commerce, as are the Incoterms noted above.

Not only will the contract for sale differ in our international sale, the bill of lading contract for shipping the goods to Bangkok will differ. The greater distance to Bangkok will involve greater risks of loss during transportation. But that is true of the greater distance to Burbank than to Brockton in the domestic sale. If ocean transportation is used, shipments to either Burbank or Bangkok will likely transit the Panama Canal. However, the Boston seller can avoid any international issues in the sale to Burbank, such as transiting the canal, by shipping the goods across the continental United States to California. Selling to Bangkok does not offer that option. The shipment to Bangkok might be on a vessel with stops in several foreign nations before reaching Bangkok, creating additional and different risks. Furthermore, the laws and rules applicable to the shipment may differ. The United States applies its Carriage of Goods at Sea Act, based on the Hague Rules, while some other nations base their shipping laws on the Hamburg Rules or the Hague-Visby Rules.

A major difference in many international transactions involves the choice of *currency*. The Boston seller probably will insist on being paid in U.S. dollars, not Thai bahts. If Thai bahts are received by the Boston seller, it can not pay suppliers with them, nor give them to workers as salary. When the seller takes Thai bahts to a Boston bank, the bank may reject them because the bank is not familiar with them, and believed it will not be able to exchange bahts for U.S. dollars. If the bank is willing to accept the bahts, it may do so only with a substantial discount, causing a projected profit from the sale to become a loss. Even if the Thai currency is freely exchangeable, the rates of conversion from bahts to dollars might change between the time of the signing of the contract and the time of the exchange, causing either an unexpected gain or an unwelcome loss. Even if the Bangkok buyer agreed to pay in dollars, the Thai government might impose exchange restrictions prohibiting the removal of hard currency from Thailand.

Not only the currency but the *language* of the contract will have to be decided. Even if the contract terms are expressed in English, as preferred by the Boston seller, the Bangkok buyer may believe the contract terms say something quite different than the view of the Boston seller. While differences in the meaning of terms may also occur in the domestic transactions, the likelihood and magnitude of differences in the international transaction are likely to be more extensive.

If the sale from Boston is to Beijing rather than to Bangkok, the Boston seller will address most of the same issues as noted above with the sale to Bangkok, plus issues of dealing with a economy which possesses some *nonmarket* economy characteristics. There are fewer nonmarket economies today than a decade ago, and many nonmarket economies are in a stage of transition to market economies, including China. Thus there may be a question regarding the character or nature of the buyer's economy. It may be a nonmarket economy and also a developing nation, such as Cuba. It may be an advanced developing country (ADC) or newly industrializing country (NIC), but still be a nonmarket economy, such as China (if it is fair to currently characterize the PRC as beyond a mere developing nation). It may be a nonmarket economy trying to become a market economy, but having difficulty overcoming decades of central planning and government involvement in the production and distribution of goods. This is true of some of the nations in Eastern Europe and the former USSR. Or it may be a nonmarket economy which prefers to remain a nonmarket economy, but which finds it necessary to do business with market economies and opens the door to market economy characteristics only enough to achieve specific goals. That is the policy of Cuba.

Where the buyer is located in a nonmarket economy, a major difference is that the purchaser may be the government rather than a private entity. Furthermore, the purchaser may not be the end user of the goods, but a centralized government agency, frequently called a foreign or state trading organization (FTO or STO). Most nonmarket economies have very strictly controlled currencies. The currencies tend to be nonexchangeable in international currency markets, and are usually artificial in value. They are sometimes so strictly controlled that they may not be removed from the country.

Unable to obtain scarce dollars from the buyer's nation, and unwilling to accept that nation's currency, the Boston seller may be asked to find local goods to accept in exchange. This is *countertrade,* a modern variation of barter. The Boston seller receives goods instead of currency, and may have to search the other country for goods of value. The Boston seller might find goods it may use in its own operations. But if it is unable to use those goods in its own operations, it will have to market those goods. This additional and often complex aspect of what was to be a simple sale to the foreign country involves two sales, and probably three contracts. The first sale is from the Boston seller to the foreign buyer. The second sale is the purchase of goods by the Boston party from that foreign nation. Two sales probably means the use of two contracts and two letters of credit. Because the two contracts are linked, there will have to be a third contract establishing the interrelationships between the parties. Often called the protocol contract, it may include penalties against the Boston seller if it does not find foreign goods to purchase within a certain time period.

Countertrade has many faces. It includes the exchange outlined above, usually called "counter-purchase". More complex forms may appear if the Boston seller wants to establish a factory in the foreign nation, and in lieu of profits agrees to accept a percentage of the foreign production—a form called "compensation" or "buy-back". In whatever face it appears, it is usually involuntary on the part of the U.S. seller or investor. Countertrade adds costs to the transaction, which will be passed on to the foreign buyer. Often countertrade occurs because the foreign nation's products are not of sufficient quality to be competitive in international trade. But sometimes traditional trade patterns tend to lock-out such products even when they are very good quality, and countertrade may thus be a way of forcing open a market. Some countertrade is voluntary, especially the above noted compensation or buy-back forms. Whatever form countertrade assumes, it has been around for much longer than currency, and it will continue to play some role in international trade.

We have noted only a few differences in a commercial sale of goods where the seller and buyer are in different countries. There are many other new issues to confront. The differences noted above tend to be attributable to different legal and economic systems in the two nations. There also may be differences in the cultures of the two nations which affect the transaction. Misunderstandings of cultural norms may create minor embarrassments, or constitute serious improprieties that terminate negotiations. The result is lost business. If the Boston seller or its counsel has gone to Bangkok or to Beijing to negotiate or sign the contract, what conduct is expected? Do people greet each other by shaking hands, or is touching inappropriate? Is it proper to discuss business over breakfast? Should spouses be invited to a business dinner? Should one sit with legs crossed? Are nominal gifts appropriate or distasteful? What transpires during the negotiations may involve one of the nation's laws which attempt to govern moral conduct, such as the U.S. Foreign Corrupt Practices Act (FCPA), which prohibits many payments or gifts intended to influence foreign officials' decisions.

Our Boston seller may begin to sell sufficient products to Bangkok or Beijing that it decides to establish some form of agency or distributorship abroad. It may have experience with the use of agents or distributors in its sales to Brockton or Burbank. The buyer might have used an *agent* to represent it. The agent would not possess title to the goods; title would pass directly from the Boston seller to the buyer. The agent would be said to have had the goods "on consignment". Or the Boston seller might have used a *distributor*. The distributor takes title to the goods, and passes that title upon the sale to the buyer. The same decision between an agent or a distributor will have to be made when selling abroad, but the Boston seller may learn that there are quite different laws governing such sales. The foreign nation may have a special distributorship law, which reduces some of the seller's choices available in U.S. law. The foreign law is likely to favor the local distributor, especially regarding matters of the right to, and rights upon, termination. Even where there is no special distributorship law, the applicable laws may be different. Those laws may be included among the many provisions of the local civil or commercial code, if the foreign nation has a civil law legal system. Establishing a foreign distributorship also may raise issues of questionable trade restraints under the foreign law, when the distributor becomes the exclusive agent, or is limited to certain territory, or must sell at seller established prices.

Depending upon the form chosen for the sale of goods abroad, the Boston seller may become enough of an employer in the foreign country to be subject to the foreign nation's labor law. Labor law in many foreign nations differs dramatically from labor law in the United States. Nations are often protective of their workforce, and the Boston seller may encounter far stricter rules regulating the employment relationship, especially termination. A "once hired, can't be fired" rule is perhaps the most troublesome for employers. In addition to the foreign labor law, the Boston seller will have to deal with the movement of business persons across borders. Even a brief *business* visit to Bangkok or Beijing may require entry papers far more complex than a tourist visa. Much business is undertaken using tourist visas, but such use may create a risk if a contract is breached. As business persons cross borders for longer stays, visa requirements are likely to increase. But it is not only the immigration rules of Bangkok and Beijing which may appear to constitute an impenetrable maze to the Boston seller, it is also the U.S. immigration rules which create obstacles. The Boston seller may wish to bring Bangkok or Beijing business associates to Boston for training. That may require a business visa, or perhaps an education visa.

As our Boston client's trade evolves and increases, from an isolated sale, to occasional sales, and perhaps to the creation of a distributorship agreement, thought may be given to the manufacture of the products abroad. Manufacture abroad may follow the major step of creating a direct foreign investment, or perhaps by licensing a foreign producer in Bangkok or Beijing to manufacture the goods. Licensing production to a company in Brockton or Burbank would involve only the negotiation of the licensing agreement by the Boston licensor and the Brockton or Burbank licensee. But if the Boston seller licenses the production to a developing or nonmarket economy nation, the transfer of technology agreement may be subject to careful scrutiny by the host government. The Boston licensor will be most concerned with protecting its intellectual property, while the foreign government may be more concerned with regulation of the transfer of technology.

Even if the foreign licensee is a privately owned enterprise, the government may mandate that all

technology agreements be registered, and sometimes subjected to review for approval, to ensure
that they do not include provisions considered detri-
mental to the economic development of the nation.
Those concerns reach such issues as duration of the
agreement, royalty amount, grant-back requirements, territory restrictions on sales, rejection of
technology "adequately" available locally, and
choice of law and forum. Not all developing nations and nonmarket economies have such requirements, which developed nations consider trade restrictive and which are generally inconsistent with
contemporary rules on intellectual property, which
focus more on protection of intellectual property
than restrictions on its transfer.

The Boston licensor of the technology is very
concerned about the existence and adequacy of laws
protecting intellectual property in the foreign country. The Boston licensor has invested considerable
time and money in developing its products, and
wants the fullest protection offered by patent,
trademark, copyright and trade secret laws. If the
products are licensed to be manufactured by a
Brockton or Burbank licensee, the Boston company
is protected by a scheme of mostly federal law
protecting intellectual property. But if the license
is to Bangkok or Beijing, the licensor may confront
very different views about rights to intellectual
property. Such rights may not be recognized at all,
because they are considered not subject to private
ownership, but to constitute part of the national
patrimony or the property of mankind. Even if

intellectual property is acknowledged to be private property, if the foreign nation's gross national product depends to a sufficient degree on counterfeit production and exports that loss of such production may cause economic dislocations, it may refuse to adopt or actively enforce laws protecting intellectual property rights.

The above business transactions illustrate some of the differences in selling to or licensing the production of goods in foreign nations. These differences occur everyday in international business. The differences may create additional transaction costs. One transaction cost all business persons hope to avoid is the cost of resolving disputes. That is accomplished by avoiding them. But we are yet to find a way to assure that all transactions will occur without conflict, and thus must be prepared to assume some costs of dispute resolution, and to understand the nature of dispute settlement in international transactions.

If a conflict arises between the seller and the buyer, the choice of law and choice of forum issues are very possibly extremely important to each party. It should come as no surprise to the Boston lawyer and client that the contract law of Thailand differs from that of Massachusetts much more than did the contract law of California. Furthermore, the legal system of Thailand, including procedural law, may have very different characteristics than the legal system of Massachusetts. But as more nations become parties to the 1980 Convention on Contracts for the International Sale of Goods (CISG), the applicable contract rules will be the same. While they may be the same, a Bangkok court will use a copy of the law in Thai, while a Boston court will use one in English. Different meanings to terms may result from different translations. Furthermore, the method of judicial interpretation in Bangkok will differ from that in Boston, far more so than judicial interpretation in Brockton or Burbank. The Bangkok court will interpret the statutory provision, with some assistance from scholarly treatises, but with less attention to Thai cases then the Boston lawyer may expect. The Boston court is likely to focus on past Massachusetts decisions, and, if none are found, decisions of other states, which interpret the particular provision. Harmonization of law does not mean harmonization of the legal systems and therefore of methods of judicial interpretation.

Because of the very different attitudes towards dispute resolution, the parties may choose to include a provision in their contract for mandatory arbitration. Considered essential when dealing with some nations because of inefficient or corrupt judicial systems, and the failure to enforce foreign judgments, arbitration is often chosen when judicial systems function honestly. Court back-logs, cost of litigation and more relaxed rules of evidence are often the reasons arbitration is used in a domestic setting, for example for disputes arising in the sale from Boston to Brockton, or Boston to Burbank. Those same reasons exist in the international setting, plus a sense of fairness provided by third party arbitration.

International litigation and arbitration add many new dimensions to the same issues when part of domestic litigation. Choosing Burbank (i.e., California) law rather than Boston (i.e., Massachusetts) law is a much less significant decision than choosing Bangkok (i.e., Thailand) law or Beijing (i.e., PRC) law rather than Boston law. The same is true in choosing a forum. Initiating a suit in a foreign country is likely to introduce us to different rules of jurisdiction, including not recognizing the distinction between subject matter and personal jurisdiction.. Service of process in many foreign nations is a more formal process than in the United States, and is unlikely to be linked to personal jurisdiction so as to allow jurisdiction based on service. The extensive process of discovery in the United States is essentially nonexistent abroad, and has few admirers sitting on the bench in foreign courts and asked to honor a U.S. court order for discovery in their nations. If the Boston seller is able to obtain jurisdiction over the Bangkok or Beijing buyer in a Boston court, and obtains a judgment, it may have little value unless the courts in Bangkok or Beijing will recognize and enforce the Boston judgment. Recognition and enforcement rules vary throughout the world. In the United States recognition and enforcement varies state-to-state, often confusing to foreign lawyers. But that variance from state-to-state in the United States is with respect to recognition of a judgment granted in a foreign *nation* rather than in a sister foreign state. Full faith and credit mandates recognition of sister state judgments. Thus the Boston judgment creditor will have an easier time enforcing the judgment in a Brockton or Burbank court, than in a Bangkok or Beijing court.

The participation of foreign officials in the transaction adds new dimensions beyond the possible questionable payments which may violate the Foreign Corrupt Practices Act. If the buyer is the foreign government, or an instrumentality of the government, special problems may arise if litigation over the contract ensues. What if the sale is canceled by the Bangkok or Beijing government agency, and the Boston seller sues, only to be confronted with a defense of sovereign immunity? The foreign government would be saying that it is the sovereign and is immune to suit anywhere. But that immunity is increasingly limited to *government* actions, rather than to *commercial* actions conducted by a government. Drawing the line between what is a government act and what is a commercial act is not easy. The United States, after decades of following the *absolute* theory of foreign state immunity, enacted the Foreign Sovereign Immunities Act (FSIA) in 1976, which adopts the *restrictive* theory—that foreign states are not immune when the transaction is commercial. That may help our Boston seller if the sales are commercial sales to foreign states, or to their agencies or instrumentalities.

A second defense our Boston seller may encounter when suing a foreign state is that the foreign act was an "act of state". The courts of one nation tend not to want to sit in judgment of acts of a foreign government which took place in the territory of that foreign government. This theory developed in case law, and unlike the above noted codification of state immunity theory in the FSIA, the act of state doctrine remains based in U.S. case law. That law has yet to clearly conclude whether or not a commercial action exception exists to the act of state doctrine. The doctrine as a whole has been partly restricted by the Supreme Court. Whatever the outcome of the commercial exception is, our Boston seller might be wise to insist on arbitration, or an express waiver of these defenses, in any contract to sell to the government in Bangkok or Beijing.

Even if the sale is to a private buyer, the government may interfere with the sale for such reasons as the scarcity of reserves which limits access to foreign currency, or the prohibition or limitation of entry of the products of the Boston seller into the nation. Would these reasons constitute *force majeure* and allow the buyer to avoid performance because of a frustration of performance? What if the buyer is an agency of the government and the purchase is canceled by order of the executive? Is the agency sufficiently separate from the executive to be entitled to present a *force majeure* defense?

Our Boston client has entered the world of international business transactions, and has learned quickly of the complexities of dealing with Bangkok or Beijing rather than Brockton or Burbank. It might decide not to deal with developing nations or nonmarket economies, but to sell to, or license or establish a direct foreign investment in, only those nations which are more developed and which are market economies. For example it may sell to buyers in Brussels. In selling goods to a Brussels buyer it will not confront import licenses; it will receive a strong, convertible currency; and it will not be asked to accept countertrade. But it may have to deal in another language and, depending on the nature of the product, it may confront European Union tariff and nontariff barriers absent in domestic U.S. sales. If the Boston company licenses a Brussels firm to make its products, it will have its intellectual property protected, but with some variations from the form of protection received in the United States. If it creates a subsidiary in Belgium it will not have to adopt a joint venture. But it will face civil law tradition corporate concepts and possibly some workers' rights not present in the United States. The company will have to learn something about dealing in an economically integrated market, in this case the European Union. The similarities with dealing in Brockton or Burbank are as prevalent as the disparities in dealing with Bangkok or Beijing. That is partly why a very large part of U.S. trade and investment abroad is with developed, market economy nations.

What follows in the chapters ahead is an introduction to some of the laws and policies, the organizations and entities, and the people that are involved in some of the activities that we believe are

included in the term "international business transactions". Because that term includes, as noted
above, the trade of goods across borders, licensing,
foreign investment, the role of governments in the
use of tariff and nontariff barriers, as well as such
other areas as controls on exports, the taking of
foreign property by governments, insuring foreign
investment, the increasing implementation of bilateral and multilateral trade agreements, and forms
and procedures of dispute resolution in all of these
international business transactions, this 8th edition
of the International Business Transactions Nutshell
will share some of these areas with its companion
volume, by the same authors, the International
Trade and Economic Relations Nutshell, 4th edition. This Nutshell focuses on the documentary
sale and use of letters of credit, E-commerce, technology transfers, foreign investment transactions,
expropriations and remedies, EU business competition law, extraterritorial antitrust, and international business dispute settlement. The International
Trade and Economic Relations Nutshell covers the
government imposed restrictions on imports and
exports, the GATT/WTO, free trade agreements and
customs unions, and economic integration with an
emphasis on the European Union and the North
American Free Trade Agreement. The two Nutshells are intended to provide a broad introduction
to the people and institutions who practice international business transactions, and the government
and multilateral organizations which both encourage and restrict trade.

CHAPTER ONE

INTERNATIONAL SALES OF GOODS

Most students who have taken the first-year Contracts course believe that Uniform Commercial Code (UCC) Article 2 is the United States law that governs all contracts for the sale of goods, both domestic and international. However, there is a U.S. federal law which governs contracts for the international sale of goods, and which pre-empts state laws like the UCC. This federal law on sales of goods was created by the ratification by the United Nations Convention on Contracts for the International Sale of Goods (1980). The parties to a contract can "opt out" of that convention, but it must be the starting point for any analysis of international sales law.

THE U.N. CONVENTION ON CONTRACTS FOR THE INTERNATIONAL SALE OF GOODS (CISG)

The United Nations Convention on Contracts for the International Sale of Goods (1980)(hereafter CISG) governs the sale of goods between parties in the United States and parties in seventy other countries, unless the parties to the sale contract have expressly "opted out" of the Convention. CISG entered into force on January 1, 1988, thirteen months after the United States had ratified the Convention and deposited its instruments of ratification with the United Nations. As a self-executing treaty, no separate implementing legislation is needed. As federal law, it pre-empts Article 2 of the UCC where it is applicable. CISG is available to be used by private parties in ordinary commercial litigation before both federal and state courts in the United States.

At the time of ratification, the United States declared one reservation, a reservation under Article 95 that the United States is not bound by Article 1(1)(b). The effect of this reservation is that the courts of the United States are bound under international law to use CISG only when the places of business of both parties to the sale contract are each in different States, and both of those different States are Contracting States to CISG. Thus, CISG governs all contracts for the international sale of goods (unless the parties "opt out" under Article 6) between parties whose principal places of business are in the United States and other Contracting States.

As of July 1, 2004, there were sixty-two Contracting States to CISG representing two thirds of the world's trade in goods. In addition to the United States, they included: Argentina, Australia, Austria, Belarus, Belgium, Bosnia and Herzegovina, Bulgaria, Burundi, Canada, Chile, China, Columbia, Croatia, Cuba, Czech Republic, Denmark, Ecuador,

Egypt, El Salvador, Estonia, Finland, France, Gabon, Georgia, Germany, Greece, Guinea, Honduras, Hungary, Iceland, Iraq, Israel, Italy, Japan, Kyrgyzstan, Latvia, Lesotho, Liberia, Lithuania, Luxembourg, Macedonia, Mauritania, Mexico, Moldova, Mongolia, Montenegro, the Netherlands, New Zealand, Norway, Paraguay, Peru, Poland, Republic of Korea, Romania, the Russian Federation, Saint Vincent and Grenadines, Serbia, Singapore, Slovakia, Slovenia, Spain, Sweden, Switzerland, Syria, Uganda, Ukraine, Uruguay, Uzbekistan, and Zambia. There are now over 2,000 cases interpreting CISG.

Other states are expected to ratify or adopt CISG in the near future. This will increase the impact and effectiveness of CISG in unifying international sales law. A current and complete list of Contracting States to this Convention can be obtained on the internet at www.uncitral.org.

CISG was drafted by the United Nations Commission on International Trade Law (UNCITRAL), and adopted and opened for signature and ratification by a U.N.–sponsored diplomatic conference held at Vienna in 1980. The mandate of UNCITRAL is the unification and harmonization of international trade law. The purpose of such unification is to reduce legal obstacles to international trade, and to promote the orderly development of new legal concepts to assist further growth in international trade.

In addition to CISG, UNCITRAL has adopted the UNCITRAL Model Law on International Commercial Arbitration (1985), which has been enacted in 28 nations and four states in the United States; the UNICITRAL Model Law on Electronic Commerce (1996), which has influenced more than twenty enactment laws to date, including uniform acts in Canada and the U.S., and EU directives; and a Legal Guide on Drawing Up International Contracts for Construction of Industrial Works, which has been widely used in LDC development projects, even before its final adoption by UNCITRAL, because of its perceived balance, fairness and attention to detail. UNCITRAL is continuing its tradition of promoting unification in "unconventional" areas of commercial law, such as government procurement law.

UNCITRAL is not the only international organization currently making proposals for the unification and harmonization of international law. The International Institute for the Unification of Private Law (UNIDROIT) held a diplomatic conference in Toronto in 1988 to adopt the Convention on International Lease Financing, which has eight Contracting States and entered into force in 1995, and the Convention on International Factoring, which has six Contracting States and entered into force in 1995. These two conventions, together with CISG, may form an alternative source of law in international transactions for issues now analyzed under UCC Articles 2 and 9. The OAS has also been active in this field on a hemisphere-wide basis.

In addition, UNIDROIT has prepared and issued in 1994 the Principles of International Commercial

Contracts. The Principles are applicable to all contracts, not just sales of goods, and their provisions are set forth in more general terms. If CISG is the international analogue to UCC Article 2 in the United States law, then the Principles are the international analogue to the Restatement of Contracts in U.S. law. They are not intended to be adopted as a convention or enacted as a uniform model law. Instead, they are expected to be used by international commercial arbitrators, and even by judges where local law is ambiguous. Some of the specific concepts are discussed later in this chapter. The substantive rules of the Principles are often different from those of CISG, because the Principles were not drafted by official delegations of governments, and the individual drafters could adopt what they considered to be "best practices" in commerce.

THE SPHERE OF APPLICATION OF CISG

CISG entered into force on January 1, 1988, and the U.S. was one of the twelve original Contracting States. UNCITRAL has placed the substantive sales law rules into the text of the Convention itself, so that the "private law" rules are part of the Convention, and are directly adopted by ratification. Thus, CISG is a "self-executing" treaty, and in the United States ratification of CISG meant the automatic adoption of the substantive provisions on sales, without any need for separate implementing legislation. The main purpose of CISG is to avoid conflicts of law problems, not to aggravate them. Thus, it is important that the scope of application of CISG be clear, both as to the circumstances where it does apply, and those where it does not.

The first six articles of CISG define its sphere of application. Article 1 requires that a sale of goods contract be both "international" and also bear a stated relation to a Contracting State before the contract can be governed by the Convention. In determining whether "a contract is for the international sale of goods," CISG does not define "contract," "sale," or "goods," but Article 1 does define "international." The transaction must be "between parties whose places of business are in different states." Neither the location of the goods themselves, nor the location of negotiations between the parties, is necessarily dispositive. Instead, the "place of business" of each party must be located, and be in a different State.

This "place of business" criterion will cause difficulty whenever one or both parties have more than one place of business. However, CISG Article 10(a) provides some help in such situations by specifying which "place of business" is to be considered. Unfortunately, Article 10(a) does not define what a "place of business" is, although the drafting history of the Convention suggests that a permanent establishment is required and that neither a warehouse nor the office of a seller's agent qualifies as a "place of business." Caselaw has established that a branch can be a "place of business."

Article 10(a) does specify which one of multiple offices is to be used in determining the internationality of a transaction, but even this is subject to ambiguity—"the place of business is that which has the closest relationship to the contract *and* its performance" (emphasis added). Thus, where one office is more closely associated with the formation of the contract and a second office is more closely associated with a party's performance of its contractual obligations, there is an unresolved issue concerning which of those offices is the relevant "place of business." However, Article 10(a) does limit the usable facts in making a choice between multiple offices to those circumstances known to "the parties" before a binding contract is formed. This should permit well-advised parties to resolve possible ambiguities by stating in the contract which office of each party they believe to have "the closest relationship to the contract."

The Convention does not, however, govern all contracts for the international sale of goods, but only those contracts which have a substantial relation to one or more Contracting States—that is, States which ratified, accepted, approved or acceded to the Convention so as to become parties to the Convention. CISG Article 1 makes the Convention applicable to sales contracts where the places of business of the parties are in different States, and either (a) both states are Contracting States, or (b) only one State is a Contracting State and private international law choice-of-law rules lead to the application of the law of a Contracting State. Thus,

CISG will govern a contract of sale between parties, where one party has its place of business in the United States and the other party has its place of business in France, China, Italy or any of the other Contracting States—*unless* the parties expressly "exclude the application of the Convention" under Article 6. This "opt-out" capacity is always available to the parties.

When it ratified CISG, the United States declared a reservation under Article 95 that it would not be bound by Article 1(1)(b). Thus, the United States' version of the Convention is that it is not applicable when a contract is between parties having places of business in different States and only one State is a Contracting State, even though choice-of-law rules lead to the application of the law of the Contracting State. A contract of sale between a United States party and another party in N, a non-Contracting State, will not be governed by CISG, even though United States law is applicable under usual choice-of-law rules. If United States law applies, but CISG does not, what law does govern the contract? Instead of CISG, United States law for domestic sales transactions would govern, which means the Uniform Commercial Code (UCC) is applicable in forty-nine states (all but Louisiana).

This reservation was included at the insistence of the United States delegation, because it was believed that the UCC is superior as a sales law to CISG. Therefore CISG was considered helpful to United States interests only where it provided a clear resolution of choice-of-law issues. It was believed that, if a court first had to resolve such choice-of-law issues and determined that United States law applied, it might as well apply the "best" United States law—the UCC. The drafting history of the reservation indicates that the sales contract between a United States party and another party in N, a non-Contracting State, will not be governed by CISG, even if the litigation is in France, a Contracting State which has made no such reservation. For the purposes of interpreting Article 1(1)(b), the United States is not a "Contracting State."

CHOICE OF LAW CLAUSES

Under CISG Article 6, the parties may expressly determine not to be governed by ("opt out of") the Convention. However, if such a decision is made, care must be used in drafting such a statement of exclusion. A simple statement that a contract "shall be governed by New York law" is ambiguous, but a court is likely to hold that the New York law concerning international sales is CISG, through federal pre-emption doctrines. Thus, if the parties decide to exclude the Convention, it should be expressly excluded by language which states that it does not apply *and* also states what law shall govern the contract. ("This contract shall not be governed by the United Nations Convention on Contracts for the International Sale of Goods, 1980, but shall be governed by the New York Uniform Commercial Code for domestic sales of goods and other New York laws.") Note that it is necessary to designate the law of a particular jurisdiction, in addition to CISG, in any choice of law clause, because CISG, like any other single statute, will not furnish a complete legal regime.

There are many attorneys who will seek to "opt out" of CISG for all contracts under all conditions, simply because they do not understand it as well as they understand the UCC. However, such action may be a disservice to the clients' interests. There may be many circumstances when a seller of goods in an international transaction will be placed in a much more awkward position by the UCC and its "perfect tender" and "rejection" rules than it will be under the rules of CISG. In such transactions, automatic rejection of CISG should be resisted, unless the attorney is willing to write comparable seller-friendly rules into the contract as express terms of the contract. At least one author has stated that negotiating an international sales contract, or automatically opting out of CISG, without understanding how it affects the client's interests, constitutes malpractice.

OTHER SCOPE ISSUES

CISG Article 3 expressly includes contracts for the sale of goods not yet produced, unless the "buyer" undertakes to supply "a substantial part" of the necessary materials. Sales involving a combination of goods and services are always a potential problem, and Article 3 includes such contracts unless "the preponderant part" of seller's obligation concerns "labour or other services."

The Convention does not define "goods," but Article 2 does expressly exclude contracts for the sale of commercial paper, investment securities, ships, aircraft, hovercraft and electricity. The implications of these express exclusions on further construction of a definition of "goods" is unclear. Under the UCC, commercial paper and investment securities would be considered "intangibles," and not subject to a statute on sales of goods. Express exclusions may be interpreted to include other intangibles not expressly excluded. Ships can be considered "immovables," and likewise excluded; but a more likely reason is that they are usually subject to registration and regulatory legislation—as are aircraft, etc. But timber to be cut, growing crops and railroad rolling stock are subject to the same conceptual and regulatory difficulties, and they are not expressly dealt with. Thus, the term "goods" is unclear, and Article 2 does not seem to help clarify it. The most important ambiguity may concern software. The cases under CISG have indicated that, discs bought off the shelf from a store may be "goods," but there is a conflict over whether a contract to develop software is a contract for the sale of "goods" or not. The status of software bought and downloaded over the net is unclear.

On the other hand, CISG Article 2 expressly excludes international sales of goods to consumers, so that the Convention would not conflict with consumer protection laws, which are often "mandatory law." Execution sales and auctions are also expressly excluded, probably on similar reasoning.

Further, CISG Article 5 provides that the Convention does not govern causes of action against the seller "for death or personal injury," even though arising out of a sales transaction, because any provisions on such causes of action would conflict with "mandatory law" of many jurisdictions.

One further limitation on the application of CISG is that its provisions do not govern all of the issues which may arise under a contract which is subject to the Convention. Under CISG Article 4, the Convention states that it governs "only the formation of the contract" and the "rights and obligations" of the parties to the contract. Thus, CISG has been held to pre-empt state law on promissory estoppel, but not tort law.

CISG does not govern the "validity" of the contract, or its effect on title to the goods, including presumably most rights and obligations of third parties to the contract. The restriction concerning "validity" was provided because CISG was not designed to police sales contracts for fairness. Originally created to avoid conflicts with regulatory law, the caselaw indicates that it also includes at least issues arising out of fraud, negligent misrepresentation, duress, illegality and mistake. Whether it also includes unconscionability, good faith, gross unfairness and the particular regulations of the form of disclaimers of warranty is debated by the authorities. The cases are often decided contrary to European scholarly writings.

The Convention does not define "contract of sale," so that its application to some types of transactions is problematic. Known problems include "consignments," in which the "buyer" may return any goods which cannot be sold, barter transactions or "countertrade," in which goods are exchanged for other goods and not for money, and "conditional sales," in which the seller retains title to secured payment. There is a split of authority under the caselaw as to whether the parties to a "distribution" contract may "opt in" to governance by CISG. Cases in the U.S. and abroad have held that CISG does not apply to "turnkey project" contracts. Separate UNCITRAL reports on countertrade indicate that it may not be regarded as a contract of sale. CISG may cover the sales aspects of a conditional sale, but not its secured transaction aspects.

GENERAL PROVISIONS OF CISG

Articles 7–13 contain its "general principles." These provisions deal with interpretation of the Convention and filling gaps in its provisions (Article 7); interpretation of international sales contracts (Article 9); a few definitions (Articles 10 and 13); and a replacement for the Statute of Frauds (Articles 11 and 12). Article 7 is designed to assist in interpretation of the Convention itself, while Articles 8 and 9 are designed to assist in interpretation of the contract terms. Article 8 concentrates on statements and conduct by the parties themselves as indications of contract terms, while Article 9 concentrates on sources external to the parties, such as trade usage.

CISG Article 7(1) is intended to inhibit local courts which decide disputes under the Convention from applying local law to these international disputes, rather than the Convention. Thus, in interpreting the concepts stated in the Convention, such as "reasonable time," regard for the "international character" of the Convention is imposed upon courts to attempt to lead them to use international practice rather than domestic practice or precedent. This preference for international practice is stressed further by the directive "to promote uniformity of its application." The latter is intended to establish foreign decisions under CISG as more persuasive than local decisions on domestic sales law. Even the doctrine of "good faith," well-known in most local law, is muted. Although UCC § 1–203 imposes an obligation of good faith on each of the parties to a sale, CISG Article 7(1) only refers to good faith in relation to interpretation of the Convention, not of the contract, by courts.

Article 7(2) continues this approach in regard to supplementary principles of law, or "gap-fillers." Unlike the corresponding provision in the UCC, these supplementary principles are not to be gathered from United States domestic law, but either from "general principles" found within the Convention or international law or, if none can be found, from principles found in the law applicable under normal choice-of-law rules. The danger to uniform application is that local courts will discover many "gaps," no usable "general principles" derivable from the Convention, choose their own law as applicable, and easily fall back on their own familiar supplementary principles of law.

Article 8 attempts to establish rules for interpreting the contract itself, and its terms. It establishes a three-tier hierarchy: (1) Where the parties have a common understanding or intent concerning the meaning of a provision, that common understanding is to be used in any interpretation. (2) Where the understandings or intent of the parties diverge, and one party "knew or could not have been unaware" of the other party's intent, under Article 8(1) the latter party's interpretation prevails. And (3), where the parties were unaware of the divergence, their statements and conduct are each to be subjected to a "reasonable person" standard under Article 8(2). The Convention does not attempt to resolve the interpretation problems created if each party's understanding of the other's statements is possible under this "reasonable person" scrutiny. In evaluating party conduct and statements under Article 8(3), a court can look to the negotiating history of the contract and to the actual administration of the terms of the contract by the parties. (Termed "course of performance" in UCC § 2–208.)

In *MCC-Marble Ceramic Center, Inc. v. Ceramica Nuova d'Agostino, S.p.A.,*, 144 F.3d 1384 (11th Cir. 1998), Article 8(1) was interpreted to require the U.S. courts to consider subjective intent while interpreting both the statements and the conduct of the parties. Article 8(3) also can direct a court to a very different approach to contract interpretation than is usual in other U.S. contract cases. Its requirement that a court give consideration to all relevant circumstances is a clear direction to consider parol evidence, even when there is a subsequent written agreement. It has also been suggested that both provisions can be used to promote the actual intent of the parties in the battle of the forms transaction, to avoid the "last shot" doctrine.

Article 9(1) allows the parties to include "any usage" to which they have agreed. The drafting history indicates that this paragraph refers only to express agreements to include usage, although the express agreement need not be written. Further, "any" usage may be so incorporated, including local ones, not just international usage. If so incorporated, usage is considered to be part of the express contract items, but is not the governing law of the contract. However, since Article 6 allows the express terms of the contract to carry the provisions of the Convention, agreed usages will prevail over CISG provisions where CISG is the governing law. The one exception to the last statement is Article 12, which is applicable only if one of the parties has its place of business in a Contracting State which has declared a reservation under Article 96. Under that reservation, which is considered to be "mandatory law" and may not be derogated by the contract terms, contracts must be evidenced by writing if so required by the local law of the Contracting State.

Article 9(2) concerns the incorporation of usages by implication. Both less developed countries

(LDCs) and nonmarket economies (NMEs) sought to limit the application by implication of usage. Thus, if the parties do not expressly agree to incorporate a usage, it is available in interpreting the contract only if "the parties knew or ought to have known" of it, it must be a usage in international (not merely local) trade, it must be widely known to others in this international trade, and it must be "regularly observed" in that trade. This seems to set a very high standard for any party assuming the burden of proof, although the principle issue in litigation is likely to concern the delineation of the specific "trade" involved.

Article 11 provides that a contract for the international sale of goods is enforceable, even though it is not written, and may be proven by any means. Thus, there is no equivalent in the Convention of the common law Statute of Frauds. However, Articles 12 and 96 allow a Contracting State to declare a reservation that the local law of that Contracting State shall govern the form requirements of the sale contract "where any party has his place of business in that State." Such a reservation may be declared at any time, but it is applicable only to the extent that the domestic law of the State making the reservation "requires contracts of sale" to be in writing. The United States has not made this declaration, so its Statute of Frauds provisions in UCC § 2–201 are not applicable to contracts under the Convention. However, the local law of parties from other States may be applicable if they have the required local legislation. The former Soviet Union was the strongest proponent of the Article 96 reservation, and the Russian Federation, Belarus and the Ukraine made this declaration when they adopted the Convention.

If the Article 96 reservation has been declared, the parties may not agree otherwise under Article 10. This gives the local law the effect of "mandatory law" under the Convention. However, it should be noted that a telex or a telegram can be used under Article 13 to satisfy the "writing" requirement. Further, a telex or a telegram qualify as a "writing" regardless of the formal requirements of the local law. Articles 12 and 96 only make unenforceable those contracts which are "other than in writing" (a Convention term), and Article 13 then defines "writing," as used in CISG, to include a telex or telegram.

CONTRACT FORMATION

The contract formation provisions (Articles 14–24) form a separate "part" of CISG—Part II. Under Article 92 a Contracting State may declare a reservation at the time of ratification that it will not be bound by Part II, even though it is bound by the rest of CISG.

Although every first-year American law student studies about "offer, acceptance and consideration," those three elements of contract formation are not present in other legal systems. Civil law emphasizes the agreement process, and does not include a "consideration" requirement. An examination of most commercial transactions will show that there is no real issue concerning consideration in most of them. An examination of most "consideration" cases will show that few of them are commercial contracts—rather, they are aunts attempting to induce nephews not to smoke. Thus, it should not be surprising to learn that CISG has no requirements of "consideration" in its contract formation provisions.

As was discussed in the previous section, the writing requirements of the Statute of Frauds are also not applicable, unless one of the parties has a place of business in a Contracting State which has declared a reservation under Article 96. Further, the "integration" concepts of the parol evidence rule are not applicable under Article 8(1).

Part II of CISG focuses on "offer" (Articles 14–17) and "acceptance" (Articles 18–22). In Convention terminology, under Article 23 a contract "is concluded" (becomes binding) "when an acceptance of an offer becomes effective." There is no need for consideration, and no formal requirements.

Article 14 defines "offer" with three requirements. First, it must be "a proposal for concluding a contract," which is a standard provision. Second, it must indicate "an intention to be bound in case of acceptance," which will distinguish an offer from a general sales catalogue or advertisement or a purchase inquiry. Article 14(2) elaborates this concept by making proposals addressed to the general public presumptively not offers "unless the contrary is clearly indicated." Third, an offer must be "sufficiently definite." This provision is directed toward only three contract terms: the description of the goods, their quantity and their price. Other terms can be left open, but not those three. The criteria for judging definiteness are somewhat ambiguous. The offer is definite enough if the goods are "indicated," which does not seem to require that they be described with any particularity. Similarly, an offer *is* definite if it "expressly or impliedly fixes or makes provision for determining the quantity and the price."

This provision seems more restrictive than the comparable UCC provision on open, or flexible, price contracts (§ 2–305), and was so intended because many civil law states do not recognize such contracts. Article 55 might seem to be helpful, but its provisions may be available only where a contract has already been "validly concluded," which assumes a valid offer. The Convention language is flexible enough, however, to authorize most forms of flexible pricing. Thus, the contract does "make provision for determining the price" where the price is to follow an index specified in the contract, or has an escalator clause or is to be set by a third party. Arguably, the latter would include "lowest price to others" clauses. The principal problem not resolved under the foregoing analysis may be only the order for a replacement part in which no price is stated. It is here that Article 55 is certainly useful. The offeror may have "implicitly" agreed to pay seller's current price for such goods, and Article

55 fixes the price as that generally charged at the time the contract is "concluded." One case has enforced a price-less contract, but the court found that the parties had established a payment practice under prior contracts.

Open quantity contracts, such as those for requirements, output and exclusive dealings, may cause less difficulty. In each such contract, there arguably is a "provision for determining the quantity" through facts which will exists after the parties become bound, even if the precise number cannot be fixed in advance. However, in view of the requirements of CISG Article 14, it is usually preferable to include either estimated quantity amounts or minimum quantity amounts, to assure that there is a fixed or determinable quantity provision.

Assortment is a final problem concerning "definiteness." (Compare UCC § 2–311.) However, a clause which permits either the buyer or the seller to specify a changing assortment during the period of the contract would seem to make a provision for determining both quantity and type of goods. The major hurdle in such cases is the requirement that the offer "indicate the goods" and be "sufficiently definite." But Article 14(1) does not require that the offer "specify" the goods, and so clauses which allow later selection of assortment are presumably authorized, if the parties take care in describing the type of goods from which the assortment will be selected. In a case involving aircraft engines, where seller's offer stipulated one set of engines if a Boeing aircraft were selected by the buyer, and a different set of engines if Airbus was selected, the court held that this was not an offer under CISG Article 14. Thus, a contract was not concluded even though a Letter of Intention had been signed by the parties.

One of the consequences of the abandonment of the "consideration" requirement is that there is no foundation for the traditional common law analysis of the revocability of an unaccepted offer. The traditional common law doctrine made an offer revocable at will until accepted, unless there was an agreement supported by consideration to keep it open (such as an option). In German law, an offer is binding unless the offeror states that it is revocable. These two approaches are opposites, and the compromise adopted by CISG uses neither of the approaches.

Under Article 16, an offer originating under the Convention is revocable unless "it indicates" that it is not revocable. In adopting this position, the Convention rejects both the common law rule that an offer is always revocable and the German civil law rule that an offer is not revocable unless it is expressly stated to be revocable. This basic concept is similar to that used in creating a "firm offer" under UCC § 2–205, but no "signed writing" is required. There are two ways in which an offer can become irrevocable under Article 16: through the offeror's statements and through reasonable reliance by the offeree. However, such an irrevocable offer must also meet the Article 14 requirements, including the fixed or determinable price, quantity and assortment terms discussed above.

An offeror can indicate that an offer is irrevocable "by stating a fixed time for acceptance or otherwise." The first reference seems relatively clear, and would include a statement that an offer will be held open for a specified period and no longer. The "or otherwise" language may include reliance, using the criteria for irrevocability of an offer after reasonable reliance by an offeror under United States caselaw and the Second Restatement of Contracts, Section 87.

Article 18(1) defines "acceptance" as either a statement or "other conduct" by an offeree "indicating assent to an offer." Silence is not necessarily acceptance, although the negotiations and other prior conduct of the parties may establish an implicit understanding that lengthy silence followed by affirmative conduct is acceptance.

Article 18(2) determines when an "indication of acceptance" is effective for "concluding" the contract. Thus, along with Articles 16(1) and 22, it forms the Convention's analog to "the mailbox rule"—except that the CISG rules are different. At common law, "the mailbox rule" passed the risk of loss or delay in transmission of an acceptance to the offeror once the offeree has dispatched the acceptance. It also chose that point in time to terminate the offeror's power to revoke an offer and to terminate the offeree's power to withdraw the acceptance. Under CISG Article 18(2), however, an acceptance is not effective until it "reaches" (is delivered to) the offeror. Thus, risk of loss or delay in transmission is on the offeree, who must now inquire if the acceptance is not acknowledged. On the other hand, the offeror's power to revoke under CISG Article 16(1) is terminated upon dispatch of the acceptance—which is the common law rule. However, the offeree's power to withdraw the acceptance terminates only when the acceptance reaches the offeror. Thus, an acceptance sent by a slow transmission method allows the offeree to speculate for a day or two while the offeror is bound. An email message will release the offeree from the acceptance.

Even though Article 18(1) states that acceptance by conduct alone is possible, the remaining paragraphs of Article 18 seem to imply that in the usual case the offeree must notify the offeror that acceptance by conduct is forthcoming. Notification of the acceptance may reach the offeror indirectly through third parties, such as banks or carriers. Article 18(3) indicates that acceptance by conduct without notice is possible only when that procedure is allowed by the offer, by usage or by the parties' prior course of performance. If so allowed, the acceptance by conduct, such as shipping the goods without notice, is effective upon dispatch of the goods, rather than upon their delivery to the offeror.

The traditional analysis of the CISG approach to the "battle of the forms" is quite different than that of the UCC, and closer to the common law "mirror-image" analysis. Under Article 19, if the buyer's purchase order form and the seller's order acknowledgment form differ as to any material term, there is no offer and acceptance. Instead, there is an offer, followed by a rejection of that offer and a counter offer (usually the seller's order acknowledgement form). The rejection of the original offer terminates it under CISG Article 17. Thus, the parties do not "conclude" a contract by exchanging forms, and if one party reneges on its obligations, before performance, it probably is not bound to perform.

However, the vast majority of transactions involving exchanges of such forms are performed by the parties, despite the lack of a contract formed by the exchange of forms. Once the goods have been shipped, accepted and paid for, there has been a transaction, and a contract underlying that transaction has been formed by the parties—what are its terms? To put the same question in a different way, is the seller's shipment of the contract "conduct" by the seller which accepts the terms in the buyer's purchase order? Or, is the buyer's acceptance and payment for the goods "conduct" which accepts the terms in the seller's order acknowledgement form? The common law analysis would make the terms of the form last sent to another party controlling, since that last form (usually seller's) would be a counter offer and a rejection and termination of all prior unaccepted offers. This is the "last shot" principle, and CISG Articles 17, 18(3) and 19 seem to follow it.

The cases indicate a reluctance by judges to follow this 19th Century legal reasoning. There are a

French and several German court decision expressly adopting the "knock out" rule, in which conflicting boilerplate clauses in forms do not become part of the contract, and the gaps are filled by CISG provisions. Other courts have disregarded Article 19(3), and stretched the concept of "non-materiality" to find a mirror-image acceptance. On the other hand, a few courts have used the mirror-image and last-shot doctrines, and have ignored the more sophisticated analytical tools available for resolving the battle of forms.

In summary and in comparison to the UCC, CISG reduces the flexibility of the parties by prohibiting some open price terms; CISG expands the "firm offer" concept and applies it to more offers; and in the battle of the forms, CISG may delay the formation of a contract through the "mirror image" rule, and may use the "last shot" principle to make the offeree's (usually seller's) terms control the transaction. However, on the last points, both the courts and the authors who have written on the subject have suggested ways of avoiding this traditional analysis.

SELLER'S OBLIGATIONS

Under CISG Article 30 the seller is obligated to deliver the goods and any related documents and to transfer "the property in the goods" to the buyer. In addition, the seller is obligated to deliver goods which conform to the contract as to quantity, quality and title.

Some of these obligations are governed by domestic law, and not the Convention, because under Article 4(b) the Convention "is not concerned with" the effect of the contract on "the property in the goods sold." Domestic law, therefore, determines whether "the property" passes from seller to buyer at the "conclusion" (formation) of the contract, upon delivery, or at some other time; whether a certificate of title is required; and whether seller may retain title as security for the purchase price or other debts.

"Delivery" under CISG is a limited concept, relating to transfer of possession or control of the goods. The CISG draftsmen did not attempt to consolidate all the incidents of sale—physical delivery, passing of risk of loss, passing of title, liability for the price, and ability to obtain specific performance, etc.—into a single concept or make them turn on a single event, as has been done in many sales statutes. Instead, they followed the format of the UCC in providing separate provisions for each of these concepts.

As to the place of delivery, CISG recognizes four distinct types of delivery terms: (1) delivery contracts in which the seller must deliver to the place specified in the contract; (2) shipment contracts, in which the contract "involves carriage of the goods", but does not require delivery to any particular place; (3) sales of goods at a known location which are not expected to be transported; and (4) sales of goods whose location is not known or specified, and which are not expected to be transported. CISG Article 31.

In delivery contracts, seller may be obligated to deliver the goods to buyer's place, or to a sub-buyer's place, or to any location specified. However, it should be noted that CISG has no provisions directly describing seller's duties in such contracts, for they are expressly excluded from Article 31, and all interpretation left to contract terms only. The goods must be conforming when delivered, not merely when shipped, unless performance is excused by force majeure under CISG Articles 79 and 69.

In a shipment contract, seller has no obligation to deliver the goods to any particular place, but it is clear that transportation of the goods by an independent third party carrier is involved. The usual reference to such a contract is through commercial terms like "FOB" or "CIF." Since the goods are to be "handed over" to the carrier and not to the buyer, transactions involving carriage by the buyer seem excluded from this provision.

The shipment contract may require seller to take more than one action to accomplish its obligation of "delivery." First, under Article 31(a), the seller must transfer ("hand over") the goods to a carrier—the first independent carrier. Second, under Article 32(3), depending upon the sale contract terms, seller must either "effect insurance" coverage of the goods during transit or, at buyer's request, give buyer the information necessary to effect insurance. Third, under Article 32(1), if the goods are not "clearly identified to the contract" by the shipping documents or by their own markings, seller must notify buyer of the consignment specifying the goods. Finally, the contract may require seller to arrange for the transportation of the goods, in which case seller must contract for "appropriate" carriage under "usual terms" under Article 32(2).

Where carriage of the goods is not "involved," the buyer may or may not be told where the goods are or will be. Absent a contrary provision in the contract, in such a transaction if buyer is told the location of the goods he is expected to pick them up at that location; otherwise at seller's place of business. Under Article 31(b) and (c), the seller's obligation under CISG is to put the goods "at buyer's disposal" at the appropriate place. The Convention is not clear as to whether this requires notification to buyer, but it would require notification to any third party bailees to allow buyer to take possession.

Where the delivery of the goods is to be accomplished by tender or delivery of documents, Article 34 merely requires that the seller conform to the terms of the contract. The second and third sentences of Article 34 establish the principle that a seller who delivers defective documents early may cure the defects until the date due under the contract, if possible, and buyer must take the cured documents, even though the original tender and cure has caused damage to buyer.

The time requirements for seller's performance are stated in Article 33. They all relate to the contract terms: the goods or documents must be delivered on or before a stated or determinable date set in the contract, within a stated or determinable span of time specified in the contract, or, if no date or span of time is set, within a "reasonable time." "Reasonable time" is not defined, and will depend on trade usage, but at least it precludes demands for immediate delivery.

The Convention has no provisions concerning seller's duties in regard of export and import licenses and taxes, but leaves the determination of these incidents of delivery to the contract terms, or usage. Where these issues are not covered by the contract terms or usage, the authorities give conflicting analyses as to what rules may be derived from the general principles of CISG.

CISG Article 35 obligates the seller to deliver goods of the quantity, quality, description and packaging required by the contract. In determining whether the quality of the goods conforms to the contract, the Convention eschews such separate and independent doctrines as "warranty" and "strict product liability" from the common law analysis, as well as "fault" or "negligence" from civil law. Instead, CISG focuses on the simpler concept that the seller is obligated to deliver the goods as described in the contract, and then elaborates on the connotations of that contractual description. This approach, however, produces results which are comparable to the "warranty" structure of the UCC.

Thus, Article 35(2)(a) and (d) require that the goods be fit for ordinary use and properly packaged (comparable to UCC § 2–314), 35(2)(b) requires that they be fit for any particular use made known to the seller (comparable to UCC § 2–315), and 35(2)(c) requires that they conform to any goods which seller has held as a sample or model (comparable to UCC § 2–313(1)(c)). Each of these obligations, however, arises out of the contract, so that the parties may "agree otherwise" and limit seller's obligations concerning quality (comparable to "disclaimers of warranty" under UCC § 2–316(2)).

There are no conditions on the imposition on seller of the obligation of fitness for ordinary use. All the contracts governed by CISG will be commercial contracts, so that there is no need for the UCC limitation to "merchant" seller. One issue not expressly resolved is whether the "ordinary use" is defined by seller's location or by buyer's location, if "ordinary use" in each is different. Although it has been argued that the standards of buyer's location govern, an alternative analysis is that any such disparity in usage means that neither usage is international in scope, and therefore neither usage can qualify as "ordinary." Instead, any use not recognized as "ordinary" in international trade must be analyzed under the criteria for fitness for a "particular purpose."

The obligation of fitness for a particular purpose arises only if buyer makes the particular purpose known to seller (expressly or impliedly) at or before the "conclusion of the contract," and buyer also relies on seller's skill and judgment, and such reliance is reasonable. There is no express requirement that buyer inform seller of buyer's reliance but only of the particular purpose. More importantly, there is no requirement that buyer inform seller of any of the difficulties which buyer may know are involved in designating or designing goods to accomplish this particular use. However, it is likely that courts can avoid any abuse of these gaps in the statute by the "reasonable reliance" criterion and through the assignment of burdens of proof.

Seller is relieved of any of the obligations under Article 35(2) against defects in quality whenever buyer is aware or "could not have been unaware" of a defect at the time the contract is "concluded." However, knowledge gained at the time of delivery or inspection of the goods will not affect seller's obligation. The "could not have been unaware" language is the subject of much dispute among common law and civil law authorities. Most common law authorities consider it to be "subjective" and relate to buyer's actual state of mind, rather than to impose "constructive knowledge" on buyer for items he should have learned.

Medical Marketing Int'l, Inc. v. Internazionale Medico Scientifica, S.R.L., 1999 WL 311945 (E.D. La.1999) held that, under CISG Art. 35, a seller is generally not obligated to supply goods that conform to the public laws and regulations in the buyer's state. It also held that there are at least three exceptions to this general rule. First, if those laws and regulations are identical to those in the seller's state, the goods must conform to them. Second, if the buyer informs the seller about the laws and regulations in its state, the goods must conform to them. And, third, if the seller knew or should have known of the laws and regulations in the buyer's state due to special circumstances, such as having a branch office in buyer's state, then the goods must conform to them.

Under CISG Article 36(1) states that these obligations begin under CISG "at the time when the risk [of loss] passes to the buyer"—a concept explored in depth later. Any nonconformity concerning the quality of the goods which exists at the time the risk of loss passes is actionable, even if discovered later. Thus, the buyer is still able to recover for any nonconformity which becomes apparent long after delivery, but the buyer may have to prove that the defect was present at delivery and was not caused by buyer's use, maintenance or protection of the goods. The buyer need not prove what caused the goods to be defective, only that they are, in fact, defective.

CISG Article 40 seems to create another obligation on seller—the obligation to notify buyer of any nonconformity known to seller, or of which "he could not have been unaware." If seller does know of a defect and does not notify, then seller may not be able to rely on buyer's failure to inspect the goods quickly or notify seller of any discovered defects. Thus, even though buyer may lose its right to rely on a nonconformity because buyer did not inspect the goods "within as short a time as is practicable" under Article 38, or did not under

Article 39 notify seller of any defects, specifying the nature of the defects, within a reasonable time after it discovered or "ought to have discovered" them, buyer's right to rely on the nonconformity revives if seller, in turn, knew of the nonconformity and did not notify buyer of it.

Can seller exclude these obligations concerning the quality of the goods by terms in the contract—and, if so, how? CISG Article 6 states that the parties may, by agreement, derogate from any provision of the Convention, and Article 35(2) supports that ability to limit obligations concerning the quality of the goods. However, it is also clear that the standard formulation in domestic contracts—disclaiming implied warranties—will be inapposite, since the CISG obligations are neither "warranties" nor "implied." New verbal formulations must be found, which deal directly with the description of the goods and their expected use.

The major unresolved issue is the extent to which local law regulating disclaimers will impact on the international contracts governed by CISG. Such local law covers a spectrum from prohibitions on disclaimers in printed standard terms to the "how to do it manual" set out in UCC 2–316. There seems to be agreement that the former raises a question of "validity," and therefore governs contracts arising under CISG; and that the UCC provisions do not raise questions of "validity," and therefore do not govern CISG contracts. The distinction drawn seems to depend upon whether the local public policy prohibits conduct completely, or allows it but only within certain conditions. Whether the United States courts will accept such a distinction is conjectural at this point. However, they should, at the least, draw a distinction between UCC provisions, which require language to be "conspicuous" and those provisions which require a particular linguistic formula, such as use of the word "merchantability." As is shown above, the latter is inapposite under CISG.

Seller's obligation under CISG Article 41 concerning title to the goods under CISG is to deliver the goods not only free from any encumbrances on their title, but also free from any claim of a third party. Thus, like UCC § 2–312, seller is obligated to transfer "quiet possession" of the goods. Although the obligation is very broad, it probably is not breached by claims which are frivolous on their face or by state restrictions on use of the goods. The parties may derogate from the terms of these provisions of CISG by agreement, but buyer's knowledge that the goods are subject to a bailee's lien does not necessarily imply such an agreement. Instead, buyer may expect seller to discharge the lien before tender of delivery.

In addition to good title, seller is obligated to deliver the goods free from patent, trademark and copyright claims assertable under the law of the "buyer's place of business" or the place where both parties expect the goods to be used or resold. This obligation is, however, subject to multiple qualifications. First, seller obligations arise only with respect to claims of which "seller knew or could not have been unaware." Second, seller has no obligation with respect to intellectual property rights or claims of which buyer had knowledge when the contract was formed. Third, seller is not liable for claims which arise out of its use of technical drawings, designs or other specifications furnished by buyer, if seller action is in "compliance with" buyer's specifications. It is clear that this provision applies when seller is following specifications required by the contract, but its application is not clear when seller is merely following "suggestions" of buyer as to how best to meet more general contract provisions. Fourth, seller is excused from these obligations if buyer does not give notice of breach under Article 42—unless seller knew of the claim, which knowledge may be required under Article 41(1) in order to create liability initially. Finally, it has been argued that mistake of law will excuse seller, or at least that seller has performed its obligations concerning intellectual property rights if it has relied on trustworthy information of a lawyer that there are no such rights which might be infringed by use or resale of the goods, because seller could not then "know" of the possible claims of infringement.

REMEDIES FOR SELLER'S BREACH

If seller breaches any of its obligations, buyer has three basic types of remedies: specific performance, "avoidance" of the contract, and an action for damages. In addition, there is a potential self-help remedy under Article 50. All this is roughly comparable to the remedies available to an aggrieved buyer under the UCC. The difficulty facing the drafters of the Convention is illustrated by two facts: First, specific performance is the preferred remedy at civil law, while the action for damages is preferred at common law. Second, at civil law, a finding of "fault" is usually required for imposition of any recovery of damages, while the common law aggrieved party need show only "nonconformity." CISG to bridges both gaps.

As to specific performance, CISG Article 46 gives buyer who has not received delivery a right to specific performance, subject to two qualifications: buyer must not have resorted to an "inconsistent" remedy, and buyer should not bring its action for specific performance in a common law court. This provision gives buyer the right to seek specific performance, rather than damages, but does not force him to do so. Thus, any preference for this remedy must arise from buyer's perspective, not from the court's. Even in civil law jurisdictions, buyers will often prefer damages and purchase of substitute goods, because of the expense and delays inherent in litigation. Even if the court prefers specific performance, buyer can terminate this option by declaring the contract "avoided," which is an inconsistent remedy.

Where the goods have been delivered, but are not conforming to the contract, buyer may require specific performance in the form of delivery of conforming substitute goods only if the nonconformity amounts to a "fundamental breach." Likewise, buyer may require seller to repair the goods only if that is reasonable, "having regard to all the circumstances." While no one quite knows what a "fundamental breach" is, it is defined in Article 25 as a breach whose results "substantially deprive [the aggrieved party] of what he is entitled to expect under the contract," unless the results were both foreseen and unforeseeable. Caselaw illustrations include the machine represented as "good-as-new", which was rusty and did not operate when delivered, and goods which were ordered off the market after delivery. The concept clearly requires more than the common law "nonconformity."

As to "avoidance of the contract," which is comparable to "cancellation of the contract" at common law and under UCC § 2–106(4), CISG permits buyer to use this remedy only if there has been a "fundamental breach" by seller, regardless of when the breach occurs. Thus, CISG does not adopt the distinctions between "acceptance of the goods," rejection and "revocation of acceptance" contained in the UCC. Also note that "avoidance of the contract" under CISG is a different concept than "avoidance" under the UCC (§ 2–613). The drafting history of CISG indicates that "fundamental breach" seems to impose a stricter standard on buyer than the "substantial impairment" test of the UCC.

Given the uncertainties of the "fundamental breach" test, it will be very difficult for buyer, or buyer's attorney, to know how to react to any particular breach—and whether "avoidance" (cancellation) of the contract is permissible or not. Incorrect analysis could put buyer in the position of making a fundamental breach through its response. CISG Articles 47 and 49(1)(b) attempt to cure these uncertainties by offering buyer a method of formulating a supposedly strict standard for performance. Buyer may notify seller that performance is due by a stated new date (after the contract date for performance), and seller's failure to perform by the new date is a fundamental breach. (Derived from the German *Nachfrist* notice.) However, this *Nachfrist* provision seems to be available only for nondelivery by seller, not for delivery of nonconforming goods, and avoidance is available only if seller does not deliver during the additional period allowed by the notice.

How long an additional period must buyer give seller? Article 47 requires that it be "of reasonable length," but unless there is a custom on this issue buyer has no certainty that the period given in the *Nachfrist* notice is long enough, especially if long distances are involved. In one German decision, the buyer fixed an additional period of 11 days under CISG Art. 47(1), which was "too short to organize carriage by sea." The buyer's declaration of avoidance seven weeks after delivery of the non-conforming goods was approved by the court because seller had offered only a partial delivery of the conforming goods in the interim.

Even if buyer seeks to "avoid the contract" after a "fundamental breach" by seller, seller has a right to "cure" any defect in its performance before avoidance is declared under CISG Article 48(1). If seller's nonconforming tender is early, seller may cure by making a conforming tender up to the delivery date in the contract, whether the nonconformity would create a fundamental breach or not. The seller's right to cure survives buyer's declaration of "avoidance of the contract," because it will be very difficult to sustain a finding of fundamental beach where seller has made a timely offer of cure.

If seller's tender or offer of cure is made after the delivery date in the contract, seller still has a right to cure through late performance, but only if it can be done "without unreasonable delay," inconvenience or uncertainty of reimbursement expenses. Must performance offered as cure meet a strict "nonconformity" test, or is it still subject to the "fundamental breach" test? CISG has no provisions on this issue. However, it has been held that, if the seller's offer of cure is defective, the buyer may procure cure on its own. Thus, the entire thrust of these CISG provisions on buyer's remedies is to require cooperation between the parties in resolving disputes over timeliness of delivery and quality of goods.

For buyer to have any remedy for nonconforming goods tendered by seller, buyer must inspect the goods in "as short a [time] as is practicable" (Article 38); notify seller of the nonconformity "within a reasonable time" (Articles 39, 49); and permit seller to attempt to cure any nonconformity, if the cure does not cause "unreasonable delay" or "inconvenience" (Article 48).

There has been more litigation over the effectiveness of such notices than over any other single issue. Although early German cases required inspection and notification within a few days, more recent cases have established one month as a presumptive deadline. The nature of the goods is also important. One U.S. case indicated that, for a complicated piece of machinery, notice "within a matter of weeks" was not practicable. In one early case, where buyer notified seller that the goods (shoes) had "poor workmanship and improper fitting," the court held that the notice was defective because it was not specific enough. However, that case is now regarded as an aberration.

In addition, for a fundamental breach permitting avoidance, the buyer must determine and be able to prove that the result of the nonconformity is "substantially to deprive him of what he [was] entitled to expect under the contract" (Article 25). After the contract has been properly avoided, the buyer can still get its money back, even if it has already paid for the goods, under the restitutionary provisions of Article 81; but it must also return the goods "substantially in the condition which he received them" under Article 82(1).

In addition to rejection of the goods through "avoidance" (cancellation) of the contract, the aggrieved buyer has one other informal remedy which appears to give it the power of self-help. Under

CISG Article 50, the buyer who receives nonconforming goods "may reduce the price" it pays to
seller. There is no requirement of prior notice to
seller, and there is little guidance on how to determine the amount of the reduction, or what evidence
of diminution in value should be sent to seller. The
provision, therefore, seems best suited to deliveries
which are defective as to quantity, rather than
quality, although at least one author has suggested
that it is available only for defective quality. A
buyer attempting to use this self-help remedy *must*
allow seller to attempt to cure, if seller so requests.
This type of self-help provision is familiar at civil
law, and also appears in the UCC (§ 2–717), but
seems not widely used by common law attorneys. If
the buyer resells the defective goods, the resale
price is evidence of their value at the time of
delivery.

CISG Articles 74–78 provide the aggrieved buyer
with an action for damages, and damages can be
available when the contract has been "avoided"
(cancelled) and also even when seller has successfully cured defects in its performance. There is no
requirement that buyer prove seller was at "fault"
as a prerequisite to damage recovery. Nor is there a
requirement that buyer prove what caused the defect, only that the goods were defective. Both direct
and consequential damages are recoverable; and
expectancy, reliance and restitutionary interests are
all protected. Under *Delchi Carrier SpA v. Rotorex
Corp.*, 71 F.3d 1024 (2nd Cir.1995) a buyer who
planned to resell the goods and properly rejects

them does recover the profits from any lost sales, measured by the price less variable costs only–and the variable costs do not include fixed overhead costs. Consequential damages are limited in the familiar manner that losses may not be recovered, which were neither actually foreseen nor should have been foreseen. However, this may not be the same as the common law *Hadley v. Baxendale*, 156 Eng. Rep. 145 (Ex. Ct. 1854) test, because recovery is available if the loss suffered is foreseeable as a "possible consequence of the breach." The aggrieved buyer must take "reasonable measures" to mitigate its damages under Article 77. Incidental damages relating to interest are covered separately in Article 78.

Where similar goods may be purchased in the market, the most usual measures of the aggrieved buyer's damages are either (1) the difference between the price of "cover" (substitute goods actually purchased) and the contract price, or (2) the difference between the market price for the goods and the contract price. The Convention provides for the recovery of each of these measures of damages, but if buyer does purchase cover supposedly only the first measure is available. The Convention gives no guidance on how to determine whether any particular purchase by buyer is a purchase of cover, or is ordinary inventory build-up. Where the market price differential is used, the market price is to be measured at the time of "avoidance" (cancellation), unless buyer has "taken over" the goods before cancelling, in which case, the market price is measured at the time of "taking over."

In most civil law nations, the litigation loser pays part of the winner's attorney's fees, according to a statutory schedule. This is regarded as part of the damages necessary to make the aggrieved party whole. Such an award has been rejected by a U.S. court on the ground that rules relating to attorney's fees are procedural, not substantive. The decision has been criticized.

Note that the seller of goods may be in a significantly better position under CISG than under the UCC, if the buyer claims a relatively minor fault in the goods. Although seller has a right to cure any defects under either statute, this right under the UCC has either time limitations or expectation requirements not stated in CISG. Rejection merely because of a tender which is not "perfect" seems to be available under the UCC, but is definitely not available under CISG. Thus, the seller is less likely to find the goods rejected for an asserted minor non-conformity, and stranded an ocean or continent away, without any effective legal remedy.

BUYER'S OBLIGATIONS

Buyer has two primary obligations in a sale contract under Article 53: to pay the price, and to take delivery of the goods. The former duty is the more important of the two. In addition, there are several derivative preliminary duties called "enabling steps."

Unless the sale contract expressly grants credit to buyer, the sale is a cash sale, and payment and delivery are concurrent conditions. Further, under Article 58(1), payment is due when seller places the goods, or their documents of title, "at buyer's disposal according to the contract." If the sales contract involves carriage of the goods, seller may ship the goods under negotiable documents of title and demand payment against those documents under Article 58(2), even though no particular method of payment was actually agreed upon by the parties. In such circumstances, buyer still has a right of inspection before payment. If, however, buyer has expressly agreed to "pay against documents" (such as through the use of CFR or CIF term), the buyer has agreed to pay upon tender of the documents, regardless of whether the goods have yet arrived, and without inspection of the goods. Article 58(3).

If buyer is to pay against "handing over" of the documents, or handing over the goods, the place of "handing over" is the place of payment. Otherwise, the place of seller's business is the place of payment, unless the contract provides otherwise. Article 57. Such a provision requires buyer to "export" the funds to seller, which is a critical issue when buyer is from a country with a "soft" currency, or with other restrictions on the transfer of funds. In addition buyer has an obligation under Article 54 to cooperate and take all necessary steps to enable payment to be made, including whatever formalities may be imposed by buyer's country to obtain administrative authorization to make a payment abroad. Failure to take such steps may create a breach by buyer even before payment is due.

The buyer's second obligation, to take delivery, also poses duties of cooperation. It includes a duty to make the expected preparations to permit seller to make delivery and may include such acts as providing for containers, transportation, unloading and import licenses. Article 60.

RISK OF LOSS

The basic rule, under CISG and domestic law, is that buyer bears the risk of loss to the goods during their transportation by a carrier, unless the contract provides otherwise. Article 67. The contract will often contain a term which expressly allocates the risk of loss, such as "FOB" or "CIF," and such terms supersede the CISG provisions. If there is no such delivery term, under CISG the risk in a shipment contract passes to buyer when the goods are "handed over" by the seller to the first carrier. They need not be on board the means of transportation, or even pass a ship's rail—any receipt by a carrier will do. Further, they need not be "handed over" to an ocean-going or international carrier—possession by the local trucker who will haul them to the port is sufficient. However, if the seller uses its own vehicle to transport the goods, seller bears the risk until the goods are handed over to an independent carrier, or to buyer.

Where the contract requires that the seller deliver the goods to buyer at buyer's location, or that seller provide part of the transportation and then "hand the goods over to a carrier at a particular place," seller bears the risk of loss to that location or particular place. Thus, in a contract between a Buffalo, N.Y., seller and Beijing, China, buyer: (1) in a shipment contract (FCA Buffalo), the risk would pass to buyer when the goods were delivered to the first carrier in Buffalo; (2) in a destination contract (DES Beijing), the seller would bear the risk during transit, and the risk would not pass to buyer until the goods were delivered in Beijing; and (3) in a transshipment contract (FAS New York City), the seller would bear the risk from Buffalo to "along side" a ship in New York harbor, and buyer would bear the risk thereafter.

If the goods are not to be transported by a carrier (e.g., when buyer or an agent are close to seller and will pick up the goods), the risk passes to buyer when he picks them up or, if he is late in doing so, when the goods are "at his disposal" and his delay in picking them up causes a breach of contract. Article 69. The goods cannot, however, be "at his disposal" until they have first been identified to the contract.

In most situations, title and risk are treated separately. Thus, manipulation of title through the use of documents of title, such as negotiable bills of lading, is irrelevant and has no effect on the point of transfer of risk of loss. However, under Article 68, if the goods are already in transit when sold, the risk passes when the contract is "concluded." This rule reflects a use of "title" concepts in risk allocation, even though it may be practically impossible to determine whether damage to goods in a ship's cargo hold occurred before or after a sale contract was signed.

Just as title and risk are treated separately, so also breach and risk are treated separately. If seller is in breach of contract when the goods are shipped, these basic risk of loss rules are not changed, which is contrary to the position of UCC § 2–510. Thus, a breach by seller, whether it is a "fundamental beach" under Article 25 or not, is irrelevant to determine risk allocation or the point when the risk of loss passes to buyer. However, if seller does commit a fundamental breach in shipment contract, further damage to the goods during transit will not deprive buyer of its right to avoid the contract under CISG Article 79. Likewise, a nonfundamental breach in a shipment contract, plus damage in transit, will not create a right for buyer to avoid the contract.

REMEDIES FOR BUYER'S BREACH

The preferred remedy for an aggrieved seller, if buyer should breach, is a cause of action for the price, which is seller's functional equivalent of an action for specific performance. A cause of action for damages, but not the price, is distinctly secondary. In addition, seller may wish to reclaim the goods if they are delivered or obtain some protection for them if the contract is "avoided" and they are rejected.

As to seller's recovery of the price, CISG Article 62 gives the seller an unqualified right to require buyer to pay the price, but no CISG article expressly states that the seller has a cause of action for payment of the price. Of course, there are implicit conditions on this right, first, that seller has itself performed to the extent required by the terms of the contract (Article 30) and, second, that payment of the price is due (Article 58). However, if seller has an action for the price, it may be an action "for specific performance" under Article 28. If it is an action for specific performance, then an aggrieved seller would have to meet the requirements of UCC § 2–709, as well as CISG Article 62, before a United States court would order buyer to pay the price rather than damages. However, if an action for the price does not require the entry of a "judgment for specific performance," then CISG Article 28 would seem to be inapplicable; and seller need meet only the requisites of CISG Article 62. On the issue of the applicability of Article 28, Professors Honnold and Farnsworth publicly disagree, so the question would seem to be open at this time.

If an unpaid seller is unable (for any reason) to obtain the price, can he get his goods back from the defaulting buyer, *after* delivery, by "avoiding" the contract and seeking to reclaim them? Such reclamation is difficult at common law (see, e.g., UCC §§ 2–507 and 2–702). The Convention, however, seems to allow such reclamation, because Article 64, which gives seller the power to declare the contract "avoided," does not distinguish between pre-and post-delivery situations and Article 81 requires "restitution ... of whatever the first party has supplied" after avoidance. This analysis, however, is available only so long as third parties (buyer's creditors and trustees in bankruptcy) are not involved, for CISG does not affect title to the goods and third party rights (Article 4), and does not require a court to order "specific performance" which it would not order under its own law. (Article 28).

As to damages, CISG Articles 74–78 provide the unpaid seller (as well as an aggrieved buyer) with an action for damages and the general principles are the same as in the discussion of buyer's remedies for seller's breach. The most usual measures of an unpaid seller's damages are either (1) the difference between the contract price and the resale price if the goods were actually resold or (2) the difference between the contract price and the market price for the goods at the time of avoidance of the contract. The Convention provides for recovery of each of these measures of damages, but if seller resells the goods only the first measure is available.

The major practical problem concerning unpaid sellers is that the "lost volume" seller is not adequately protected by the above two measures of damages. However, the CISG provisions which establish these measures state that they are not exclusive, and the CISG cases have used Article 74 to include recovery of lost profits as "direct" damages. Thus, the courts have granted full protection to the lost volume seller by awarding "lost profits" damages, and measuring them by subtracting from the contract price only those variable costs saved by the termination of the sale.

A Buyer who rejected goods after they have been received must take "reasonable" steps to preserve them (Article 85), which may include depositing the goods in a warehouse at seller's expense. Article 87. If seller has no agent in buyer's location, a buyer who rejects goods which have been "placed at his disposal at their destination" must take possession of them "on behalf of the seller" if this can be done without payment of the price (i.e., through paying for a negotiable bill of lading) and without "unreasonable inconvenience" or expense. After such a taking of possession on behalf of seller, buyer must again take "reasonable" steps to preserve them. If the goods are perishable, a rejecting buyer in possession may have to try to sell them and remit any proceeds to seller, less buyer's expenses of preserving and selling them. CISG does not, however, contain any provisions which require a buyer in possession who has rejected the seller's tender to follow seller's instructions, such as to resell on seller's behalf, whether seemingly reasonable or not.

THE UNIDROIT PRINCIPLES OF INTERNATIONAL COMMERCIAL CONTRACTS

The UNIDROIT Principles for International Commercial Contracts represent a different approach to unification and harmonization of international commercial law. CISG and its comparable conventions in other fields attempt to regulate the law of specific subjects in international transactions, and only by adopting rules which can gain "concensus" approval of national governments. Thus, this approach is much like that of the National Conference of Commissioners on Uniform State Laws (the drafters of the UCC). On the other hand, UNIDROIT (The International Institute for the Unification of Private Law in Rome) has proposed something quite different, which is the equivalent of a "Restatement of Contracts" for international commercial contracts. It is not limited as to types of such contracts and will not be proposed for ratification as a convention, and so does not need approval of any national government.

In transactions to which CISG is applicable, the courts will usually apply the rules of CISG. However, where CISG is silent or ambiguous, courts are instructed by CISG Art. 7(2) to consult the "general principles" of international commercial law, and the UNIDROIT Principles are one source of such general principles. In 2007, there were 150 decisionsreferencing the Principles. In addition, it is expected that arbitrators may use the Principles in the absence of any choice of law by the parties, or that the parties themselves may expressly choose the Principles as the law to govern their contract. Finally, the drafters hoped that the Principles might serve as a model law, especially for LDCs. Note that, in all these uses, the effectiveness of UNIDROIT's Principles depend upon their persuasive value.

To promote maximization of their persuasive value, UNIDROIT assembled individual experts and requested that they draft the Principles to reflect current trade practices. These practices could be reflected either in conventions, such as CISG, or in private contracts, such as general conditions or (international) standard form contracts in use by industry. Where there was no existing common trade practice, the drafters were instructed to formulate solutions which are best adapted to international commercial transactions, whether they were in fact part of any existing legal regime or not. Thus, they do not necessarily represent the national rule of a majority of states.

The principles were drafted over a period of 20 years, and were adopted by UNIDROIT's Governing Council in May, 1994. They are more comprehensive than CISG. For example, they include new provisions on how a contract may be formed, on confirmation of documents, on contracts with open term clauses, on negotiations in bad faith, on the duty of confidentiality, on merger clauses, on use of standard forms, and on the battle of the forms. There are also new concepts proposed, such as "gross disparity" as an element of the analysis of validity and "hardship" as an element of excuse of performance. There are provisions on payment, not only by "cheque," but also by funds transfers and other methods and on the currency to be paid in the absence of specification.

This Nutshell cannot provide a detailed, comprehensive description of the Principles, but it will provide three examples as illustrations of their approach to three known problems: the battle of the forms, the unilateral use of standard form contracts, and excuse of performance by changed circumstances.

In the battle of the forms, Art. 2.22 of the Principle eschews the "mirror-image" and the "last-shot" traditional rules. Instead of the mirror image rule, it provides that a contract is concluded where the parties reach an agreement on all the terms of the contract, except for those incorporated in "standard terms." There will be a problem in identifying what terms are standard terms in the modern world of computer-generated contract clauses inserted into electronic communications between the parties, but this provision will at least make sense of the transaction involving exchanges of printed forms. It also attempts to deal with the standard use of clauses which insist that no agreement is formed unless that form's terms are accepted ("my way or the highway" clauses). If such a clause is contained in the standard terms, it is ineffective, but its use in "non-standard terms" would prevent the formation of the contract. Thus, the rationale of the Principles' provision is that, where the parties agree on terms which they are willing to raise individually and negotiate, they should be bound to a contract.

What are the terms of that contract? Instead of adopting the traditional "last shot" doctrine, or even the modified "first shot" doctrine of the UCC, the Principles adopt the "knock-out" rule. The terms of the contract include (1) the "non-standard" terms, which presumably have all been expressly agreed upon by the parties; (2) those standard terms which are "common in substance," unless objected to; and (3) the default rules of the Principles. Thus, the rationale of the Principles is that, where the parties agree on terms which they are willing to raise individually and negotiate, those agreed terms are the terms of the contract. The identification of which terms are "standard terms" in an electronic communication environment will become an increasingly more difficult and important issue.

Where there is use of a standard form by only one party, there is no "battle" of forms, but such forms may be one-sided. Under Art. 2.20 of the Principles, a standard term is not "effective" if the "other party could not reasonably have expected it." A term is a standard term if it was prepared in advance for general and repeated use. Thus, the Principles relates such terms to the expectations of the non-drafting, and presumably non-reading, party, adopting as a norm the prevalent conduct today that standard terms are rarely read.

However, the Comments to the Principles indicate that the non-drafting, non-reading party is bound to many, but not all, terms which are standard in an industry. One example in the Comments of a "surprising" term would be a standard term in a travel agency tour package contract that the agency is not liable for the hotel accommodations, but is merely an agent of the hotelkeeper; after it had advertised that it was selling a complete tour package. Other examples include choice of forum clauses which choose courts or arbitral tribunals which are located outside the jurisdiction of the immediate parties to the contract. Thus, unexpected terms can be surprising *either* because of their content *or* their manner of presentation. This resembles the unconscionability doctrine, but there is less emphasis on finding both "harsh terms" and an "unfair surprise" in the contracting process.

The Principles provide two distinctly different paths for asserting excuse from performance by changed circumstances. One is labelled "Force Majeure" and the other is labelled "Hardship." These two paths are not the equivalent of the common law doctrines of impossibility and impracticability. Instead, the concepts in the Principles have civil law foundations.

The *force majeure* provisions in Art. 7.1.7 are similar to those in CISG Art. 79, and include the use of the concept "impediment." The non-performance must be due to an impediment which the nonperforming party "could not control" and "could not reasonably be expected to have taken . . . into account." Thus, complete impossibility seems to be required for excuse under these provisions, and mere impracticability is not sufficient. The nonperforming party must give notice "of the impediment", and is liable for a failure to notify, but the Principles do not specify when the notice must be given.

The "hardship" provisions in Arts. 6.2, however, are completely different from any concepts in CISG or in the common law. Hardship occurs when "events fundamentally alter" the cost or value of a promised performance. Illustrations include a tenfold increase in prices of products to be supplied or a 99% decline in the currency of payment, but there may be a consensus that a 50% change is sufficient to trigger the application of the doctrine. This would be in line with many of the "price unconscionability" cases in the U.S.

However, under the Principles, "hardship" does not by itself excuse performance. Instead, under Art. 6.2.3, the effect of hardship is to compel renegotiation of the contract, if the disadvantaged party so requests. If the attempt to renegotiate fails, either party may seek intervention by "the court." Which courts would have such jurisdiction is left unstated. Also, whether intervention by an arbitral tribunal is available as an alternative is not expressly stated. A court which finds the hardship criteria to be satisfied can "adapt" the contract so as to restore its "equilibrium," or may even terminate the contract.

COMMERCIAL TERMS

Where the goods are to be carried from one location to another as part of the sale transaction, the parties will often adopt a commercial term to state the delivery obligation of the seller. Such terms include F.O.B. (Free on Board), F.A.S. (Free

Alongside) and C.I.F. (Cost, Insurance and Freight). These terms are defined in the UCC (§§ 2–319, 2–320), but the UCC definitions are seldom used intentionally in international trade. In fact the UCC definitions are becoming obsolescent because the statutory terms do not include the new terminology associated with air freight, containerization, or multi-modal transportation practices. Thus, in the proposed amendments to UCC Article 2, adopted by the Uniform Commissioners, these statutory definitions of commercial terms are deleted. However, to date, no state has enacted those proposed amendments.

In international commerce the dominant source of definitions for commercial delivery terms is "Incoterms," published by the International Chamber of Commerce (I.C.C.) and last revised by them in 2000. Incoterms is an acronym for International Commercial Terms, and provides rules for determining the obligations of both seller and buyer when different commercial terms (like F.O.B. or C.I.F.) are used. They state what acts seller must do to deliver, what acts buyer must do to accommodate delivery, what costs each party must bear, and at what point in the delivery process the risk of loss passes from seller to buyer. Each of these obligations may be different for different commercial terms. Thus, the obligations, costs, and risks of seller and buyer are different under F.O.B. than they are under C.I.F.

There are other sources of such definitions, in addition to the UCC and Incoterms, such as the American Revised Foreign Trade Definitions (1941).

It has been widely used in Pacific Ocean trade, but may be replaced by the more recently revised Incoterms.

Since the I.C.C. is a non-governmental entity, Incoterms is neither a national legislation nor an international treaty. Thus, it cannot be "the governing law" of any contract. Instead, it is a written form of custom and usage in the trade, which can be, and often is, expressly incorporated by a party or the parties to an international contract for the sale of goods. Alternatively, if it is not expressly incorporated in the contract, Incoterms can also be made an implicit term of the contract as part of international custom. Courts in the U.S., France and Germany have done so, describing Incoterms as a widely-observed usage for commercial terms. This description has allowed Incoterms to qualify under CISG Article 9(2) as a "usage . . . which in international trade is widely known to, and regularly observed by, parties to" international sales contracts, even if the usage is not global.

Although the UCC has definitions for some commercial terms (e.g., F.O.B., F.A.S., C.I.F.), these definitions are expressly subject to "agreement otherwise." Thus, an express reference to Incoterms will supercede the UCC provisions, and United States courts have so held. Such incorporation by express reference is often made in American international sales contracts, especially in Atlantic Ocean trade. If there is no express term, and the UCC is the governing law rather than CISG, Incoterms can still be applicable as a "usage of trade" under UCC § 1–205(2). The UCC criteria for such a usage is "a practice.... having such regularity of observance ... as to justify an expectation that it will be observed with respect to the transaction in question." A usage need not be "universal" nor "ancient," just "currently observed by the great majority of decent dealers."

Incoterms gives the parties a menu of thirteen different commercial terms to describe the delivery obligations of the seller and the reciprocal obligations of the buyer to accommodate delivery. They include:

1) EXW (Ex Works)

2) FCA (Free Carrier)

3) FAS (Free Alongside Ship)

4) FOB (Free On Board)

5) CFR (Cost and Freight)

6) CIF (Cost, Insurance and Freight)

7) CPT (Carriage Paid To)

8) CIP (Carriage and Insurance Paid To)

9) DAF (Delivered at Frontier)

10) DES (Delivered Ex Ship)

11) DEQ (Delivered Ex Quay)

12) DDU (Delivered Duty Unpaid)

13) DDP (Delivered Duty Paid)

There are several types of divisions which one may make of these thirteen different terms. One is a division between the one term which does not assume that a carrier will be involved (EXW), and all the twelve other terms. A second division is between those six terms which require the involvement of water-borne transportation (FAS, FOB, CFR, CIF, DES and DEQ) and those six other terms which are applicable to any mode of transportation, including multi-modal transportation (FCA, CPT, CIP, DAF, DDU, and DDP). The UCC has none of the latter six terms, although the types of transactions they are designed for arise routinely, and can be handled under the UCC designations "F.O.B. place of shipment," "C. & F.", "C.I.F.," and "F.O.B. named place of destination."

The twelve terms requiring transportation can also be divided into "shipment contract" terms (FCA, FAS, FOB, CFR, CIF, CPT, and CIP) and "destination contract" terms (DAF, DES, DEQ, DDU, and DDP.). The UCC and CISG both use this terminology. CISG Art. 31. The underlying concept is that, in shipment contracts seller puts the goods in the hands of a carrier and arranges for their transportation, but transportation is at buyer's risk and expense. (UCC § 2–504). On the other hand, in destination contracts seller is responsible to put the goods in the hands of the carrier, arrange their transportation, and bear the cost and risk of transportation. Unfortunately, many aspects of transportation usages have changed since 1952, and the UCC concepts do not always fit the practices now described in Incoterms.

The I.C.C. suggests that these thirteen commercial terms be divided into four principal categories, one for each of the different first letters of the constituent terms, E, F, C and D. The "E" term (EXW) is where the goods are made available to buyer, but use of a carrier is not expressly required. All other terms require the use of a carrier. The "F" terms (FCA, FAS, FOB) require seller only to assume the risks and costs to deliver the goods to a carrier, and to a carrier nominated by the buyer. The "C" terms require seller to assume the risks and costs to deliver the goods to a carrier, arrange and pay for the "main transportation" (and sometimes insurance), but without assuming additional risks due to post-shipment events. Thus, under "C" terms, seller bears risks until one point in the transportation (delivery to a carrier), but pays costs to a different point in the transportation (the agreed destination). The "D" terms (DAF, DES, DEQ, DDU and DDP) require the seller to deliver the goods to a carrier, arrange for their transportation, and assume the risks and costs until the arrival of the goods at an agreed country of destination.

Incoterms are periodically revised, lately about once every ten years. The last revision was in 2000 and is set forth in I.C.C. Publication No. 560. In the latest revision, the I.C.C. included references to electronic messages and to new types of transport documents, such as air waybills, railway and road consignment notes, and "multimodal transport documents." The I.C.C. explained that these changes were needed because of "the increasing use of electronic data interchange (EDI)" and "changed transportation techniques," including "containers, multi-modal transport and roll on-roll off traffic."

The following is a brief discussion of each of the Incoterms commercial terms.

Under the Incoterms Ex Works (EXW) commercial term (including Ex Factory and Ex Warehouse), the seller needs only to "tender" the goods to the buyer by placing them at buyer's disposal at a named place of delivery. Thus, seller has no obligation to deliver the goods to a carrier or to load the goods on any vehicle. Seller must also notify buyer when and where the goods will be tendered, but has no obligation to arrange for transportation or insurance. The risk of loss transfers to buyer at the time the goods are placed at its disposal. Seller will normally provide a commercial invoice or its equivalent electronic message, but has no obligation to obtain a document of title or an export license. The Incoterms definition has no effect upon either payment or inspection obligations under the contract, except to require buyer to pay for pre-shipment inspection. The Incoterms risk of loss provision is contrary to the default rules of both the UCC (§ 2–509) and CISG (Art. 69), which delay passing the risk until buyer's receipt of the goods, both because seller is more likely to have insurance and because seller has a greater ability to protect the goods.

Under the Incoterms Free Carrier (FCA) commercial term, the seller is obligated to deliver the goods into the custody of a carrier, usually the first carrier in a multi-modal transportation scheme. The Incoterms definition of "carrier" includes freight forwarders. Seller has no obligation to pay for transportation costs or insurance. Usually the carrier will be named by, and arranged by, the buyer. However, seller "may" arrange transportation at buyer's expense if requested by the buyer, or if it is "commercial practice" for seller to do so. But, even under such circumstances, seller may refuse to make such arrangements as long as it so notifies buyer. Even if seller does arrange transportation, it has no obligation to arrange for insurance coverage during transportation, and need only notify buyer "that the goods *have been* delivered into the custody of the carrier" (emphasis added). The risk of loss transfers to buyer upon delivery to the carrier, but buyer may not receive notice until after that time. The seller must provide a commercial invoice or its equivalent electronic message, any necessary export license, and usually a transport document that will allow buyer to take delivery—or an equivalent electronic data interchange message. The Incoterms definition has no provisions on either payment or post-shipment inspection terms under the contract.

This FCA term is the Incoterms commercial term which is most comparable to the UCC's "F.O.B. place of shipment" term under § 2–319(1)(a). However, there are two levels of confusion. One is that Incoterms has an "FOB" term which is different, and the UCC "F.O.B." term is more likely to be compared with the Incoterms "FOB" term. The other is that the obligations under FCA and the UCC "F.O.B. place of shipment" term are, in fact, different. The norm under the UCC's "F.O.B." is for seller to arrange transportation, while seller need do so under FCA only in special circumstances. (UCC §§ 2–319, 2–504.) Further, if seller does ship, under UCC § 2–504 seller usually must also arrange insurance coverage, unless instructed otherwise by buyer. Under Incoterms FCA, seller does not seem ever to have any obligation to arrange for insurance coverage. Traditionally, under both the 1980 version of Incoterms FAS and the UCC "F.O.B. place of shipment" term, there is no implied special payment or inspection terms, no implied requirement of payment against documents or payment before inspection. This would also seem to be a preferable interpretation of the current Incoterms FCA term.

Under the Incoterms Free Alongside Ship (FAS) commercial term, the seller is obligated to deliver the goods alongside a ship arranged for and named by the buyer at a named port of shipment. Thus, it is appropriate only for water-borne transportation, and seller must bear the costs and risks of inland transportation to the named port of shipment. Seller has no obligation to arrange transportation or insurance for the "main" (or water-borne) part of the carriage, but does have a duty to notify buyer "that the goods have been delivered alongside the ship." The risk of loss will transfer to the buyer also at the time the goods are delivered alongside the ship. Seller must provide a commercial invoice and usually a transport document that will allow buyer to take delivery, or the electronic equivalent of either. But seller has no obligation to provide an export license, only an obligation to render assistance to buyer to obtain one.

The Incoterms definition has no provisions on either payment or post-shipment inspection terms under the contract. Under the UCC (§ 2–319), the term "F.A.S. vessel" requires the buyer to pay against a tender of documents, such as a negotiable bill of lading, before the goods arrive at their destination and before buyer has any post-shipment opportunity to inspect the goods. UCC § 2–319(4). Otherwise, the UCC "F.A.S." term is similar to the Incoterms "FAS" term, including obligating the seller only to deliver the goods alongside a named vessel and not obligating the seller to arrange transportation to a final destination. The Incoterms FAS is not intended to require payment against documents, to restrict inspection before payment, or to be used with negotiable bills of lading.

Under the Incoterms Free on Board (FOB) commercial term, the seller is obligated to deliver the goods on board a ship arranged for and named by the buyer at a named port of shipment. Thus, this term is also appropriate only for water-borne transportation, and seller must bear the costs and risks of inland transportation to the named port of shipment, and also of loading the goods on the ship (until "they have passed the ship's rail"). Seller has no obligation to arrange transportation or insurance, but does have a duty to notify buyer "that the goods have been delivered on board" the ship. The risk of loss will transfer to the buyer also at the time the goods have "passed the ship's rail." The seller must provide a commercial invoice, or its equivalent electronic message, any necessary export license, and usually a transport document that will allow buyer to take delivery—or an equivalent electronic data interchange message.

The Incoterms definition has no provisions on either payment or post-shipment inspection terms under the contract. The UCC does define "F.O.B.," but it is not a term requiring water-borne transportation. Thus, as has been discussed above, the UCC "F.O.B." is more closely linked to the Incoterms FCA term. But the UCC also has a term "F.O.B. vessel," which does relate only to water-borne transportation, and therefore is most closely linked to the Incoterms FOB term. Under the UCC, the term "F.O.B. vessel" requires the buyer to pay against a tender of documents, such as a negotiable bill of lading, before the goods arrive at their destination and before buyer has any post-shipment opportunity to inspect the goods. UCC § 2–319(4). Otherwise, the UCC "F.O.B. vessel" term is similar to the Incoterms "FOB" term, including obligating the seller only to deliver the goods to a named ship's rail and not obligating the seller to arrange transportation to a final destination. The Incoterms FOB is not intended to require payment against documents or to restrict inspection before payment, unless such a term is expressly added or there is a known custom in a particular trade. In addition, it is more likely that negotiable bills of lading are not intended to be used with Incoterms FOB shipments, unless the parties specify "payment against documents" in the sale contract.

Under the Incoterms Cost, Insurance and Freight (CIF) commercial term, the seller is obligated to arrange for both transportation and insurance to a named destination port and then to deliver the goods on board the ship arranged for by the seller. Thus, the term is appropriate only for water-borne transportation. Seller must arrange the transportation, and pay the freight costs to the *destination port*, but has completed its delivery obligations when the goods have "passed the ship's rail" at the *port of shipment*. Seller must arrange and pay for insurance during transportation to the *port of destination*, but the risk of loss transfers to the buyer at the time the goods pass the ship's rail at the *port of shipment*. Seller must notify buyer "that the goods have been delivered on board" the ship to enable buyer to receive the goods. Seller must provide a commercial invoice, or its equivalent electronic message, any necessary export license, and "the usual transport documents" for the destination port.

The Incoterms definition has no provisions on either payment or post-shipment inspection terms under the contract. However, it does require that the transportation document "must ... enable the buyer to sell the goods in transit by the transfer of the document to a subsequent buyer ... or by notification to the carrier," unless otherwise agreed. As is explained below in the materials on bills of lading, the traditional manner of enabling buyer to do this, in either the "payment against documents" transaction or the letter of credit transaction, is for seller to obtain a negotiable bill of lading from the carrier and to tender that negotiable document to buyer through a series of banks. The banks allow buyer to obtain possession of the document (and control of the goods) only after buyer pays for the goods. Thus, buyer "pays against documents," while the goods are at sea, and pays for them before any post-shipment inspection of the goods is possible.

The UCC also has a definition of "C.I.F." which requires the buyer to "make payment against tender of the required documents." UCC § 2–320(4). The UCC "C.I.F." term is otherwise similar to Incoterms CIF, in that it requires seller to deliver to carrier at the port of shipment and bear the risk of loss only to that port, but to pay freight costs and insurance to the port of destination.

The Incoterms Cost and Freight (CFR) commercial term is similar to the CIF term, except that seller has no obligations with respect to either arranging or paying for insurance coverage of the goods during transportation. Under the CFR term, the seller is obligated to arrange for transportation to a named destination point and then to deliver the goods on board the ship arranged for by the seller. Thus, the term is appropriate only for water-borne transportation. Seller must arrange the transportation and pay the freight costs to the *destination port*, but has completed its delivery obligations when the goods have "passed the ship's rail" at the *port of shipment*. Seller has no express obligation to arrange or pay for insurance on the goods during transportation, and the risk of loss transfers to the buyer at the time the goods pass the ship's rail at the *port of shipment*. Seller must notify buyer "that the goods *have been delivered* on board" the ship (emphasis added) to enable buyer to receive the goods. Seller must provide a commercial invoice, or its equivalent electronic message, any necessary export license, and "the usual transport document" for the destination port. As with CIF, the Incoterms CFR definition has no provisions on either payment or post-shipment inspection terms under the contract. However, it does require that the transport document "must ... enable the buyer to sell the goods in transit by the transfer of the document to a subsequent buyer," which has traditionally meant use of a negotiable bill of lading and payment against documents. Both the UCC and prior versions of Incoterms regarded this term as requiring payment against documents while the goods were still at sea, thus restricting port-shipment inspection of the goods before payment. These provisions should still be regarded as the norm under Incoterms CFR.

The Incoterms Carriage and Insurance Paid To (CIP) and Carriage Paid To (CPT) commercial terms are similar to its CIF and CFR terms, except that they may be used for any type of transportation, including multimodal transportation, and not just for waterborne transportation. Under the CIP term, seller is obligated to arrange and pay for both transportation and insurance to a named *destina-*

tion place. However, Seller completes its delivery obligations, and the risk of loss passes to the buyer, upon delivery to the first carrier at the place of *shipment*. Thus, the term is appropriate for multi-modal transportation. The CPT commercial term is similar, except that seller has no duty to arrange or pay for insurance coverage of the goods during transportation.

Under both CIP and CPT, seller must notify buyer "that the goods have been delivered" to the first carrier, and also give any other notice required to enable buyer "to take the goods." Under both, seller must also provide a commercial invoice, or its equivalent electronic message, any necessary export license, and "the usual transport document." A list of acceptable transport documents is given, and there is no requirement that the document enable buyer to sell the goods in transit. There are no payment or post-shipment inspection provisions in the Incoterms definitions, and the UCC does not define these terms. Further, the Introduction to Incoterms contrasts CIP and CPT with CIF and CFR, indicating that there is no requirement to provide a negotiable bill of lading with CIP or CPT terms. Thus, unless the parties expressly agree to a "payment against documents" term, it is more likely that the CIP or CPT commercial terms are not intended to require payment against documents or to restrict inspection before payment.

Incoterms provides five different commercial terms for "destination" or "arrival" contracts. Two of them, Delivered Ex Ship (DES) and Delivered Ex

Quay (DEQ) should only be used for waterborne transportation. The other three, Delivered At Frontier (DAF), Delivered Duty Unpaid (DDU) and Delivered Duty Paid (DDP), can all be used with any type of transportation, including multimodal transport. In all of them, seller is required to arrange transportation, pay the freight costs and bear the risk of loss to a named destination point. Although these definitions have no provisions on insurance during transportation, since seller bears the risk of loss during that event, seller must either arrange and pay for insurance or act as a self-insuror during transportation. There are also no provisions on payment or post-shipment inspection, but there is no requirement for use of a negotiable bill of lading, and delivery occurs only after arrival of the goods. Thus, there is no reason to imply a "payment against documents" requirement if none is expressly stated. On the other hand, the parties are free to agree expressly on both a destination commercial term and a payment against documents term.

Under the Incoterms DES commercial term, delivery occurs and the risk of loss passes when the goods are placed at buyer's disposal on board ship at the named destination port. To be "at buyer's disposal", the goods must be placed (at seller's risk and expense) so that it can be removed by "appropriate" unloading equipment. However, the goods need not be cleared for importation by customs officials; that is buyer's obligation. [Under the UCC, the term "ex ship" requires seller also to unload the goods.] Under the DEQ commercial term, the goods must be placed at buyer's disposal on the quay or wharf at the named destination port. However, the parties who use a DEQ term should further specify either "Duty Paid" or "Duty Unpaid," because both DEQ (Duty Paid) and DEQ (Duty Unpaid) terms are in use. If "Duty Paid" is specified, or there is no specification, seller must "pay the costs of customs formalities ... duties, taxes ... payable upon ... importation of the goods, unless otherwise agreed."

In both DES and DEQ shipments, seller must notify buyer of the estimated time of arrival of a named vessel at a named destination port. Also, in both DES and DEQ shipments, seller must provide buyer with a commercial invoice or the equivalent electronic message, "a delivery order and/or the usual transport document", and an export license. For DEQ shipments, seller must also provide an import license, unless otherwise agreed.

Under the Incoterms DAF commercial term, which is most appropriately used with rail or road transportation, delivery occurs and the risk of loss passes when the goods are placed at buyer's disposal at a named place at the frontier, but before the customs frontier of the importing country. Under the DDU commercial term, delivery occurs and the risk of loss passes when the goods are placed at buyer's disposal at "the agreed point at the named point of destination" in the country of importation. However, seller has no obligation to pay import duties or charges. Under the Incoterms DDP commercial term, delivery occurs and the risk of loss passes when the goods are placed at buyer's disposal at the named place in the country of destination, cleared for importation into that country. Seller must pay all import duties and charges and complete customs formalities at its risk and expense. The only UCC destination term is "F.O.B. destination," § 2–319(1)(b), which seems similar to "DDU," but without much of the detail and precision.

In each of these terms DAF, DDU and DDP, seller must notify buyer of the dispatch of the goods and give any other notice necessary for buyer "to take the goods." In each type of shipment, seller must provide a commercial invoice or its equivalent electronic message. In a DAF shipment, seller must also provide "the usual document or other evidence of the delivery" and an export license. In a DDU shipment, seller must also provide a "delivery order and/or the usual transport document" and an export license. In a DDP shipment, seller must provide the delivery order or transport document and both an export license and an import license.

INTERNATIONAL ELECTRONIC COMMERCE

The recent phenomenal growth of E Commerce caught the legal regimes of the world unprepared. None was ready for the legal problems caused by the new forms of contract-making, payment, performance and information exchange. They have done their best to adapt traditional rules to new transaction patterns, but each legal regime has adapted in a different manner. Thus, there is little consistency in the rules applicable to E Commerce transactions which cross national borders.

Such a lack of consistency is not new, but the problems are magnified by another aspect of E Commerce. The parties often do not know when an E Commerce transaction is in fact across national boundaries. A website with a ".com" address may literally be located anywhere in the world. Thus, the website address of each party, which may be the only information each has of the other, may not reveal the transborder nature of the transaction.

The new contracts issues created by E Commerce include how to satisfy requirements for agreements in writing and signatures, authentication and attribution without personal contact, security and integrity of electronic messages, and express and implied terms and conditions for both commercial and consumer contracts. It also raises jurisdiction issues, ranging from choice of law to presence in a jurisdiction for purposes of being sued in a civil action to presence in a jurisdiction for purposes of regulation by public authorities. The public authorities not only wish to prevent fraud and deception by E Merchants, but also to regulate privacy, intellectual property and taxation issues, among others. In all these areas, there are very few statutory rules or decided cases; and, where there are, the existing rules and approaches to E Commerce differ from one legal regime to another.

Thus, there is a perceived need, not only for statutory rules to facilitate E Commerce, but for such rules to be similar across national borders, since it is not usually clear where the parties are located. Promoting similar rules could be accomplished by either an international multilateral treaty or proposed model legislation. Because the practices of E Commerce are still developing, UNCITRAL (the organization which developed CISG) has also developed a Model Law on Electronic Commerce, which it adopted in 1996. The Model Law is a minimalist approach to legislation, seeking to facilitate E Commerce transactions and not to regulate them. This Model Law is now available to all legal regimes for enactment to provide guidance for E Merchants and their customers.

In its general provisions, the UNCITRAL Model Law provides equality of treatment for paper documents and electronic messages. It provides that "data messages" are not to be denied legal effect because they are electronic, and that any "writing" requirement is satisfied by a data message which is accessible for subsequent reference. Legal requirements for a "signature" are met by a data message if there is a method which is "reasonable for the circumstances" to identify both the identity of the person sending the message and that person's approval of the message. An electronic data message is allowed to satisfy evidentiary requirements, and an evidentiary requirement for "an original document" is satisfied by an electronic data message whose information integrity can be assured, and whose

information can be displayed. Finally, record retention requirements may be satisfied for data messages by appropriate electronic retention.

The UNCITRAL Model Law also contains more
specialized rules, which may be varied by agreement
between the parties. These rules concern contract
formation, attribution of messages, and acknowledgment and time of receipt of data messages. As to
attribution, a message is deemed to be sent by a
designated originator if it is sent either by an authorized person or by a machine that is pro-
grammed by the originator to operate automatically. The addressee of the data message is authorized
to rely on it as being from the originator if either an
agreed-upon security procedure has been used or
the originator enabled the actual sender to gain
access to a message identification method.

A major problem with electronic data messages is
that they get lost much more often than messages
sent through the U.S. Post Office. Thus, acknowledgment of receipt of electronic messages is much
more important to the parties than is acknowledgment of paper-based messages, and the parties often
stipulate in their agreements that data messages
must be acknowledged. If they so agree, under the
UNCITRAL Model Law, acknowledgment can be
accomplished either by the method agreed upon or,
where no specific acknowledgment method has been
agreed, any communication or conduct can be sufficient. Even where the parties have not agreed to
require acknowledgment, the originator of a data
message may unilaterally require it by stating in

the body of the message that it is conditional on acknowledgment. Such a message is deemed "never been sent" until acknowledgment is received. Receipt of a message generally requires that the message enter an information system outside the control of the originator or its agents.

There are other provisions in the UNCITRAL Model Law which are specific to the contracts for the carriage of goods and to transportation documents. These provisions generally permit electronic data messages to replace bills of lading and waybills, even where local statutes require a writing on a paper document. They also provide that legal rules which compel the use of paper documents in carriage contracts are satisfied by such data messages.

The UNCITRAL Model Law on Electronic Commerce has been enacted by twenty nations, and the state of Illinois, as of August 1, 2004, and was a model for uniform acts in the United States and Canada. Further enactments are expected. In the United States, the National Conference of Commissioners on Uniform State Laws has adopted two different proposed uniform acts to facilitate electronic commerce. One is the Uniform Electronic Transactions Act (UETA), which is similar in scope and substance to the UNCITRAL Model Law. It applies to all types of electronic messages and contracts, and seeks to validate and facilitate their use at a very basic level. The second is the Uniform Computer Information Transactions Act (UCITA) which applies primarily only to software licensing transactions, and incorporates very detailed provisions concerning every aspect of the transaction. Its format is similar to UCC Article 2 on sales of goods, and at one time was intended to be UCC Article 2B, until it was rejected by the American Law Institute as not sufficiently balanced.

UCITA also rejects many of the concepts in both the UNCITRAL Model Law and UETA. Thus, the Uniform Commissioners have proposed two different uniform acts whose provisions conflict on such basic terms as authentication and attribution. The introduction and adoption of differing state, national and international legislation with conflicting provisions to govern E Commerce is likely to create difficulties for all the participants in a transaction where the location of the parties is unknown. These difficulties are likely to grow as more non-U.S. parties participate in E Commerce, and a greater proportion of such transactions are across national boundaries.

THE "PAYMENT AGAINST DOCUMENTS" TRANSACTION

How does the "payment against documents" transaction work? When buyer and seller are forming their contract for the sale of the goods, seller will insist that buyer "pay against the documents", rather than after delivery and inspection of the goods themselves. Such a payment term must be bargained for and expressed in the sales contract. It will not normally be implied.

Seller will then pack the goods and prepare a commercial invoice. If the commercial term requires it (e.g., under a "CIF" term) seller will also procure an insurance certificate (another form of contract) covering the goods during transit. Seller then delivers the goods to the carrier, which issues a negotiable bill of lading as a combination receipt and contract. This bill of lading will commonly require carrier to deliver the goods only "to seller or order"—i.e., only to seller or a person seller may designate by an appropriate endorsement.

Under the terms of the bill of lading contract, in return for payment of the freight charge, carrier promises to deliver the goods to either (1) the named "consignee" in a "straight" (or non-negotiable) bill of lading, or (2) the person in possession ("holder") of a properly indorsed "order" (or negotiable) bill of lading. The order (negotiable) bill of lading should be used in the payment against documents sale, so that the buyer is able to obtain delivery of goods *only if* buyer has physical possession of a properly endorsed bill of lading. Such a bill of lading controls access to and delivery of the goods, so that the bill of lading is also a "document of title."

Further, if it is a negotiable bill of lading, it also controls the right to obtain the goods from carrier. Thus, a negotiable bill of lading delivered by seller to the collecting banks will assure buyer and seller that: (1) the goods have been delivered to carrier, (2) they are destined for buyer and not some third party, and (3) the collecting banks can control carrier's delivery of the goods to buyer by simply retaining possession of the order bill of lading. In other words, when a bank undertakes to collect funds from the buyer for the seller, it receives from seller a "document of title" (the bill of lading), issued by carrier which gives the bank control of carrier's delivery of the goods. Buyer cannot obtain possession of the goods from a carrier without physical possession of the negotiable bill of lading, so after the banks have received that piece of paper from seller, they can obtain payment (or assurances that buyer will pay them) before buyer receives the ability to obtain the goods from carrier.

Once the seller has obtained a negotiable bill of lading to his own order, how does he obtain payment? First, he attaches a "draft" to it, together with an invoice and any other documents required by the sales contract. Then he uses the banking system as a collection agent. A "draft" (sometimes also called a "bill of exchange") will usually be a "sight draft," which is payable "on demand" when presented to buyer. The draft is drawn for the amount due under the sales contract, and it is payable to seller's order.

At the bank, the seller endorses both the draft and the negotiable bill of lading to Seller's Bank, and will also transfer the other documents to it. If no letter of credit is involved in the transaction, the bank will usually take these documents only "for collection," although it is also possible for the bank to "discount," or buy, the documents outright and become the owner.

To understand the collection transaction by the banking system, consult the flow chart on page ___. Seller's Bank is required to send the draft and its accompanying documents for presentment to the buyer which is usually done by sending them through "customary banking channels." Seller's Bank deals with "for collection" items individually, without assuming that they will be honored, and therefore without giving seller a provisional credit in the seller's account until the buyer pays the draft.

The draft, with its attached documents, will pass through "customary banking channels" to Buyer's Bank (the "presenting bank"), which will notify the buyer of the arrival of the documents. Buyer's Bank will demand that the buyer "honor" the draft which means paying the amount of a demand draft, or "accepting" (promising to pay later) a time draft. The buyer may require the bank to "exhibit" the draft and documents to it to allow the buyer to determine whether they conform to the contract. The buyer has three banking days after the notice was sent to decide whether to "honor" the draft, if mere notice is sent. However, if the draft and documents are exhibited directly to the buyer, the buyer must decide whether to honor the draft or not by the close of business on that same day, unless there are extenuating circumstances.

Buyer must "pay against the documents" and not the goods themselves, which is why it is preferable to specify the terms of the documents in the original contract for the sale of goods. Once buyer has paid, or arranged to pay, Buyer's Bank, it will obtain possession of the bill of lading and only then will it be entitled to obtain the goods from carrier. Buyer never sees the goods, only the documents—so it inspects the documents rigorously to determine that they comply exactly with the requirements of the sale contract. Substantial performance by seller in the tender of documents is not acceptable.

DIAGRAM OF AN INTERNATIONAL DOCUMENTARY SALE

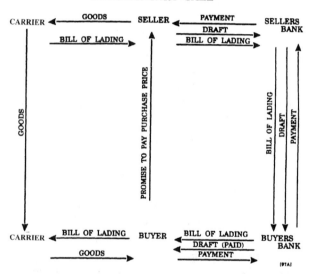

An international sale of goods involving payment against documents is diagramed on this page.

Note the risks to each party. If the seller ships conforming goods, it will be paid before the documents or the goods are released to the buyer. Thus, seller will not lose control of the goods without being paid for them. If buyer pays Buyer's Bank, the proceeds are remitted immediately and automatically to seller's bank account in seller's nation.

What can go wrong from the seller's point of view? Seller has shipped the goods to a foreign buyer without being paid before shipping them, and with no guarantee of payment from anyone other than the buyer. The buyer may refuse to pay the sight draft, with documents attached, when it arrives. This would give the seller a cause of action, but often it is usable only in the buyer's jurisdiction, which means bringing a suit abroad with its extra expense, delay and uncertainty. In particular, a plaintiff could feel that it will be the target of discrimination in the courts of another nation.

The seller would still have control of the goods, because after dishonor of the draft the bill of lading will be returned to the seller. However, the goods would now be at a foreign destination—one at which the seller has no agents, and no particular prospects for resale. In addition, if the seller wished to bring the goods back to its base of operations (and normal sales territory), it would have to pay a second transportation charge, and this may be substantial in relation to the value of the goods. Thus, the dishonor of the draft and rejection of the goods by the buyer can create economic circumstances where seller's only rational option is a distress sale in buyer's nation. This risk to seller is inherent in the payment against documents transaction, unless seller requires that buyer also procure the issuance of a letter of credit. (See Chapter 2 for a complete description and discussion of the letter of credit transaction.)

On the other hand, for its payment of the price, buyer has a document from carrier entitling it to delivery of the goods, an insurance certificate protecting buyer against casualty loss and perhaps an inspection certificate warranting that the goods conform to the sale contract. In other words, buyer should receive what it bargained for—delivery of conforming goods or insurance proceeds sufficient to cover any loss. However, without the ability to inspect the actual goods before payment, buyer cannot be absolutely assured that they conform to the contract.

What can go wrong from the buyer's point of view? There are *at least* six problems which could arise:

(a) The goods could be lost or stolen.

(b) The carrier could stow the goods or operate so negligently that they are damaged in transit.

(c) The goods shipped could be non-conforming to the sales contract. The non-conformity could range from (1) the seller shipping scrap paper to (2) the labelling on the packaging being incorrect (which can cause problems with customs agents in both countries).

(d) The bill of lading and attached draft could be stolen and presented to buyer by a thief— with any necessary indorsements having been forged.

(e) The goods could fail to conform to the bill of lading, so that the documents state that goods of a particular description will be delivered, and the goods actually delivered are of a different description.

(f) The bill of lading could be forged—and no goods were shipped.

Some of these problems are recognized and dealt with in the standard handling of the "payment against documents" transaction. For example, insuring the goods against loss or theft is standard practice in the CIF transaction. Other problems, such as payment before inspection, make buyers feel unprotected, and they have searched for devices within the transaction which can afford them more protection. Such a device, in common use in modern transactions, is the Inspection Certificate.

Three of these problems are uniquely related to any transaction using a bill of lading, and will be considered in the materials below:

(a) The loss of the bill of lading, followed by the forgery of a necessary indorsement and carrier's misdelivery (delivery of the goods to the wrong person under a bill of lading).

(b) The misdescription of the goods by the shipper and in the bill of lading followed by carrier's delivery of goods which do not conform to the description in the bill of lading.

(c) The forgery of a complete bill of lading by shipper without carrier's knowledge.

BILLS OF LADING

As to regulation of the transfer of the bill of lading, UCC Article 7 would appear to regulate these relationships, but in fact, except for intrastate transactions, the UCC is preempted by federal law. The Federal Bill of Lading Act (formerly called the Pomerene Act), 49 U.S.C.A. §§ 80101–80116, governs the transfer and transferability of all bills of lading generated to cover both international and interstate shipments. The form and content of bills of lading are also governed by the Harter Act, 46 U.S.C.A. §§ 190–196, and the Carriage of Goods by Sea Act, 46 U.S.C.A. App. §§ 1300–1315. With this multiplicity of statutes governing the terms of the bill of lading and its use, conflicting concepts from overlapping statutes should be expected. Congress has recently recodified the Federal Bill of Lading Act. It did not intend to change the substance of the Act, but it did reorganize, reword and consolidate the prior provisions and change all the section numbers.

The Federal Bill of Lading Act governs all interstate and international shipments which use a bill of lading issued by a common carrier. By its terms, the statute governs the bill of lading if the goods are shipped from the United States to another country. The word "carrier" is not defined, so it is not clear whether documents issued by freight forwarders are covered. Further, the term "bill of lading" is not defined, so it is not clear whether air waybills or inland waterway documents are included.

There are two different types of bills of lading—a "straight," or non-negotiable, bill of lading, and an "order," or negotiable, bill of lading. (These are also known in the trade as "white" and "yellow" for the different colors of paper on which they are often printed.) Each usually represents the shipper's contract with the carrier, and will set forth the terms of that contract expressly or incorporate a carrier's terms and tariffs by reference.

MISDELIVERY

A non-negotiable, or "straight," bill of lading is issued to a named person, the consignee. Under a non-negotiable bill of lading, the carrier obligates itself to deliver the goods at the destination point to the consignee named in the bill of lading. 49 U.S.C.A. § 80110. Possession of the actual straight bill of lading does not confer rights over the goods or against the carrier to a person in possession of the paper who is not the consignee. Further, indorsements on such a straight bill of lading are irrelevant to making the bill negotiable or to giving rights to the indorsee. In short, the carrier is liable to the consignee of a straight bill of lading for misdelivery if it delivers the goods to anyone but the consignee or a person whom the consignee delegates to receive them. Thus, straight bills of lading are not appropriate for a "payment against documents" transaction, and the case reporters are full of litigation where an attorney tried a short-cut using a straight bill of lading as the "easy" way to do this transaction—and sacrificed the client's interests. Straight bills of lading are also called "air waybills," "sea waybills" and "freight receipts," depending upon the intended method of main transportation for the goods.

An "order," or negotiable, bill of lading is issued to a named person "or order." This allows the named person (the consignee) to indorse the bill of lading to "order" delivery of the goods to others. If possession of the bill of lading is transferred to a third party, and the bill of lading is indorsed to that third party (either specially or in blank), then the third party becomes a "holder" of the bill of lading. Under a negotiable bill of lading, the carrier obligates itself to deliver the goods to the "holder" of the bill of lading at the destination point. 46 U.S.C.A. § 80110. Thus, possession of the negotiable bill of lading becomes crucial. The carrier must see the actual bill of lading both to determine who has possession and to determine to whom the indorsements run.

Therefore, possession of the actual negotiable bill of lading, properly indorsed, does confer rights over the goods and against the carrier to the person in possession of the paper, the "holder." The original consignee may indorse the negotiable bill of lading either "in blank" by a bare signature ("Ralph Folsom") or by a "special indorsement," which specifies the name of the intended holder ("Deliver the goods to Michael Gordon, or order. Ralph Folsom"). 46 U.S.C.A. § 80104. Under a blank indorsement, any person in possession becomes a holder, and is entitled to demand delivery from the carrier. Under a special indorsement, only the named indorsee can become a holder, and only that person can demand delivery from the carrier or indorse the bill of lading to another party so as to make it a holder. Thus, the special indorsement protects the interests of the parties from thieves and forgers much better than a blank indorsement.

In short, the carrier is liable to the holder of a negotiable bill of lading for misdelivery if it delivers the goods to anyone but the holder. In this sense the negotiable bill of lading is a "document of title," because possession of it, properly indorsed, controls title to the document, title to the goods, and the direct obligation of the carrier to hold the goods and deliver them to the holder of the document. For this reason, the negotiable bill of lading is appropriate for a "payment against documents" transaction. The collecting banks can use their possession of such bills of lading to control title to both the goods and the document until they have collected the price from the buyer. Some other commercial nations have only "straight" bills of lading and not negotiable bills of lading, but most commentators believe the United States' system is preferable.

The holder of the bill of lading does not have absolute title to the goods in all cases, but nearly so. If the shipper is not the owner of the goods, for example if the goods have been stolen at gunpoint from the "true owner," then no holder of the bill of lading will have title because the shipper's claim of title was void. However, if the owner voluntarily parted with the goods but was defrauded by the shipper (a "cash sale" in which the check bounces later), then the shipper obtains voidable title (UCC § 2–403) and can pass good title to a holder of the document who purchases it in good faith for value without notice. The rights of such a good faith holder for value are also superior to any seller's lien or right to stop delivery of the goods in transit.

Under the Federal Bill of Lading Act, as under the UCC, any forgery of a necessary indorsement is not effective to create or transfer rights, whether the forgery is perfect or inept. Further, any unauthorized signature by an agent is treated as a forgery, as long as it was made without actual, implied or apparent authority. The protection is illustrated in the situation where a thief steals a negotiable bill of lading from the holder who was in possession of the document under a special indorsement. As such, the holder's indorsement is necessary to transfer rights to the document or goods to any other party. Without that indorsement, the thief is not a holder and has no rights to the document or goods. If the thief forges the holder's signature, that forgery is ineffective, and the thief is still not a holder and still has no rights. If the thief transfers the document to another party, that party also is not a holder and cannot obtain rights under the document without the holder's signature. *Adel Precision Products Corp. v. Grand Trunk Western R. Co.*, 51 N.W.2d 922 (Mich. 1952). The carrier is still obligated to deliver the goods only to the holder, the victim of the theft.

Thus, if a collecting bank or other party takes the document under a special indorsement, it is protected from loss from theft of the paper and forgery, and even from unauthorized transfer by an agent.

If the carrier does deliver to the forger, or to someone who received the document from the forger without the holder's indorsement, the carrier is liable for misdelivery under 49 U.S.C.A. § 80111. The forger is also liable, if he can be found. The person who received the goods and other transferees have all made warranties under 49 U.S.C.A. § 80107 that they had "a right to transfer the bill and title to the goods," when they had no such rights or title.

The concept is that each person who takes the bill of lading should "know your indorser." If the goods are misdelivered, the party most easily found is the one who received the goods, and that party is liable. That party then has a warranty action against its transferor—and it is the person involved most likely to be able to find that transferor. The transferor, in turn, has a warranty action against its transferor— and so on back up the chain of transfers. This is not very efficient, but the purpose is to push liability back up the chain of transfers to the person who took from the forger, or even to the forger himself. (In the meantime, the holder collects from the misdelivering carrier, which collects from its insuror.)

Collecting banks which transfer the document for value can be subject to this warranty liability. If the buyer pays, and those funds are transmitted to the forger, then the collecting banks have received value. However, such banks have several potential escape valves. One is to disclaim such warranty liability when indorsing the negotiable bill of lading. The statutory warranties do not arise if "a contrary intention appears." Thus, an indorsement "XYZ Bank Prior indorsements not guaranteed" would clearly disclaim liability for such a warranty. A second avenue is to claim that the bank is only holding the document "as security for a debt," for the statute exempts such holders from warranty liability. The difficulty with this avenue is that a collecting bank does not pay the seller until after it receives payment, so it never becomes a creditor, secured or otherwise. Also banks may argue that banking custom relieves them from any duty to examine documents, so that this custom provides an implicit blanket "contrary intention" under the statute. Any bank found to have warranty liability can pass this liability back to its transferor, as long as it can identify that transferor.

MISDESCRIPTION

The carrier in a shipment transaction has no privity with the contract between buyer and seller for the sale of goods, and therefore has no obligation to deliver goods that conform to the sale contract. However, the goods are described in the bill of lading which constitutes part of the carriage contract. Thus, the carrier does have an obligation to deliver goods which conform to the description in the bill of lading. Under the Federal Bills of Lading

Act, a carrier is liable for any failure to deliver goods which correspond to the description in the bill of lading, either as to quantity or as to quality. 49 U.S.C.A. § 80113. This obligation is owed the owner of the goods under a straight bill of lading and to the holder of a negotiable bill of lading.

The problem with this obligation is that the carrier usually does not know what it is carrying, since the goods are often in containers. Thus, the carrier knows that it received a container which was labelled "100 IBM word-processing computers." It will not, and is not expected to, open the container to check whether it contains computers, or to count how many items there are in it. Even if it opened the container, it would not be expected to check whether each computer is in working order. Even if it did so check, it is not likely to have the expertise to determine whether each computer can perform the necessary routines to be a word processor. Thus, the carrier is not expected to warrant the description and capability of packaged goods given to it to transport.

To solve this problem, carriers are allowed, under the Federal Bills of Lading Act, to effectively disclaim their obligations to deliver goods which conform to the description. Appropriate disclaimer language is set forth in the statute, and includes:

"contents or condition of contents of packages unknown",

"said to contain", and

"shipper's weight, load, and count".

Other language conveying the same meaning can be used; the statutory linguistic formulas are not required.

The disclaimers are not effective if the carrier knows that the goods do not conform. The protection is available only to the uninformed carrier. However, when goods are loaded by a carrier, the carrier is obligated to count the number of packages and is expected to note the condition of the packages. The carrier is also obligated to "determine the kind and quantity" (but not the quality) of any bulk freight that it loads. For bulk freight, even where it is loaded by the shipper, the carrier must still determine the kind and quantity of the freight if the shipper so requests and provides adequate facilities for the carrier to weigh the freight. In situations where the carrier must count packages or weigh the goods, disclaimers (such as "shipper's weight, load, and count") will not be effective.

Thus, what is established is a system in which the carrier is responsible for checking some quantity terms, the number of cartons and the weight of a shipment. These are items which the carrier is likely to check in any event, to be certain that some cartons are not inadvertently left behind, and to determine the appropriate freight charge. However, the carrier is not required to check most quality terms, such as what goods are in a container and whether they are in operating condition or not. In the latter case, it can truthfully say that it has received 100 cartons "said to contain" IBM word processing computers, without opening the cartons;

but it does need to count the number of cartons. The intersection of these rules arises when the carrier accepts a sealed container supposed to contain 2000 tin ingots weighing 35 tons, and issues a bill of lading for a container "said to contain 2000 tin ingots." If the container is empty, weighs less than a ton and the carrier does not weigh it, the carrier's disclaimer is not likely to protect it. *Berisford Metals Corp. v. S/S Salvador*, 779 F.2d 841 (2nd Cir. 1985).

According to the statutory provision, all of these disclaimers are effective only if the seller loads the goods. This restriction seems appropriate for disclaimers of the "shipper's weight, load, and count" variety, but seems inapposite for disclaimers of the "said to contain" or "contents or condition of contents of packages unknown" variety. There are cases which require shipper actually to load, however, in the sense that the carrier is liable for misdescription despite "shipper's weight, load and count," if carrier issues a bill of lading and the shipper has in fact never loaded anything on board the carrier's cars.

THE FORGED BILL OF LADING

If the carrier issues a bill of lading for which there are no goods, the carrier is likely to be liable to the holder. However, suppose the carrier never issued any bill of lading. Instead, a person unrelated to the carrier created (forged) the bill of lading, with no authority from the carrier. The buyer who purchases such a forged bill of lading has paid funds to a forger, probably through a series of banks, and finds that the carrier has no goods to deliver. There is no misdelivery or misdescription claim against the carrier, for there never were any goods delivered to the carrier for it to redeliver or to describe. If the carrier did not issue the bill of lading and its "signature" is a forgery or unauthorized, that signature is not "effective," and carrier will not be liable on the bill, absent some sort of actionable negligence.

The forger is liable for the fraud, if he can be found. Unlike the forged indorsement situation, there is no one who has received any goods, for there never were any goods to deliver. However, like the forged indorsement situation, each party that transferred the bill of lading for value makes warranties to later parties, and the first warranty is that "the bill is genuine." If the bill of lading itself is forged that warranty is breached. Thus, all parties who transferred the bill and received payment funds can be liable to breach of warranty actions against them by later parties. The concept is that the last person to purchase the bill will "know its indorser," and be able to recover against its transferor. That transferor can, in turn, recover against *its* transferor, and so on up the chain of transfers, until the loss falls either on the forger or upon the person who dealt with and took the bill from the forger.

Collecting banks which have transferred the document for value can be subject to this warranty liability, but have the same three potential escape values discussed under forged indorsements. (1) A disclaimer of warranty through making "a contrary intention appear." (2) A claim that the bank is holding the document only "as security for a debt." (3) The limitation in the I.C.C. Collection Rules that banks need examine only the appearance of the documents. Each of these approaches has analytical difficulties, but they may indicate a corporate, blanket intention to disclaim the statutory warranties implicitly. Any bank which is found to have warranty liability can pass this liability back to its transferor, as long as it can identify and find that transferor.

ELECTRONIC BILLS OF LADING

The Federal Bills of Lading Act does not define "bill of lading" and does not require that it be written on a piece of paper or signed by anyone. Thus, use of electronic bills of lading would seem to be a technical possibility. However, all of the primary rules of the federal law are filled with an implicit assumption that the bill of lading is a paper document. The references to indorsement (in blank or to a specified person), transfer by delivery and "person in possession" (holder) make sense only in a paper document transaction.

However, telecommunications technology can provide electronic messages which perform the main functions of the bill of lading: as a receipt, transport contract and document of title. Thus, several types of bill of lading equivalents are currently in use, but most of them are used only as receipts for the goods generated by the carrier. Their utility is enhanced where a "straight," or non-negotiable, bill of lading (or waybill) does not need to be presented to a carrier to obtain possession of the goods. Unfortunately, the Federal Bills of Lading Act requires the carrier to deliver the goods only to a person who "has possession of the bill," even under a straight bill of lading (49 U.S.C.A. § 80110(a)(2)), and makes the carrier liable for damages if it does not take and cancel the bill when delivering the goods. These requirements are often ignored by carriers in practice, and the parties merely exchange printed forms, but the statutory requirements do inhibit the acceptance of electronic bills of lading in the United States.

Despite these requirements, the Interstate Commerce Commission now authorizes the use of uniform electronic bills of lading, both negotiable and non-negotiable, for both motor carrier and rail carrier use. These have been authorized since 1982 and 1988 respectively. There is an assumption that such electronic bills of lading merely communicate information about the goods, the shipper and the consignee. There are no provisions defining the rights and obligations of the parties to the electronic bill. Thus, the bills do not allow for further sale or rerouting of the goods in transit, or for using the bills of lading to finance the transaction. Under the regulations, negotiable uniform electronic bills of lading must "provide for endorsement on the back portion," but there is no explanation of how an electronic message has a "back portion," or how "endorsement" is to be effected.

There have been several programs to create electronic carrier-issued international receipts for goods. Atlantic Container Lines used dedicated lines between terminals at its offices in different ports to send messages between those offices. It generated a Data Freight Receipt which was given to the consignee or notify party. Such a receipt was not negotiable and gave buyers and banks little protection from further sale or rerouting of the goods by shipper in transit. The Cargo Key Receipt was similar, but also an advance over the prior approach, because it included a "no disposal" term in the shipper-carrier contract. Thus, this electronic message protected buyer from further sale or rerouting by seller in transit. It still could not be used to finance the transfer, however, because the electronic receipt, even if it named a bank as consignee, was not formally a negotiable document of title. The receipt was believed to give the bank only the right to prevent delivery to the buyer, not a positive right to take control of the goods for itself.

The Chase Manhattan Bank created the SEADOCS Registry which was intended to create a negotiable electronic bill of lading for oil shipments. The Registry acted as custodian for an actual paper negotiable bill of lading issued by a carrier, and maintained a registry of transfers of that bill from the original shipper to the ultimate "holder." The transfers were made by a series of electronic messages, each of which could be authenticated by "test keys", or identification numbers, generated by SEA-DOCS. SEADOCS would then, as agent, endorse the paper bill of lading in its custody. At the end, SEADOCS would electronically deliver a paper copy of the negotiable bill of lading to the last endorsee to enable it to obtain the goods from the carrier. While SEADOCS was a legal success, showing that such a program was technically feasible; it was not a commercial success, lasting less than a year.

The Comite Maritime International (CMI) has adopted Rules for Electronic Bills of Lading (1990). Under those rules, any carrier can issue an electronic bill of lading as long as it will act as a clearinghouse for subsequent transfers. Upon receiving goods, the carrier sends an electronic message to the shipper describing the goods, the contract terms and a "private key" which can be used to transfer shipper's rights to a third party. Under the CMI Rules, the shipper now has the "right of control and transfer" over the goods, and is called a "holder." Under Rules 4 and 7, an electronic message from shipper which includes the private key can be used to transfer the shipper's rights to a third party, who then becomes a new holder. The carrier then cancels the shipper's "private key" and issues a different private key to the new holder. Upon arrival, the carrier will deliver the goods to the then-current holder or a consignee designated by the holder.

The original parties to the transaction agree that the CMI Rules will govern the "communications" aspects of the transaction. All parties also agree that electronic messages satisfy any national law requirements that a bill of lading be in writing. This is an attempt to create an "electronic" writing which is a negotiable document of title by contract and estoppel. Some commentators have observed that this is an attempt by private parties to create a negotiable document, a power usually reserved to legislatures.

The Commission of the European Committees has sponsored the BOLERO electronic bill of lading initiative, which is based on the CMI Rules. However, under the BOLERO system, neither a bank nor a carrier is the repository of the sensitive information of who has bought and sold the cargo covered by the electronic bills of lading. Instead BOLERO establishes a third party who is independent of the shipper, the carrier, the ultimate buyer and all intermediate parties as the operator of the central registry.

American bankers have been skeptical of the device created by the CMI Rules. The registries maintained by each carrier do not have the same level of security associated with SWIFT procedures. (See "Electronic Letters of Credit" in Chapter 2.) In addition to fraudulent transactions, there is a risk of misdirected messages. Thus, a bank could find itself relying on "non-existent rights based upon fraudulent information in a receipt message transmitted to it by someone pretending to be the carrier." The banks are concerned as to whether carriers will accept liability in their new role as electronic registrars for losses due to such fraudulent practices. The banks are also concerned that the full terms and conditions of the contract of carriage are not available to subsequent "holders." Thus, use of the CMI Rules does not yet seem to be widely adopted in the United States, and bills of lading are still primarily paper-based in both the "payment against documents" and letter of credit transactions.

CHAPTER TWO

FINANCING THE INTERNATIONAL SALE OF GOODS

THE INTERNATIONAL DOCUMENTARY SALE AND DOCUMENTARY LETTER OF CREDIT

THE PROBLEM

Unlike most domestic sales transactions, in a sale of goods across national borders the exporter-seller and importer-buyer may not have previously dealt with one another; or each may know nothing about the other, or the other's national legal system. The seller does not know: (1) whether buyer is creditworthy or trustworthy; (2) whether information received on these subjects from buyer's associates is reliable; (3) whether exchange controls will hinder movement of the payment funds (especially if in "hard currency"); (4) how great is the exchange risk if payment in buyer's currency is permitted, and (5) what delays may be involved in receiving unencumbered funds from buyer.

On the other hand, buyer does not know: (1) whether seller can be trusted to ship the goods if buyer prepays; (2) whether the goods shipped will be of the quantity and quality contracted for; (3)

whether the goods will be shipped by an appropriate carrier and properly insured; (4) whether the goods may be damaged in transit; (5) whether the seller will furnish to buyer sufficient ownership documentation covering the goods to allow buyer to claim them from the customs officials; (6) whether seller will provide the documentation necessary to satisfy export control regulations and import customs and valuation regulations (e.g., country of origin certificates, health and other inspection certificates); and (7) what delays may be involved in receiving unencumbered possession and use of the goods in the buyer-importer's location.

Where the parties are strangers, these risks are significant, possibly overwhelming. Since they operate at a distance from each other, seller and buyer cannot concurrently exchange the goods for the payment funds *without the help of third parties.* The documentary sale, involving the use of a letter of credit, illustrates how these potentially large risks can be distributed to third parties who have special knowledge, can properly evaluate each risk assumed, and thereby can reduce the transaction risks to insignificance.

THE DOCUMENTARY SALE TRANSACTION

The third party intermediaries enlisted are banks (at least one in buyer's nation and usually a second one in seller's nation) and at least one carrier. Thus, the parties involved are: (1) a buyer, who is also presumably a "customer" of (2) Buyer's Bank,

(3) a seller, (4) a bank with an office in seller's nation (hereafter "Seller's Bank"), and (5) at least one carrier. Among them, these parties are able to take a large risk which is not subject to any firm evaluation, and divide it into several small, calculable risks, each of which is easily borne by one party. Thus, the documentary sale is an example that not all risk allocation is a "zero sum game," but may in fact create a "win-win" situation.

These parties will be related by a series of contracts—but not all of the parties to the transaction will be parties to each contract. The contracts include (A) the sale of goods contract between buyer and seller; (B) the bill of lading, a receipt and contract issued by the carrier; and (C) the letter of credit, a promise by Buyer's Bank (and, if confirmed, also by Seller's Bank) to pay seller under certain conditions concerning proof that seller has shipped the goods.

(A) The contract underlying the entire series of transactions is the contract for the sale of goods from buyer to seller. Buyer and seller are parties to this contract, but the banks and the carrier are not parties. Seller is responsible to deliver the contracted quantity and quality of goods, and buyer is responsible for taking the goods and paying the stated price. (For conditions and further elaborations on this point, see the discussion of the Convention on Contracts for the International Sale of Goods in Chapter 1.)

(B) In documentary sales, buyers and sellers are usually distant from each other, and the goods must be moved. Thus, an international carrier of the goods is usually employed, and either seller or buyer will make a contract with the carrier to transport the goods. (For our illustration, seller will make that contract.) Seller (or, in the language of a contract of carriage, "shipper") makes a contract with carrier that the goods will be transported to buyer's ("consignee's") location.

This second contract in our transaction will be expressed in the "bill of lading" issued by the carrier. Under the terms of the bill of lading contract, in return for payment of the freight charge, carrier promises to deliver the goods to either (1) the named "consignee" in a "straight" (or non-negotiable) bill of lading, or (2) the person in possession ("holder") of an "order" (or negotiable) bill of lading. The order (negotiable) bill of lading should be used in the documentary sale (letter of credit transaction), so that the buyer is able to obtain delivery of goods *only if* buyer has physical possession of the bill of lading. Such a bill of lading controls access to and delivery of the goods, so that the bill of lading is also a "document of title."

(C) Before seller ("shipper") delivers the goods to the carrier, seller wants assurance that payment will be forthcoming. A promise from buyer may not be sufficient. Even a promise from a bank in buyer's nation may not be sufficient, because seller does not know them or know about them. Instead, seller wants a promise from a bank known to it, and preferably in seller's location.

What seller wants is the third contract in our transaction—a confirmed, irrevocable letter of credit. A letter of credit is a contract—a promise by a bank (usually Buyer's Bank) that it will pay to seller (or, "will honor drafts drawn on this bank by seller for") the amount of the contract price. The bank's promise is conditioned upon seller's presenting evidence that the goods have been shipped via carrier to arrive in buyer's port, along with any other documents required by the contract for the sale of goods. What would furnish such evidence? The bill of lading between seller and carrier, the second contract in our transaction, furnishes the evidence that seller has shipped the goods.

Further, if it is a negotiable bill of lading, it also controls the right to obtain the goods from carrier. Thus, a negotiable bill of lading delivered by seller to Seller's Bank will assure Bank that: (1) the goods have been delivered to carrier, (2) they are destined for buyer and not some third party, and (3) Bank can control carrier's delivery of the goods to buyer by simply retaining possession of the order bill of lading. In other words, when a bank pays seller, it receives from seller a "document of title" issued by carrier which gives the bank control of carrier's delivery of the goods. Buyer cannot obtain possession of the goods from a carrier without physical possession of the bill of lading, so after the banks have paid seller for that piece of paper, they can obtain payment (or assurances that buyer will pay

them) before buyer receives the ability to obtain the
goods from carrier.

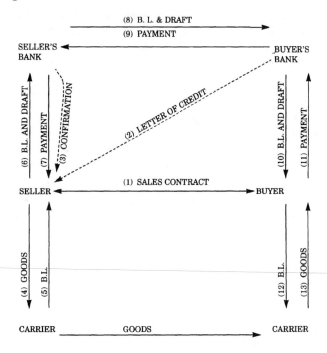

How does the international documentary sales
transaction work? An international documentary
sale is diagramed above. When buyer and seller are
forming their contract for the sale of the goods,
seller will insist that the contract have both a
"Price" term and a "Payment" term. For maximum protection, seller will seek payment to be by
"Confirmed, Irrevocable Letter of Credit," and
should specify what documents are required with

great detail. The reason for putting this payment term in the sales contract is that, since buyer is expected to establish a letter of credit and "to pay against the documents," rather than after delivery and inspection of the goods themselves, that payment term must be bargained for and expressed in the sales contract. It will not normally be implied.

What documents will be required? Usually, they include the:

(1) negotiable bill of lading (showing transportation company's receipt of the goods to be shipped and obligation to deliver them only to the holder of the document)

(2) commercial invoice (which sets out the terms of purchase such as grade and number of goods, price, etc.)

(3) policy of marine insurance (if goods are to go by sea)

(4) certificate of inspection (issued by a commercial inspecting firm and confirming that the required number and type of goods are being shipped)

(5) export license and/or health inspection certificate (showing that the goods are cleared for export)

(6) certificate of origin (relevant to the rules of origin used by customs personnel in importer's country for determining tariff assessments).

If buyer agrees to a letter of credit payment term, buyer (or, in the language of the letter of credit, the "account party" or "customer") will contract with Buyer's Bank ("issuer" or "issuing bank") to issue a letter of credit ("credit") to seller ("beneficiary"). The letter of credit is a direct promise by the issuing bank that it will pay the contract price to seller ("beneficiary"), if seller presents to it the documents specified in the letter of credit (and previously in the sales contract). Buyer's Bank will be aware of buyer's creditworthiness, and will make appropriate arrangements to receive the funds from buyer (through either immediate payment or future repayment of a loan). These arrangements will be made before the letter of credit is issued, for Buyer's Bank is bound to the letter of credit terms after issuance if it is irrevocable.

If seller requires an obligation of a bank known to seller, the letter of credit must be confirmed by a Seller's Bank ("confirming bank"). Buyer's Bank will forward its letter of credit to seller through another bank, Seller's Bank. By merely indicating "We confirm this credit," Seller's Bank makes a direct promise to seller that it will pay the contract price to seller, if seller presents the required documents to it. If no confirmation of the credit is required by the sales contract, Buyer's Bank can forward the letter of credit through a "notifying bank" or an "advising bank" which is near seller. These banks will not be obligated to seller, but will take the documents and forward them to Buyer's Bank for collection purposes only.

Once the letter of credit is issued and confirmed, seller will pack the goods and prepare a commercial invoice, and procure an insurance certificate (another form of contract) covering the goods during transit. If an inspection certificate is required, the goods will be made available to the inspector designated in the sales contract, and the inspecting firm will issue a certificate (another contract) stating that the goods conform to the description in the sales contract. Seller will also prepare the necessary documents for the customs officials in its nation (e.g., export license) and in buyer's nation (certificate of origin). Seller then sends the goods to the carrier, which issues a negotiable bill of lading as a combination receipt and contract. This bill of lading will commonly require carrier to deliver the goods only "to seller or order"—i.e., only to seller or a person seller may designate by an appropriate endorsement.

Seller now has the complete set of documents needed, and takes these documents to Seller's Bank, which (as a confirming bank) is obligated to pay seller the contract price upon presentation of the documents. To obtain payment, seller attaches a "draft" to the documents; and in the letter of credit the banks have promised to honor such a draft. The draft (sometimes also called a "bill of exchange") resembles a check written by seller and drawn on Seller's Bank or on Buyer's Bank for the amount of the contract price. A draft can be payable on demand ("at sight") in a cash sale, or payable at a later time (e.g. "30 days after sight") in a credit sale. If a "demand draft" is used, the bank will pay the amount immediately, usually by crediting seller's bank account; if a time draft is used, the bank will "accept" it (write on it the bank's promise to pay it later). In the latter case, seller can still raise funds immediately by selling the paper on the strength of the bank's credit.

Seller's Bank never sees the goods, only the documents—so the bank inspects the documents rigorously to determine that they comply exactly with the requirements of the letter of credit, for the documents are its only protection. Substantial performance by seller is not acceptable. Thus, where a credit called for "100% acrylic yarn" and the invoice stated "imported acrylic yarn", the credit was not satisfied, even though the packing list stated "100% acrylic yarn".

In return for the bank's payment, seller will endorse both the draft and the negotiable bill of lading to Seller's Bank and transfer the other documents to it. Seller's Bank, in turn, will endorse and present the draft and its accompanying documents to Buyer's Bank, which is obligated under the letter of credit to "honor" (accept) the draft and reimburse Seller's Bank if the documents attached to the draft are conforming. Buyer's Bank then contacts buyer and presents the documents to buyer for payment. Buyer, like the banks, must pay "against the documents" and not the goods themselves, which is why it is necessary to specify the terms of the documents in the original contract for the sale of goods, and then repeat those specifications precisely in the letter of credit. Once buyer has paid, or arranged to pay, Buyer's Bank, it will obtain possession of the bill of lading and only then will it be entitled to obtain the goods from carrier.

Note the limited risks to each party. If seller ships conforming goods, it has independent promises of payment from both buyer and two banks. The banks' promises are enforceable despite assertions of non-conformity of the goods, so long as the documents conform. Thus, as a practical matter, seller is at risk only if Seller's Bank fails (and also Buyer's Bank and buyer), a risk it can probably evaluate. If Seller's Bank unjustifiably refuses to perform its obligation, seller has a cause of action in a local court against a "deep pocket defendant."

Even though Seller's Bank is obligated to pay seller on the documents, it is entitled to reimbursement from Buyer's Bank and from buyer, and practically is at risk only if Buyer's Bank (and buyer) fails or refuses to perform its obligation—risks which Seller's Bank should be able to evaluate accurately. Buyer's Bank is at risk only if buyer fails or refuses to perform, risks which Buyer's Bank had an opportunity to evaluate before issuing the letter of credit, and for which it could adjust its price (interest rate).

On the other hand, for its payment of the price, buyer has a document from carrier entitling it to delivery of the goods, an insurance certificate protecting buyer against casualty loss and perhaps an inspection certificate warranting that the goods conform to the sale contract. In other words, buyer should receive what it bargained for—delivery of conforming goods or insurance proceeds sufficient to cover any loss.

THE GOVERNING RULES

The law relating to letters of credit developed before World War I principally in England, and thereafter by courts in the United States. In the United States, the governing law is usually the applicable state's version of Revised Article 5 of the Uniform Commercial Code. However, most of UCC Article 5 is not mandatory law, and therefore most Article 5 provisions defer to the contract terms of the parties as expressed in the contract. The International Chamber of Commerce (I.C.C.) has developed and published the Uniform Customs and Practices for Documentary Credits (the UCP), which is incorporated by reference in most international letters of credit. The UCP constitutes a rather detailed manual of operations for banks, but they are a restatement of "custom" in the industry, and they do not purport to be law. They are incorporated as an express statement of contract terms and banking trade usage, and the UCP contract terms furnish the rules which usually determine the actions of the parties.

Both UCC Article 5 and the UCP have recently been revised. The Revised Article 5 was adopted by the Uniform Commissioners and the American Law Institute in 1995, and has been enacted by 48 state legislatures. The most recent version of the UCP is the 2007 Revision (I.C.C. Publ. No. 600). The rules set forth in each are relatively similar, but there are some differences. The UCP provisions will have more impact on the analysis of non-fraud issues, and the Revised UCC Article 5 provisions will be used to resolve issues related to allegations of fraud. Therefore, this chapter will describe the UCP rules for all non-fraud issues, and the UCC provisions on fraud.

The UCP establishes four categories of banks in the letter of credit transaction: an issuing bank, an advising bank, a confirming bank, and a nominated bank. An issuing bank promises to honor drafts on itself, if the documents stated in the letter of credit (conforming documents) are presented to it. An advising bank advises the beneficiary (usually the Seller) of the documentary credit, but makes no promise to pay against documents. It is obligated to take "reasonable care" to check the authenticity of the credit before advising, but is not otherwise obligated. A confirming bank receives the credit from the issuing bank and adds its own promise to honor drafts presented to it if accompanied by conforming documents. A nominated bank is a bank in Seller's locality designated by the issuing bank to pay or negotiate the drafts which accompany the required documents. It may, or may not, be a confirming bank.

There are two basic principles of the letter of credit rules promulgated by the UCP (and also of UCC Article 5). One is that the banks' obligations under the letter of credit are independent of the buyer's and seller's obligations under the contract for the sale of goods. (UCP Article 4.) The second is that banks deal only with documents, and not with performance of the underlying sales contract. (UCP Article 5.) The promises of an issuing bank or a confirming bank are not subject to claims or defenses by the applicant (Buyer) that the beneficiary (Seller) has not performed its obligations under the sales contract. (UCP Article 4(a).) However, the bank's promises may still be subject to claims by the applicant (Buyer) of fraud by the beneficiary (Seller), as will be discussed below. The UCP has no provisions concerning fraud, and therefore such issues must be analyzed under Revised UCC Article 5, where U.S. law is applicable.

Since the banks pay the beneficiary (Seller) against the documents, and never see the goods, banks insist on "perfect tender" and "strict compliance" with all documentary conditions. The primary document for describing the goods in a documentary sale transaction is the commercial invoice. The description in the commercial invoice must be specific and must "correspond with the description in the credit;" descriptions in all other documents can be general and need only be "consistent" with the description in the credit. English courts gained renown by determining that "machine shelled groundnut kernels" was not the same description as "Coromandel groundnuts," even though it was agreed that the same goods were described by either label. Bankers could not be expected to know that, or to find it out. *J.H. Rayner & Co. Ltd. v. Hambro's Bank, Ltd*, 1 K.B. 36 (1943).

The more difficult litigated issues concerning the strict conformity of documents seem to arise in transportation terms. Express conditions in the credit that loading, presentment or other acts must be performed by a certain time will be strictly enforced. A credit calling for "Full Set Clean On board ocean bills of lading" is not satisfied by a tender of "truckers bills of lading," even though evidence was presented that the bills of lading were in customary Mexican form and that Mexican truckers did not specify on the bill of lading that the goods were "on board." *Marine Midland Grace Trust Co. of N.Y. v. Banco Del Pais, S.A.*, 261 F.Supp. 884 (S.D.N.Y. 1966).

However, there are circumstances in which the courts may seem to use a different standard. Suppose the seller-shipper does not prepay the freight charges on a CIF contract, but instead credits the freight charges against the amount of the invoice price, and then submits the resulting documents to the issuing bank. Should the issuing bank reject the documents, and refuse to pay the draft accompanying the documents, as non-conforming? Such documents do not strictly comply with CIF terms. However, in *Dixon, Irmaos & Cia, Ltda v. Chase Nat. Bank*, 144 F.2d 759 (2nd Cir. 1944) Dthe court held that the documents were conforming because of "ancient usage" which permitted shippers to take such action. Other types of discrepancies which seem not to warrant rejection include technically invalid clauses in bills of lading which limit the carrier's liability.

Recent cases often involve typographical errors. When the letter of credit mistakenly identified the beneficiary as Sung Jin Electronics, while the documents were correctly addressed to Sung Jun Electronics, the banks were allowed to refuse payment. But this decision has been criticized by practicing lawyers as being "too narrow." *Hanil Bank v. Pt. Bank Negara Indonesia*, 148 F.3d 127 (2nd Cir. 1998). A line of American cases which seemed to permit payment upon substantial performance by the beneficiary, has now been rejected by the Revised Article 5 (Revised § 5–108 and Comment).

Discrepancies in tendered documents are an everyday occurrence. The Preface to the UCP estimates that one half of presentations are rejected for discrepancies. Expert testimony in one case stated that discrepancies are discovered in nearly one half of all documentary transactions. Other commentary and cases indicate between one half and two thirds of all such presentations contain at least one discrepancy. That rate of error should not be surprising if one understands that the presentation in some reported cases, consists of 967 pages of documents. However, it is clear that the "strict compliance" standard itself causes problems.

Under UCP Article 14(a), banks "must examine a presentation to determine, on the basis of the documents alone, whether or not the documents appear, on their face, to constitute a complying presentation." Compliance is not defined in the UCP. This instead is left to other ICC publications which supposedly define standard international banking practices. See ICC Publ. No. 645 (2003) and 681.

When documents are tendered to an issuing or a confirming bank (or a nominated bank acting for them), it has two duties. One is to examine the documents to determine whether they conform to the terms of the letter of credit. The second is to act upon any discrepancies found.

The examination must be, not only thorough, but also quick. If the bank does discover discrepancies, it may reject the documents without consulting its customer, the applicant (Buyer). However, in many situations, the discrepancies may be trivial or typographical, and the customer may want the payment made, and the goods delivered, despite the discrepancy. Thus, UCP Article 16(b) allows, but does not require, the bank to consult the applicant, its customer, for a waiver of the discrepancies it has discovered. That provision does not permit the bank to seek help from the applicant to find further discrepancies. About 90% of the times they are consulted by the issuing bank, applicants will in fact waive the discrepancies discovered by the bank. Thus, the system seems to work because the nonbank parties (Buyer and Seller) want the transaction to be completed despite the technical difficulties imposed by the banking system.

UCP Article 14(b) gives the bank a "maximum of five banking days . . . to determine if a presentation is complying." If the bank discovers no discrepancies, there is no particular difficulty in meeting this deadline, and "the maximum" may be significantly shortened. In one case, 967 pages of documents were examined twice by the issuing bank in two and a half days. *Banco Espanol de Credito v. State Street Bank and Trust Co.*, 385 F.2d 230 (1st Cir. 1967). Once the bank has decided to accept the documents, it must notify the party from whom it received them.

If the bank discovers discrepancies, however, it may be subject to time pressures. The "five banking days" deadline includes not only time to examine the documents presented, but also time to consult the bank's customer (Buyer) about waiving the discrepancies *and* notifying the party from whom the documents were received. It is the latter two requirements which can create difficulties. There are other ICC publications which examine the time for clerks to examine documents and the time period for consulting with the customer, the applicant, and obtaining a response.

UCP Article 16(c) requires any bank which rejects a presentation of documents to state "each discrepancy" that it will rely upon in its notice to the person who presented the documents. Under UCP Article 16(f), failure to state all the discrepancies "precludes" the bank from claiming non-compliance due to any unstated discrepancy, without the necessity of proving waiver or estoppel. Thus, banks which reject documents have only one chance to identify all the discrepancies on which they can ever rely. The rationale for this rule is to inform the beneficiary (Seller) of all the discrepancies at once, so that it can determine whether they all can be cured and whether such cure is cost-effective. But the rule can also lead the issuing bank to delay notification for additional re-examinations to ensure that all defects are discovered.

Under the UCP, banks deal only in documents. (UCP Article 5.) The parties may provide conditions upon the credit, as long as compliance with those conditions can be satisfied through documentary evidence. Thus, letters of credit must state precisely the documents, and the terms of the documents, against which payment is to be made. It is the responsibility of the issuing bank and its customer, the applicant (Buyer), to ensure that satisfaction of each condition can be evidenced by documents. Otherwise, the condition need not be satisfied. UCP Article 14(h) provides that if a letter of credit contains any condition which is not satisfied by a document to be presented to evidence compliance with it, the bank can ignore that condition as though it were not written.

Although it is the commercial invoice that must "strictly conform" to the letter of credit, the most important of the documents required by a letter of credit is the transportation document. Under prior versions of the UCP, this had referred to ocean bills of lading, evidencing an assumption that the goods would be carried by sea. However, there are new developments in the transport industry and new technological applications. Thus the 1993 Revision of the UCP provides separate articles for negotiable ocean bills of lading, non-negotiable sea waybills, charter party bills of lading, multi-modal transport documents, air transport documents, road, rail or inland waterway transport documents, and courier and post receipts.

Under UCP Article 20, an ocean bill of lading must name the port of loading, the port of discharge, the carrier and specify the parties which will be acceptable signatories. Banks have no duty, however, to check the signature or initials accompanying an "on board" notation, absent a special arrangement with the bank. The bill of lading may indicate an "intended vessel." In such cases, any "on board" notation must specify the vessel on which the goods have been loaded. The medieval custom of issuing "a set" of bills of lading, and hoping one of them would arrive and be honored, is now disapproved; and the UCP seeks to have only a single original bill of lading issued as the norm.

A charter party bill of lading does not identify the carrier, and is now a permissible transport document for use with a letter of credit. UCP Article 25(b) relieves the banks from any duty to examine the terms of the charter party, under the assumption that only sophisticated parties with considerable knowledge of the trade will use them.

In multimodal transportation arrangements, the bill of lading is likely to be issued by a freight forwarder and not by a carrier. Thus, it does not name a carrier and it does not contain a receipt by the bailee (who is the carrier), which is the norm for documents of title. However, if the letter of credit authorizes the use of a signature of a named agent of the carrier, such a bill of lading may be used under UCP Article 19, if the freight forwarder issues it as a multi-modal transport document as an agent for a carrier. Otherwise, such "house bills" of freight forwarders are not acceptable transport documents for letters of credit under the UCP.

The liability of the confirming bank is separate and independent of the liability of the issuing bank. To establish the confirming bank's liability, documents may be presented by the beneficiary to the confirming bank or to any other nominated bank under UCP Article 8. This provision can create difficulties for the confirming bank by creating liability without providing it an opportunity to examine the documents. However, the letter of credit must specify both a place for presentation of the documents and an expiration date for the presentation of the documents. Thus, the confirming bank would like to insist that it be the nominated bank, but that is not always possible. Instead, the confirming bank that is not the nominated bank can insist that its office is designated as the place for presentation of the documents.

ELECTRONIC LETTERS OF CREDIT

Electronic communication has taken over some aspects of letters of credit practice, but not others. They dominate the issuance process in bank-to-bank communications, and are sometimes used by applicants to stimulate the issuance process. However, at this time they have not been able to create an entirely paperless transaction pattern for many reasons. First, the beneficiary still wants a piece of paper committing the banks to pay upon specified conditions. Second, electronic bills of lading still are not accepted in most trades as transferable documents of title for the reasons discussed in the preceding chapter. Thus, in the collection of the letter of credit, physical documents will be forwarded, while funds settlement may be electronic.

About three quarters of letter of credit communication between banks, for other banks' issuance, advice, confirmation or negotiation of letters of credit is paperless; and the communication is electronic. While bank-to-bank communication is electronic, bank-to-beneficiary (Seller) communication is still paper-based. Letter of credit issuers can now communicate directly with beneficiaries' computers, however, and use of this practice should be expected to increase. The UCP rules are now written in terms of "teletransmissions," rather than paper-based terminology, which facilitates the use of electronic practices.

Most bank-to-bank communication concerning letters of credit are routed through the dedicated lines of SWIFT (the Society for Worldwide Interstate Financial Telecommunications). SWIFT is a Belgian not-for-profit organization owned by banks as a cooperative venture for the transmission of financial transaction messages. It requires all such messages to be structured in a uniform format, and uses standardized elements for allocating message space and for message text. Thus, messages can be communicated on a computer-to-computer basis without being re-keyed.

A bank issuing a letter of credit communicates that message to the nearest SWIFT access point. The message is then routed on a dedicated data transmission line to a regional processor, where it is validated (see below). From the regional processor, it is routed over a dedicated line to one of two main switches located in either the United States or Europe. From there it is routed through a regional processor to a SWIFT access point to the receiving bank. The message switching and sometimes necessary storage can be performed by computers, if the standardization of the format of the financial messages is sufficiently developed and comprehensive. SWIFT seems to have achieved this level of uniformity.

The bank which receives a SWIFT electronic letter of credit message does not have to send a reply stating that it accepts the request to advise or the authorization to negotiate or pay the letter of credit. It needs only to perform by advising, negotiating or paying, and it is entitled to reimbursement by the issuing bank. However, the SWIFT messages only transmit the letter of credit and their authorizations and requests. SWIFT messages do not effect the settlements of letters of credit or other transfers of funds between issuing banks and other banks. SWIFT is not a clearing house for bank settlements like, for example, CHIPS (Clearing House for Interbank Payment Systems). Under the SWIFT letter of credit system, participating banks must use other arrangements (such as CHIPS) to settle their accounts and accomplish a transfer of funds.

SWIFT relies upon both incryption of messages and authentication to provide security to its users. The authentication of SWIFT messages is accomplished by the use of algorithms, which are mathematical formulas that calculate the contents of a message from header to trailer. If a SWIFT message requires authentication, and all letter of credit messages do, the issuing bank computes the contents and compiles a result based on the number of characters and data fields. At the regional processor, SWIFT checks the authentication trailer for the number of characters in the authentication. However, a more rigorous authentication will be performed by the receiving bank, using an algorithm contained in an authentication key provided by the issuing bank. The computations involving these authentication procedures will indicate a mismatch if the message is fraudulent or has been altered. There are also "log in" procedures, application-selection procedures, message numbering and error checking capabilities, and control of access to the system hardware. SWIFT also retains records of each transaction. In all, the security devices are numerous and complex.

Most SWIFT messages are delivered within minutes of their issuance by a bank, although delays of up to two hours are possible. Thus, delays in the system are slight, but present. When is the issuer of an electronic letter of credit bound? The UCP provides no set rules on the issue, but Revised UCC Article 5 establishes that such messages are effective and enforceable upon transmission by the issuer, not delivery to the receiving bank. Revised § 5–106(a) and SWIFT rules require no reply. This UCC rule conforms to the understanding of bankers involved in the trade.

Under SWIFT rules, Belgian law governs all relations between SWIFT and its users. SWIFT is liable for negligence or fraud of its own employees and agents and for those parts of the communication system that it controls, such as regional processors, main switches and the dedicated lines that connect them. But SWIFT disclaims liability for those parts of the communication system that it does not control, such as the bank computers that issue and receive messages and the dedicated lines from bank to a regional processor. Even where SWIFT is liable, its liability is limited to "direct" damages (loss of interest), and liability for indirect (consequential) damages is not available. Whether Belgian law also governs relations between SWIFT and the non-bank parties to the transaction (applicants and beneficiaries), or between banks and their customers, does not seem yet to have been tested in court.

It is now possible for an applicant (Buyer, in the documentary credit transaction) to draft a proposed electronic letter of credit. The electronic proposed credit can then be transmitted to the issuing bank for it to issue over the SWIFT system. This procedure is usually used where the applicant seeks multiple credits and there is a master agreement between the issuing bank and the applicant. The issuing bank will first check to see whether the proposed credit is authorized and contains the required security codes. Then it will determine whether it is within the previously authorized credit limits and is stated in the standardized elements and uniform format for electronic messages. Both SWIFT and UCP requirements must be analyzed, and changes in the proposed message may be necessary. Thus, the procedures are not yet fully automatic.

On the other end of the electronic communications, the beneficiary (Seller, in the documentary sale), who must be induced to part with value on the basis of the bank's promises, wants a "hard copy", a written letter of credit in the traditional form. The receiving bank therefore will convert the SWIFT electronic message into such a written, paper credit. However, the SWIFT message has been designed for bank-to-bank use, and not necessarily for use by beneficiaries, which creates some problems. First, it does not bear a signature in the traditional sense, even though it has been thoroughly authenticated within the computer-based transmission mechanisms. Thus, the beneficiary is entitled to doubt whether the sending bank is bound to the beneficiary to perform by the written credit derived from the SWIFT electronic message.

The issue if usually framed as: "Is the SWIFT message to be considered to be *the* operative credit instrument as far as the beneficiary is concerned?" The issue is of importance to beneficiaries not only in the original issuance of the credit, but also in the myriad of amendments to the credit which may follow. Under SWIFT rules, SWIFT users treat the electronic message as a binding obligation, and treat the authentication as the functional equivalent of a signature. However, the beneficiary is not a SWIFT user, and banking practice has been that a beneficiary can rely on an electronic message only after it has been issued in a paper-based format, properly signed or otherwise authenticated. Revised UCC § 5–104 states that a letter of credit "may be issued in any form," including an electronic format, but that provision does not necessarily answer the question as to whether the unsigned, paper-based transcription of a SWIFT message, generated by the recipient of that message, is the operative credit instrument and binds the issuing bank.

Under the UCP, whether an electronic message is the operative credit instrument or not depends upon the terminology in the message itself. UCP Article 11(a)(ii) provides that, if the electronic message states "full details to follow," or states that a mail confirmation will be the operative credit instrument, then the electronic message is not that instrument, and the subsequent message is. However, UCP Article 11(a)(i) states that other authenticated electronic messages to advise or amend credits *are* the operative credit instrument. In the latter transactions, mail confirmations should not be sent, and are to have no effect if sent.

However, there is some doubt as to whether SWIFT-generated transcriptions are subject to the

UCP. SWIFT internal rules provide that credits issued through its system are subject to the UCP, but the transcription into a hard copy may bear no reference to the UCP. UCP Article 1 states that the UCP provisions govern "where they are incorporated into the text of the credit." That language is deemed, in some parts of the world, to require an express reference to the UCP in the message to the beneficiary.

The attempts to create an electronic bill of lading have been discussed earlier in Chapter 1. If successful, an electronic bill of lading could help facilitate the electronic letter of credit transaction. However, to date, while electronic bills of lading have been used successfully to replace the straight (non-negotiable) bill of lading, its use to replace the negotiable bill of lading has been met with skepticism. Although SEDOCS showed that an electronic approach was technically feasible, it was not a commercial success. American bankers have been skeptical of their rights to any actual goods under electronic bills of lading issued under CMI (Comite Maritime International) Rules. However, the Commission of the European Communities has just initiated the BOLERO program under the CMI Rules, and it may prove to be more successful. It is discussed in more detail in Chapter 1.

STANDBY LETTERS OF CREDIT

Third world governments often require a financial assurance (by way of a financial guarantee) that foreign firms which undertake to supply goods or to perform a construction project will do so competently and in accordance with the terms of the contract covering the sale or project. Performance bonds can serve as an adequate assurance, but United States banks are barred from issuing insurance contracts, including performance bonds. They have, however, developed an alternative—the "standby" letter of credit, which is a second type of letter of credit transaction. It involves a letter of credit which is issued by the seller's bank and runs in favor of the buyer—truly a backwards arrangement—and payable against a writing which certifies that the seller has not performed its promises. Such a standby letter of credit is not for the purpose of ensuring payment to the seller for goods shipped. Instead, this standby letter of credit is used as a guarantee, or a performance bond, or as insurance of the seller's performance. Under federal law, banks were not allowed to issue guarantees or performance bonds or insurance policies. However, the use of stand-by letters of credit can accomplish the same results, and was not prohibited by bank regulatory agencies. The result was the creation of a new commercial device, which is now commercially accepted for its own value, and which has supplanted the performance bond in many fields of endeavor.

Below is an example of a standby letter of credit issued by seller's bank from *Dynamics Corp. of America v. Citizens & Southern Nat. Bank*, 356 F.Supp. 991 (N.D.Ga. 1973).

" ... TO: THE PRESIDENT OF INDIA

INDIA

BY ORDER OF: ELECTRONICS SYSTEMS DI-
VISION OF DYNAMICS CORPORATION OF
AMERICA

For account

of same

GENTLEMEN:

WE HEREBY ESTABLISH OUR IRREVO-
CABLE CREDIT IN YOUR FAVOR, FOR
THE ACCOUNT INDICATED ABOVE, FOR
A SUM OR SUMS NOT EXCEEDING IN
ALL FOUR HUNDRED TEN THOUSAND
FOUR HUNDRED SEVENTY TWO AND
60/100 US DOLLARS (US$410,472.60)—
AVAILABLE BY YOUR DRAFT(S) AT sight,

DRAWN ON: us

Which must be accompanied by:

1. Your signed certification as follows: "The
President of India being one of the parties to the
Agreement dated March 14, 1971 signed and exchanged between the President of India and the
Dynamics Corporation of America for the license
to manufacture, purchase and supply of radio
equipment as per Schedule I thereof for the total
contract value of $1,368,242.00, does hereby certi-

fy in the exercise of reasonable discretion and in good faith that the Dynamics Corporation of America has failed to carry out certain obligations of theirs under the said Order/Agreement.... ''

In it, the seller (account party) has contracted to have the seller's bank (issuing bank) issue an irrevocable letter of credit in favor of the third world government (beneficiary) that payment will be made upon presentation of a document which is only a simple statement by the beneficiary that the account party has failed to carry out its obligations under a contract (called a "suicide credit"). Some require no document, but provide for payment to be made upon the beneficiary's demand. This transaction is almost a mirror image of the letter of credit in the documentary sale. In the standby credit, the account party is the seller or contractor, the beneficiary is the purchaser (not the seller), and the documents do not control the goods and have no independent value of their own. Often the required documentation is a mere certification by the beneficiary that the contractor has failed to perform under the contract or, perhaps, has failed to return an advance payment.

Standby letters of credit may be governed by the UCP, and are then governed by the same rules as those applicable to documentary credits "to the extent they may be applicable." UCP Art. 1. If the documents presented conform precisely to the terms of the letter of credit, the Confirming Bank and the Issuing Bank are obligated to pay the beneficiary or to honor its draft. The beneficiary is not subject to defenses arising out of the underlying sales transaction, so the conformity of the goods is, with exceptions noted below, irrelevant to the bank's decision. The decision is to be based upon the documents alone. Further, the documents need not conform to the underlying sales contract either, so long as they comply with the letter of credit. This is the "independence principle" which underlies the legal setting for letters of credit.

Some legal commentators question whether the traditional "independence principle" of letter of credit rules should be applied to standby credits, in light of the facts that such letters do not assure an exporter about payment for goods to be shipped, but serve principally a non-payment function to assure an importer (beneficiary) about payment if an exporter (the account party) does not deliver on its contract (to supply goods, services or raw materials). However, the text of both the UCP and Revised UCC Article 5 make it clear that the drafters intended them to cover standby letters of credit, and to apply the "independence principle" to such bank obligations.

NEW INTERNATIONAL RULES FOR STANDBY LETTERS OF CREDIT

Even though both the UCP and Revised UCC Article 5 expressly include standby letters of credit within their coverage, it is clear that they were designed to cover the documentary letter of credit transaction and not the standby transaction. Thus, they impose many unnecessary document-related conditions on the use of standbys. The UCP, in particular, contains many provisions on the proper presentation of transportation documents and the requirements for drawing installment payments, both of which are irrelevant to the usual standby letter of credit transaction. The UCP also does not address several issues, such as fraud and choice of law, which are significant to standby transactions.

In response to these difficulties, the United Nations Commission on International Trade Law (UN-CITRAL) has developed the United Nations Convention on Independent Guarantees and Stand-by Letters of Credit (1995) which entered into force on January 1, 2000. For the same reason, the International Chamber of Commerce (I.C.C.) has developed the Rules on International Standby Practices (ISP 98), which became effective on January 1, 1999. The Convention currently has six Contracting States (Belarus, Ecuador, El Salvador, Kuwait, Panama and Tunisia). The ISP 98 was designed to replace the UCP and be its equivalent in international practice regarding standby letters of credit.

The U.N. Convention on standbys is limited to international undertakings by the issuing bank, so that the issuer and at least one other party must have their places of business in different nations. It also provides choice of law provisions, allowing the parties to choose the applicable law. If the parties do not specify a choice of law, the Convention provides a default rule that the law of the issuer's place of business shall govern the transaction. The Convention also provides rules for allegations of fraud and the seeking injunctive relief. Payment can be withheld from a beneficiary if a document is not genuine, or does not provide a basis for demanding payment. A court may issue an order blocking payment on freezing proceeds of a standby credit if it finds "strong evidence" of such a circumstance.

ISP 98 deletes all the provisions concerning transportation documents, but does require that any official documents be certified. It also places a floor on the amount of information a beneficiary must provide, and requires "magic words," in regard to the presentation of certificates of default under a standby. The ISP also provides rules to govern electronic demands for payment under standby letters of credit. However, since the ISP is not a statute, but merely trade terms incorporated into the contract by reference, it does not attempt to include provisions on fraud and injunctive relief. Perhaps surprisingly, it also does not include any choice of law provisions.

THE FRAUD DEFENSE

Where the documents are forged or fraudulent, or there is fraud in the transaction, however, a different analysis is applied. The "independence principle" promotes the utility of the letter of credit transaction, by offering certainty of payment to the beneficiary who complies with a credit's requirements. But, where there is fraud or forgery, rather than a "mere" breach of the underlying sales contract, a counter principle comes into play. "There is as much public interest in discouraging fraud as in encouraging the use of letters of credit." *Dynamics Corp., supra.* Where the seller's fraud has been called to the bank's attention before the drafts and documents have been presented for payment, the principle of "the independence of the bank's obligation under the letter of credit" should not be extended to protect the unscrupulous seller. *Sztejn v. J. Henry Schroder Banking Corp.*, 31 N.Y.S.2d 631 (N.Y.Sup. 1941).

Thus, there are two competing principles, and the courts have created compromises which limit the impact of the independence principle when there are forged or fraudulent documents, or fraud in the transaction. Vexing problems are raised by claims of fraud and, more particularly, of "fraud in the transaction", but the doctrine that there is a "fraud exception" to the "independence principle" seems to be generally recognized. However, there is still a significant debate about how broad and extensive the fraud exception should be.

This "fraud exception" is available where the credit is expressly subject to the UCP, even though the UCP has no specific provisions on the subject. Since the UCP is silent, the courts have generally held that the UCC provisions govern as a "gap-filling provision." The principle underlying this approach is that the courts will not allow their process to be used by a dishonest person to carry out a fraud.

While the concept of enjoining payment due to fraud has not been widely used in the documentary letter of credit transaction, it has been widely sought in the stand-by letter of credit transaction. Some limiting concepts in the documentary letter of credit transaction, such as "strict compliance" of the documents, become somewhat meaningless when the "document" becomes a mere allegation by one party that the other party failed to perform properly under the contract. When the limitations which give structure to the transaction become meaningless, the transaction can become a breeding ground for fraud.

Under Revised UCC § 5–109, there is a series of limitations on the availability of the fraud exception for use by the beneficiary. The first limitation is that "the issuer shall honor presentation, if honor is demanded by a nominated person who has given value in good faith without notice of material injury or fraud." Thus, confirming banks who have paid against the documents in good faith and without notice of any defense to, or defect in, the documents are entitled to reimbursement, despite fraud on the beneficiary. So also is an advising bank which has been authorized to pay against the documents, rather than merely to accept the documents for collection. Under the UCC, if the documents are presented by such a confirming bank, or authorized advising bank, and the documents appear on their face to comply with the credit, the issuing bank *must* pay the confirming bank, even though the documents are forged or fraudulent or there is fraud in the transaction.

A second limitation is that, if the documents are presented by anyone else (beneficiary, advising bank authorized to take for collection only, confirming bank which took with notice of defects or defenses, etc.), the issuing bank *may* still pay, even though it has been notified that the documents are forged or fraudulent, or that there is fraud in the transaction, as long as it acts in good faith. In the latter case, the issuing bank *may* also refuse to pay, but that is not very likely. Reasons for the issuing bank not refusing to pay range from its reluctance to be known as an unreliable source of funds in letter of credit transactions to its inability to evaluate the available evidence of fraud, especially on an *ex parte* basis. Banks are paid to handle documents, not to become judge and jury.

The account party is, however, given the power to obtain a court order against payment, so long as it can prove forgery, fraud or fraud in the transaction. Thus, under the UCC, if the account party obtains a court injunction against payment from a court having proper jurisdiction, the issuing bank is permitted to dishonor the presentment. But the Revised UCC Article 5 leaves only a very narrow avenue for the account party to seek and obtain judicial intervention through injunctive relief in the letter of credit transaction. To beneficiaries, the concept creates great uncertainty about prompt payment, because they know nothing about the judicial system and fear the worst. To account parties, the concept has created a theoretical argument, but there have been very few reported cases in which they were successful.

The Revised Article 5 provision limits itself in several ways:

First, the fraud must be "material," but material is not defined. The Comments to Revised § 5–109 cite some prior decisions favorably, but its meaning will be decided on a case by case basis. Second, the account party must present sufficient evidence of fraud or forgery, not merely allegations of it. Third, all the procedural requirements for injunctive or other relief must be met. Fourth, the relief can be denied if third parties are not "adequately protected," and no relief will be granted if a confirming or advising bank has paid funds to the beneficiary. However, this concept has been expanded in the Comments to include protection against incidental damages, such as legal fees, by *bond* or otherwise. All of these are limitations which have been found in the prior cases and which would be expected in an action for injunctive relief.

The principal new limitation is one stated in Revised § 5–109. A forgery or a fraud in the document may permit an injunction of payment if perpetrated by anyone, but a fraud in the underlying transaction is cognizable only if it is "committed by the beneficiary," and not by some third party, such as a carrier. The difference between the two concepts is illustrated by the approach of English and Canadian courts to the fraud exception.

The English and Canadian courts have each recognized the "fraud exception," based upon the persuasive precedent of the American cases. However, each of them, in addition to the requirements of the pre-Revision UCC, place great stress on the *scienter* requirements of common law fraud and require the account party to establish that the beneficiary itself made, or was responsible for, the misrepresentation that was the foundation for the fraud claim. A misrepresentation made by any other party to the transaction would not permit an injunction against payment of the beneficiary. Thus, the House of Lords, while recognizing the basic fraud concept, refused to extend it to protect the buyer when the fraud was committed by a third party (a loading broker) without seller's knowledge. *United City Merchants (Investments) Ltd. v. Royal Bank of Canada (The American Accord)*. Under the English–Canadian formulation: (1) Where the credit requires loading by May 15 and the bill of lading shows loading on the 16th, the bank must dishonor. (2) Where the credit requires loading on May 15, and bank knows that the beneficiary has altered a document in a non-apparent manner, the bank must dishonor. (3) But, where the credit requires loading by May 15, and bank knows that a freight forwarder has altered a document in a non-apparent manner, the bank must *honor* the credit.

Under Revised § 5–109, American courts would reach such a result if the misrepresentation was considered a fraud in the underlying transaction. However, such a misrepresentation is more likely to be considered arising out of the document itself. If so, the identity of the perpetrator would be irrelevant. Revised § 5–109 does not attempt to define fraud, which is a product of caselaw and varies widely from state to state.

The traditional difference between fraud doctrines and breach of contract concepts was that the former considered the state of mind of the seller, while breach of contract concerns only whether the goods lived up to particular objective standard set by their description. Fraud concepts have expanded enormously since 1952, and conduct which would not have been actionable during the first half of the 20th Century is now routinely within current caselaw concepts. The modern fraud doctrines often do not require any evil intent, but only that seller know that a particular fact is not true—or, that he does not know whether a particular fact is true or not when he states it—or, that he believes that a fact is true when it is not, and a court decides that he should have made a more thorough investigation before speaking.

As an outgrowth of the 1979 change of government in Iran, increased attention was given to the potential that a standby letter's beneficiary could require payment for what was characterized as "bad faith" or "arbitrary" reasons, or at least for reasons not related to the contractor's intentional failure to perform on the contract (e.g., perhaps because of conditions surrounding a civil insurrection).

Many courts have declined to enjoin payment because of insufficient evidence of fraud, or because an account party sought to expand the definition of fraud. Other courts have been willing to issue a "notice injunction" requiring issuers to give some prior notice (usually three to ten days) to the account party before transferring money to the beneficiary of a standby credit after demand for payment, while a few courts have granted preliminary injunctions of indefinite duration.

Article 19 of The United Nations Convention on Independent Guarantees and Stand-by Letters of Credit permits a court to issue a "provisional order" that the beneficiary not receive payment, or that the funds are blocked if paid, if the applicant can show that a document is not genuine, that the document shows that no payment is due, or that "the demand has no conceivable basis." The Convention also describes five illustrations of the latter principle. The Convention expressly prohibits a court from enjoining payment on any other basis. There is some doubt as to whether "fraud in the transaction" is covered by the criteria of Article 19.

OTHER LETTERS OF CREDIT: BACK TO BACK AND REVOLVING CREDITS

Although the irrevocable documentary letter of credit is used most often in international commercial transactions, documentary letters may also be "revocable," giving the beneficiary a right to payment "unless previously canceled" by the account party. A letter of credit is irrevocable from the time it is issued, under UCP Article 7.

Letters of credit may be "sight" (payable on demand) or "time" (such as, six months following presentation of documents). A time draft will grant credit to the account party, (buyer) and give the beneficiary (seller) an instrument (an accepted draft) which can be negotiated to banks to raise cash now. The confirming or issuing bank will "accept" the draft which accompanies the documents, thus making the bank primarily liable on the draft. A "general" letter of credit does not restrict the beneficiary's right to transfer its rights thereunder, while a "special" letter of credit limits permissible transferees, usually to one or more banks. A letter of credit is "fixed" if it can become "exhausted" either when drafts for payment have been drawn by beneficiary for the full amount of the letter or when the time period for drawing upon the letter has expired.

Brokers of goods have a problem because they often have two transactions in the same goods. They will sell the goods to a buyer in one transaction and then buy them from a supplier in a separate transaction. If both sales transactions involve payment by letters of credit, the broker will be the beneficiary (seller) of the letter of credit in the first transaction and the account party (buyer) in the second. If the documents required by each letter of credit are *identical,* the broker can assign its rights in the first credit to the issuing bank of the second credit. Such arrangements are facilitated if the credits specify the use of time drafts (e.g. "pay 30 days after sight"). This arrangement is a "back to back credit" and allows broker to finance its purchase of the goods from supplier with the credit of its buyer. Such arrangements work more easily using general letters of credit, although special credits can be used by giving an issuing bank a security interest in its proceeds.

However, back to back credits can also become unworkable if one of the credits is amended, and no similar amendment is made to the other credit. Thus, most banks prefer not to use the back to back letter of credit transaction. Instead, they recommend that sellers and brokers obtain financing through a "transferable letter of credit" or an "assignment of proceeds" from a letter of credit.

A transferable letter of credit is one that expressly states that it can be transferred by the original beneficiary to third parties, who become new and substitute beneficiaries. UCP Article 38. Thus, a broker who is the beneficiary of a transferable letter of credit can use its rights under that credit to finance the purchase of the goods from suppliers by transferring part of the broker's rights under the credit to the suppliers. Partial transfers are allowed, so the broker can use this device to finance purchases from several suppliers. However, although substitute commercial invoices and drafts may be used, all other necessary documents must be presented to the original account party, which will reveal the identity of the substitute beneficiary. That may compromise commercially sensitive information, and so brokers tend to avoid use of such credits.

The beneficiary of a letter of credit may irrevocably assign a portion of the credit's proceeds to a third party. If the proceeds are assigned, the advising bank notifies the assignee of the assignment. Thus, a broker who is the beneficiary of a letter of credit that permits assignment of proceeds can use its rights under that credit to finance the purchase of the goods from a supplier by assigning a part of the broker's rights under the credit to the supplier. The assignment of proceeds does not change the parties to the letter of credit. The original account party is obligated to pay only if it receives documents which conform to the credit, so the assignee will not be paid unless it ships the goods using conforming documents. The assignee is not a party to the original credit, it may not know what the terms of the credit are, and must trust the broker (the original beneficiary) to fulfill those terms. The assignment is not governed by the UCP, but by the applicable law of contract. UCP Article 39.

Rapid expansion of turn-key construction contracts (e.g., for building a complete steel mill or cement plant needing someone only to "turn a key" to begin plant operation) has expanded use of "revolving" letters of credit as a vehicle for ensuring that contractors are given progress payments promptly as initial construction phases are completed and to permit further construction phases to occur. Revolving letters of credit are usually clean (no documents required), sight letters which work in the same way and are subject to the same legal rules for fixed letters of credit. But there are differences—first, the importer (often a third world host government) pays, by way of a letter of credit, to import services (building skills) and raw materials rather than finished goods, and second the importer (account party) restores the amount of the letter (by payment to issuer) to an agreed level of further payment to beneficiary (the foreign construction company) following each time that beneficiary has drawn upon the letter for payment. Revolving letters may be documentary (requiring presentation of a certificate of construction phase completion), but "red tape" in obtaining such interim certifications prompts many contractors to seek less formal arrangements, requiring the account party to trust the contractor not to draw upon the letter before such action is appropriate. As a result, the payment ceiling (amount) of the revolving letter will usually be a modest fraction of the total value of the construction contract.

CHAPTER THREE
TECHNOLOGY TRANSFERS

Issues surrounding the transfer of knowledge across national borders have provoked intense discussions during the last decade. The discussions promise to continue unabated. At the core is the desire of third world countries (often advanced developing countries like China, Brazil, and India) to obtain protected information quickly and affordably irrespective of the proprietary rights and profit motives of current holders (usually persons from the most developed countries). Developing countries want production processes which maximize inexpensive labor but which result in products that are competitive in the international marketplace. Capital intensive production processes (e.g., robot production of automobiles) may be of less interest. MNEs may be willing to share (by way of license or sale) a good deal of proprietary information, but are reluctant to part with their "core technology."

Among the industrialized countries, efforts often occur to acquire (even by way of stealing) "leading edge" technology. One example involved attempted theft of IBM computer technology by Japanese companies ultimately caught by the F.B.I. In the United States, the Office of Export Administration uses the export license procedure to control strategic technological "diversions." But in 1984 falsification of licensing documents by prominent Norwegian and Japanese companies allowed the Soviets to obtain the technology for making vastly quieter submarine propellers. In the ensuing scandal, "anti-Toshiba" legislation was adopted in the U.S. Congress. See Section 2443 of the 1988 Omnibus Trade and Competitiveness Act. Leading Japanese executives resigned their positions, which is considered the highest form of apology in Japanese business circles.

The predominant vehicle for controlling technology transfers across national borders is the "license" or "franchise" contract. The holder of information in one country first acquires the legally protected right to own the information in another country. The holder then licenses the right, usually for a fee, to a person in that other country. The very sharing of information raises a risk that proprietary control of the technology may be lost or, at a minimum, that a competitor will be created. Absent authorized transfers, piracy of intellectual property is increasingly commonplace. Indeed, in some countries such theft has risen to the height of development strategy.

The developing nations (as a "Group of 77"), the industrialized nations and the nonmarket economy nations tried to agree in UNCTAD upon an international "Code of Conduct" for the transfer of technology. Wide disparities in attitudes toward such a Code were reflected by the developing nations' insistence that it be an "internationally legally binding Code," and the industrialized nations' position that it consist of "guidelines for the international transfer of technology." Some economics of the debate are illustrated by the fact that persons in the United States pay about one-tenth in royalties for use of imported technology than they receive in royalty payments from technology sent abroad. Many considered development of an international technology transfer Code the most important feature of the North-South dialogue. But it was not to be. Instead, to some degree, the TRIPs Agreement of the World Trade Organization functions as such a code.

THE TRIPS AGREEMENT

The World Trade Organization agreements effective January 1995 include an agreement on trade-related intellectual property rights (TRIPs). This agreement is binding upon the over 150 nations that are members of the World Trade Organization. In the United States, the TRIPs agreement was ratified and implemented by Congress in December of 1994 under the Uruguay Round Agreements Act. There is a general requirement of national and most-favored-nation treatment among the parties.

The TRIPs Code covers the gamut of intellectual property. On copyrights, there is protection for computer programs and databases, rental authorization controls for owners of computer software and sound recordings, a 50-year motion picture and sound recording copyright term, and a general obligation to comply with the Berne Convention (except for its provisions on moral rights).

On patents, the Paris Convention (1967) prevails, product and process patents are to be available for pharmaceuticals and agricultural chemicals, limits are placed on compulsory licensing, and a general 20-year patent term from the date of application is created. United States law, which previously granted 17 year patents from the date of issuance, has been amended to conform. For trademarks, internationally prominent marks receive enhanced protection, the linking of local marks with foreign trademarks is prohibited, service marks become registrable, and compulsory licensing is banned. In addition, trade secret protection is assisted by TRIPs rules enabling owners to prevent unauthorized use or disclosure. Integrated circuits are covered by rules intended to improve upon the Washington Treaty. Lastly, industrial designs and geographic indicators of alcoholic beverages (e.g., Canadian Whiskey) are also part of the TRIPs regime.

Infringement and anticounterfeiting remedies are included in the TRIPs, for both domestic and international trade protection. There are specific provisions governing injunctions, damages, customs seizures, and discovery of evidence.

Late in 2001, the Doha Round of WTO negotiations were launched. These negotiations have reconsidered the TRIPs agreement, particularly as it applies to developing nations. In addition, a Declaration on the TRIPs Agreement and Public Health was issued at the Qatar Ministerial Conference. This Declaration includes the following statement:

We agree that the TRIPs Agreement does not prevent Members from taking measures to protect public health. Accordingly, while reiterating our commitment to the TRIPs Agreement, we affirm that the Agreement can and should be interpreted and implemented in a manner supportive of WTO Members' right to protect public health and, in particular, to promote access to medicines for all.

By mid-2003, a "Medicines Agreement" was finally reached on how to implement this Declaration. Compulsory licensing and/or importation of generic copies of patented medicines needed to address developing nation public health problems are authorized. Such activities may not pursue industrial or commercial policy objectives, and different packaging and labeling must be used in an effort at minimizing the risk of diversion of the generics to developed country markets. Under pressure from the United States, a number of more advanced developing nations (such as Mexico, Singapore and Qatar) agreed not to employ compulsory licensing except in situations of national emergency or extreme urgency. Canada, on the other hand has licensed production of drugs for Rwanda and other nations incapable of pharmaceutical production.

TRIPs disputes decided by WTO Panels or the Appellate Body have required India to reform its "mailbox rule" for pharmaceutical and agricultural chemical patent applications (patentable since 2005), Canada to give 20 year terms to pre-TRIPs patents and limit its generic pharmaceutical regulatory review and stockpiling patent rights' exceptions, the European Union to amend discriminatory regulations regarding geographical indicators, and the United States to pay for "business use" of copyrighted music and to remove a prohibition against registration of Cuban confiscated trademarks without the original owner's consent (HA-VANA CLUB rum).

PATENT PROTECTION

For the most part, patents are granted to inventors according to national law. Thus, patents represent *territorial* grants of exclusive rights. The inventor receives Canadian patents, United States patents, Mexican patents, and so on. Since over one hundred countries have laws regulating patents, there are relatively few jurisdictions without some form of patent protection. However, legally protected intellectual property in one country may not be protected similarly in another country. For example, some third world nations refuse to grant patents on pharmaceuticals. These countries often assert that their public health needs require such a policy. Thailand was traditionally one such country and unlicensed or compulsory licensed "generics" have been a growth industry there, and also in Brazil and India.

Nominal patent protection in some developing nations may lack effective forms of relief-giving the appearance but not the reality of legal rights. Since international patent protection is expensive to obtain, some holders take a chance and limit their applications to those markets where they foresee demand or competition for their product. Nevertheless, U.S. nationals continue to receive tens of thousands of patents in other countries. But the reverse is also increasingly true. Residents of foreign countries now receive over 50 percent of the patents issued under United States law. In many countries, persons who deal with the issuance and protection of patents are called patent agents. In the United States, patent practice is a specialized branch of the legal profession. Obtaining international patent protection often involves retaining the services of specialists in each country.

What constitutes a "patent" and how it is protected in any country depends upon domestic law. In the United States, a patent issued by the U.S. Patent Office grants the right for 20 years to exclude everyone from making, using or selling the patented invention without the permission of the patentee. The United States grants patents to the "first to invent," not (as in many other countries) the "first to file." Patent infringement can result in injunctive and damages relief in the U.S. courts. "Exclusion orders" against foreign-made patent infringing goods are also available. Such orders are frequently issued by the International Trade Commission under Section 337 of the Tariff Act of 1930, and are enforced by the U.S. Customs Service.

A U.S. patent thus provides a short-term legal, but not necessarily economic, monopoly. For example, the exclusive legal rights conveyed by the patents held by Xerox on its photocopying machines have not given it a monopoly in the marketplace. There are many other producers of non-infringing photocopy machines with whom Xerox competes.

There are basically two types of patent systems in the world community, registration and examination. Some countries (e.g., France) grant a patent upon "registration" accompanied by appropriate documents and fees, without making an inquiry about the patentability of the invention. The validity of such a patent grant is most difficult to gauge until a time comes to defend the patent against alleged infringement in an appropriate tribunal. In other countries, the patent grant is made following a careful "examination" of the prior art and statutory criteria on patentability or a "deferred examination" is made following public notice given to permit an "opposition." The odds are increased that the validity of such a patent will be sustained in the face of an alleged infringement. The United States and Germany have examination systems.

To obtain U.S. patents, applicants must demonstrate to the satisfaction of the U.S. Patent Office that their inventions are novel, useful and nonobvious. Nevertheless, a significant number of U.S. patents have been subsequently held invalid in the courts and the Patent Office has frequently been criticized for a lax approach to issuance of patents. Much of this growth is centered in high-tech industries, including computer software and business methods patents.

The terms of a patent grant vary from country to country. For example, local law may provide for "confirmation," "importation," "introduction" or "revalidation" patents (which serve to extend limited protection to patents already existing in another country). "Inventor's certificates" and rewards are granted in some socialist countries where private ownership of the means of production is discouraged. The state owns the invention. This was the case in China, for example, but inventors now may obtain patents and exclusive private rights under the 1984 Patent Law. Some countries, such as Britain, require that a patent be "worked" (commercially applied) within a designated period of time. This requirement is so important that the British mandate a "compulsory license" to local persons if a patent is deemed unworked. Many developing nations have similar provisions in their patent laws ... the owner must use it or lose it.

INTERNATIONAL RECOGNITION OF PATENTS

The principal treaties regarding patents are the 1970 Patent Cooperation Treaty and the 1883 Convention of the Union of Paris, frequently revised and amended. To some extent, the Paris Convention also deals with trademarks, servicemarks, trade names, industrial designs, and unfair competition. Other treaties dealing with patents are the European Patent Convention (designed to permit a single office at Munich and The Hague to issue patents of all countries party to the treaty), and the proposed European Union Patent Convention (designed to create a single patent valid throughout the EU).

The Paris Convention, to which over 140 countries including the U.S. are parties, remains the basic international agreement dealing with treatment of foreigners under national patent laws. It is administered by the International Bureau of the World Intellectual Property Organization (WIPO) at Geneva. The "right of national treatment" prohibits discrimination against foreign holders of local patents and trademarks. Thus, for example, a foreigner granted a Canadian patent must receive the same legal rights and remedies accorded Canadian nationals. Furthermore, important "rights of priority" are granted to patent holders provided they file in foreign jurisdictions within twelve months of their home country patent applications. But such rights may not overcome prior filings by others in "first to file" jurisdictions.

Patent applications in foreign jurisdictions are not dependent upon success in the home country. Patentability criteria vary from country to country. Nevertheless, the Paris Convention obviates the need to file simultaneously in every country where intellectual property protection is sought. If an inventor elects not to obtain patent protection in other countries, anyone may make, use or sell the invention in that territory. The Paris Convention does not attempt to reduce the need for individual patent applications in all jurisdictions where patent protection is sought. Nor does it alter the various domestic criteria on patentability.

The Patent Cooperation Treaty (PCT), to which about 120 countries including the U.S. are parties, is designed to achieve greater uniformity and less cost in the international patent filing process, and in the examination of prior art. Instead of filing patent applications individually in each nation, filings under the PCT are done in selected countries. The national patent offices of Japan, Sweden, Russia and the United States have been designated International Searching Authorities (ISA), as has the European Patent Office at Munich and The Hague. The international application, together with the international search report, is communicated by an ISA to each national patent office where protection is sought. Nothing in this Treaty limits the freedom of each nation to establish substantive conditions of patentability and determine infringement remedies.

However, the Patent Cooperation Treaty also provides that the applicant may arrange for an international preliminary examination in order to formulate a non-binding opinion on whether the claimed invention is novel, involves an inventive step (nonobvious) and is industrially applicable. In a country without sophisticated search facilities, the report of the international preliminary examination may largely determine whether a patent will be granted. For this reason alone, the Patent Cooperation Treaty may generate considerable uniformity in world patent law. In 1986 the United States ratified the PCT provisions on preliminary examination reports, thereby supporting such uniformity.

KNOWHOW

Knowhow is commercially valuable knowledge. It may or may not be a trade secret, and may or may not be patentable. Though often technical or scientific, e.g. engineering services, knowhow can also be more general in character. Marketing and management skills as well as simply business advice can constitute knowhow. If someone is willing to pay for the information, it can be sold or licensed internationally.

Legal protection for knowhow varies from country to country and is, at best, limited. Unlike patents, copyrights and trademarks, you cannot by registration obtain exclusive legal rights to knowhow. Knowledge, like the air we breathe, is a public good. Once released in the community, knowhow can generally be used by anyone and is almost impossible to retrieve. In the absence of exclusive legal rights, preserving the confidentiality of knowhow becomes an important business strategy. If everyone knows it, who will pay for it? If your competitors have access to the knowledge, your market position is at risk. It is for these reasons that only a few people on earth ever know the Coca Cola formula, which is perhaps the world's best kept knowhow.

Protecting knowhow is mostly a function of contract, tort and trade secrets law. Employers will surround their critical knowhow with employees bound by contract to confidentiality. But some valuable knowledge leaks from or moves with these employees, e.g. when a disgruntled retired or ex-employee sells or goes public with the knowhow. The remedies at law or in equity for breach of contract are unlikely to render the employer whole. Neither is torts relief likely to be sufficient since most employees are essentially judgment proof, though they may be of more use if a competitor induced the breach of contract. Likewise, even though genuine trade secrets are protected by criminal statutes in a few jurisdictions, persuading the prosecutor to take up your business problem is not easy and criminal penalties will not recoup the trade secrets (though they may make the revelation of others less likely in the future).

The Economic Espionage Act of 1996 creates *criminal* penalties for misappropriation of trade secrets for the benefit of foreign governments or anyone. For these purposes, a "trade secret" is defined as "financial, business, scientific, technical, economic or engineering information" that the owner has taken reasonable measures to keep secret and whose "independent economic value derives from being closely held." In addition to criminal fines, forfeitures and jail terms, the Act authorizes seizure of all proceeds from the theft of trade secrets as well as property used or intended for use in the misappropriation (e.g., buildings and capital equipment).

Despite all of these legal hazards, even when certain knowhow is patentable, a desire to prolong the commercial exploitation of that knowledge may result in no patent registrations. The international chemicals industry, for example, is said to prefer trade secrets to public disclosure and patent rights with time limitations. Licensing or selling such knowhow around the globe is risky, but lucrative.

TRADEMARK PROTECTION

Virtually all countries offer some legal protection to trademarks, even when they do not have trademark registration systems. Trademark rights derived from the use of marks on goods in commerce have long been recognized at common law and remain so today in countries as diverse as the United States and the United Arab Emirates. The latter nation, for example, had no trademark registration law in 1986, but this did not prevent McDonald's from obtaining an injunction against a local business using its famous name and golden arches without authorization. However, obtaining international trademark protection requires separate registration under the law of each nation.

Roughly 50,000 trademark applications are filed each year by U.S. citizens with the appropriate authorities in other countries. In the United States, trademarks are protected at common law and by state and federal registrations. Federal registration is permitted by the U.S. Trademark Office for all marks capable of distinguishing the goods on which they appear from other goods. Unless the mark falls within a category of forbidden registrations (e.g. those that offend socialist morality in the People's Republic of China), a mark becomes valid for a term of years following registration.

In some countries (like the United States prior to 1989), marks must be used on goods before registration. In others, like France, use is not required and speculative registration of marks can occur. It is said that ESSO was obliged to purchase French trademark rights from such a speculator when it switched to EXXON in its search for the perfect global trademark. Since 1989, U.S. law has allowed applications when there is a bona fide intent to use a trademark within 12 months and, if there is good cause for the delay in actual usage, up to 24 additional months. Such filings in effect reserve the mark for the applicant. The emphasis on bona fide intent and good cause represent an attempt to control any speculative use of U.S. trademark law.

The scope of trademark protection may differ substantially from country to country. Under U.S. federal trademark law, injunctions, damages and seizures of goods by customs officials may follow infringement. Other jurisdictions may provide similar remedies on their law books, but offer little practical enforcement. Thus, trademark registration is no guarantee against trademark piracy. A pair of blue jeans labeled "Levi Strauss made in San Francisco" may have been counterfeited in Israel or Paraguay without the knowledge or consent of Levi Strauss and in spite of its trademark registrations in those countries. Trademark counterfeiting is not just a third world problem, as any visitor to a United States "flea market" can tell. Congress created criminal offenses and private treble damages remedies for the first time in the Trademark Counterfeiting Act of 1984.

In many countries trademarks (appearing on goods) may be distinguished from "service marks" used by providers of services (e.g., The Law Store), "trade names" (business names), "collective marks" (marks used by a group or organization), and "certification marks" (marks which certify a certain quality, origin, or other fact). Although national trademark schemes differ, it can be said generally that a valid trademark (e.g., a mark not "canceled," "renounced," "abandoned," "waived" or "generic") will be protected against infringing use. A trademark can be valid in one country (ASPIRIN brand tablets in Canada), but invalid because generic in another (BAYER brand aspirin in the United States). A trademark can be valid, e.g., CHEVROLET NOVA brand automobiles in the U.S. and Mexico, but diminished in value for reasons of language. If you were Mexican, would you buy a CHEVROLET promising to "no va"?

Unlike patents and copyrights, trademarks may be renewed continuously. A valid mark may be licensed, perhaps to a "registered user" or it may be assigned, in some cases only with the sale of the goodwill of a business. A growing example of international licensing of trademarks can be found in franchise agreements taken abroad. And national trademark law sometimes accompanies international licensing. The principal U.S. trademark law, the Lanham Act of 1946, has been construed to apply extraterritorially (much like the Sherman Antitrust Act) to foreign licensees engaging in deceptive practices.

Foreigners who seek a registration may be required to prove a prior and valid "home registration," and a new registration in another country may not have an existence "independent" of the continuing validity of the home country registration. Foreigners are often assisted in their registration efforts by international and regional trademark treaties.

INTERNATIONAL RECOGNITION OF TRADEMARKS

The premium placed on priority of use of a trademark is reflected in several international trademark treaties. These include the Paris Convention, the 1957 Arrangement of Nice Concerning the International Classification of Goods and Services, and the 1973 Trademark Registration Treaty done at Vienna. The treaties of widest international application are the Paris Convention and the Arrangement of Nice, as revised to 1967, to which the United States is signatory. The International Bureau of WIPO plays a central role in the administration of arrangements contemplated by these agreements.

The Paris Convention reflects an effort to internationalize some trademark rules. In addition to extending the principle of national treatment in Article 2 and providing for a right of priority of six months for trademarks (see patent discussion ante), the Convention mitigates the frequent national requirement that foreigners seeking trademark registration prove a pre-existing, valid and continuing home registration. This makes it easier to obtain foreign trademark registrations, avoids the possibility that a lapse in registration at home will cause all foreign registrations to become invalid, and allows registration abroad of entirely different (and perhaps culturally adapted) marks. Article 6 bis of the Paris Convention gives owners of "well known" trademarks the right to block or cancel the unauthorized registration of their marks. One issue that frequently arises under this provision is whether the mark needs to be well known locally or just internationally to obtain protection.

The Nice Agreement addresses the question of registration by "class" or "classification" of goods. In order to simplify internal administrative procedures relating to marks, many countries classify and thereby identify goods (and sometimes services) which have the same or similar attributes. An applicant seeking registration of a mark often is required to specify the class or classes to which the product mark belongs. However, not all countries have the same classification system and some lack any such system. Article 1 of the Nice Agreement adopts, for the purposes of the registration of marks, a single classification system for goods and services. This has brought order out of chaos in the field.

The 1973 Vienna Trademark Registration Treaty (to which the United States is a signatory) contemplates an international filing and examination scheme like that in force for patents under the Patent Cooperation Treaty. This treaty has not yet been fully implemented, but holds out the promise of reduced costs and greater uniformity when obtaining international trademark protection. Numerous European and Mediterranean countries are parties to the Madrid Agreement for International Registration of Marks (1891, as amended). Since 2002, the United States has joined in the Madrid Protocol of 1989. This Protocol permits international filings to obtain about 60 national trademark rights and is administered by WIPO. A Common Market trademark has been developed by the European Union, an alternative to national trademark registrations.

COPYRIGHT PROTECTION

Nearly one hundred nations recognize some form of copyright protection for ''authors' works.'' The scope of this coverage and available remedies varies from country to country, with some uniformity established in the roughly 80 nations participating in the Berne and Universal Copyright Conventions (below). In the United States, for example, the Copyright Act of 1976 protects all original expressions fixed in a tangible medium (now known or later developed), including literary works, musical works, dramatic works, choreographic works, graphic works, audiovisual works, sound recordings and computer programs. It is not necessary to publish a work to obtain a U.S. copyright. It is sufficient that the work is original and fixed in a tangible medium of expression. Prior to 1989, to retain a U.S. copyright, the author had to give formal notice of a reservation of rights when publishing the work. Publication of the work without such notice no longer dedicates it to free public usage.

U.S. copyright protection now extends from creation of the work to 70 years after the death of the author. The author also controls "derivative works," such as movies made from books. Only the author (or her assignees or employer in appropriate cases) may make copies, display, perform, and first sell the work. Registration with the U.S. Copyright Office is not required to obtain copyright rights, but is important to federal copyright infringement remedies. Infringers are subject to criminal penalties, injunctive relief and civil damages. Infringing works are impounded pending trial and ultimately destroyed. But educators, critics and news reporters are allowed "fair use" of the work, a traditional common law doctrine now codified in the 1976 Copyright Act.

The marketing of copyrights is sometimes accomplished through agency "clearinghouses." This is especially true of musical compositions because the many authors and potential users are dispersed. In the United States, the American Society of Composers, Authors and Publishers (ASCAP) and Broadcast Music, Inc. (BMI) are the principal clearinghouses for such rights. Thousands of these rights are sold under "blanket licenses" for fees established by the clearinghouses and later distributed to their members. Similar organizations exist in most European states. Their activities have repeatedly been scrutinized under U.S. and EU antitrust law. A Joint International Copyright Information Service run since 1981 by WIPO and UNESCO is designed to promote licensing of copyrights in the third world. This Service does not act as an agency clearinghouse for authors' rights, a deficiency sometimes said to promote copyright piracy.

Copyright protection in other countries may be more or less comprehensive or capable of adaptation to modern technologies. The copyrightability of computer programs, for example, is less certain in many jurisdictions. In some developing countries, "fair use" is a theme which is expansively construed to undermine copyright protection. But these differences seem less significant when contrasted with the worldwide problem of copyright piracy, ranging from satellite signal poaching to unlicensed music and books.

In the United States, the Copyright Felony Act of 1992 criminalized all copyright infringements. The

No Electronic Theft Act of 1997 (NET) removed the need to prove financial gain as element of copyright infringement law, thus ensuring coverage of copying done with intent to harm copyright owners or copying simply for personal use. The Digital Millennium Copyright Act of 1998 (DMCA) brought the United States into compliance with WIPO treaties and created two new copyright offenses; one for circumventing technological measures used by copyright owners to protect their works ("hacking") and a second for tampering with copyright management information (encryption). The DMCA also made it clear that "webmasters" digitally broadcasting music on the internet must pay performance royalties.

INTERNATIONAL RECOGNITION
OF COPYRIGHTS

Absent an appropriate convention, copyright registrations must be tediously acquired in each country recognizing such rights. However, copyright holders receive national treatment, translation rights and other benefits under the Universal Copyright Convention (UCC) of 1952 (U.S. adheres). Most importantly, the UCC *excuses* foreigners from registration requirements provided notice of a claim of copyright is adequately given (e.g., © Folsom, Gordon and Spanogle, 2009). Some countries like the United States took advantage of an option *not* to excuse registration requirements. The exercise of this option had the effect at that time of reinforcing the U.S. "manufacturing clause" requiring local printing of U.S. copyrighted books and prohibiting importation of foreign copies. This protectionist clause finally expired under U.S. copyright law in 1986. The UCC establishes a minimum term for copyright protection: 25 years after publication, prior registration or death of the author. It also authorizes compulsory license schemes for translation rights in all states and compulsory reprint rights and instructional usage in developing countries.

National treatment and a release from registration formalities (subject to copyright notice requirements) can be obtained in Pan-American countries under the Mexico City Convention of 1902 and the Buenos Aires Convention of 1911, the United States adhering to both. Various benefits can be had in many other countries through the Berne Convention of 1886 (as revised). Like the UCC, the Berne Convention suspends registration requirements for copyright holders from participating states. Unlike the UCC, it allows for local copyright protection independent of protection granted in the country of origin and does not require copyright notice. The Berne Convention establishes a minimum copyright term of the life of the author plus 50 years, a more generous minimum copyright than that of the UCC. It also recognizes the exclusive translation rights of authors. The Berne Convention does not contemplate compulsory licensing of translation rights. Most U.S. copyright holders previously acquired Berne Convention benefits by simultaneously publishing their works in Canada, a member country.

In 1989, the United States ratified the Berne Convention. U.S. ratification of the Berne Convention creates copyright relations with an additional 25 nations. Ratification has eliminated U.S. registration requirements (reserved under the UCC) for foreign copyright holders and required protection of the "moral rights" of authors, i.e. the rights of integrity and paternity. The right of paternity insures acknowledgment of authorship. The right of integrity conveys the ability to object to distortion, alteration or other derogation of the work. It is generally thought that unfair competition law at the federal and state levels will provide the legal basis in U.S. law for these moral rights. A limited class of visual artists explicitly receive these rights under the Visual Artists Rights Act of 1990.

FRANCHISING IN THE UNITED STATES

Franchising is an important sector in the United States economy. Thousands of franchisors have created and administer franchise systems throughout the nation. U.S. franchisees number in the hundreds of thousands. These franchisees are typically independent business persons, and their local franchise outlets employ millions of people. It has been estimated that approximately one-third of all retail sales in the United States take place through franchised outlets. Just as U.S. franchisors have found franchising particularly effective for market penetration abroad, Canadian, European and Japanese companies are increasingly penetrating the U.S. market through franchising.

Franchising is a business technique that permits rapid and flexible penetration of markets, growth and capital development. In the United States, there are traditional distinctions between product franchises and business format franchises. Product franchises involve manufacturers who actually produce the goods that are distributed through franchise agreements. For example, ice cream stores, soft drink bottling companies and gasoline retailers are often the subject of product franchises. Business format franchises are more common. These do not involve the manufacture by the franchisor of the product being sold by the franchisee. More typically, the franchisor licenses intellectual property rights in conjunction with a particular "formula for success" of the business. Fast food establishments, hotels, and a variety of service franchises are examples of business format franchising.

U.S. regulation of franchise relationships occurs at both the federal and state levels of government. Such regulation can be as specific as the Federal Trade Commission Franchising Rule and state franchise disclosure duties or as amorphous as the ever present dangers of state and federal antitrust law.

INTERNATIONAL FRANCHISING

International franchising raises a host of legal issues under intellectual property, antitrust, tax, licensing and other laws. The significance of these issues is magnified by the rapid growth of international franchising. Many U.S. franchisors start in Canada, with Japan and Britain following. Some U.S. investors have found franchising the least risky and most popular way to enter Central and Eastern Europe. U.S. franchising in China is expanding rapidly. Franchising is not just a U.S. export. Many foreign franchisors have entered the U.S. market.

Most franchisors have standard contracts which are used in their home markets and receive counsel on the myriad of laws relevant to their business operations. Such contracts need to be revised and adapted to international franchising without significantly altering the franchisor's successful business formula. Franchise fees and royalties must be specified, the provision of services, training, and control by the franchisor detailed, the term and area of the franchise negotiated ("master franchises" conveying rights in an entire country or region are common in international franchise agreements), accounting procedures agreed upon, business standards and advertising selected, insurance obtained, taxes and other liabilities allocated, and default and dispute settlement procedures decided. At the heart of all franchise agreements lies a trademark licensing clause conveying local trademark rights of the franchisor to the franchisee in return for royalty payments.

Were franchising unaffected by regulation, the attorney's role would be limited to negotiation and drafting of the agreement. But international franchising is increasingly regulated by home and host jurisdictions, including regional groups like the EU. In third world countries, especially Latin America, technology transfer laws, aimed principally at international patent and knowhow licensing, also regulate franchise agreements. These laws benefit franchisees and further development policies, e.g., conservation of hard currencies by control of royalty levels. In 1986, the European Court of Justice issued its first major opinion on the legality of franchise agreements under competition law. The *Pronuptia* decision indicates that European law can depart significantly from leading American antitrust law on market division arrangements for distributors. The Europeans subsequently implemented a comprehensive regulation on franchise agreements, which in turn was replaced by the EU "vertical restraints" Regulation No. 2790/1999.

There is often a perception of being invaded culturally that follows franchising. Local laws sometimes respond to the cultural impact of foreign franchises, as when McDonald's wishes to introduce its large golden arch into the traditional architecture of Europe. But this did not stop McDonald's from opening in Moscow with great success. In India and Mexico, nationalist feelings hostile to the appearance of foreign trademarks on franchised products have produced laws intended to remove such usage. For example, the Mexican Law of Inventions and Tradenames (1976)(repealed 1987) anticipated requiring use of culturally Mexican marks in addition to marks of foreign origin. Other nations require local materials (olive oil in the Mediterranean) to be substituted. This could, for example, alter the formula for success (and value) of fast food franchises. Still others (e.g., Alberta, Canada) mandate extensive disclosures by franchisors in a registered prospectus before agreements may be completed. Disclosure violations can trigger a range of franchisee remedies: rescission, injunction, and damages. Such laws are also found in many of the American states.

Franchise advertising must conform to local law. For example, regulations in the People's Republic of China prohibit ads which "have reactionary ... content." Antitrust and tax law are important in international franchising. Double taxation treaties, for example, will affect the level of taxation of royalties. Antitrust law will temper purchasing requirements of the franchisor, lest unlawful "tying arrangements" be undertaken. Tying arrangements involve coercion of franchisees to take supplies from the franchisor or designated sources in return for the franchise. Such arrangements must, by definition, involve two products: the tying and tied products. They are subject to a complex, not entirely consistent, body of case law under the U.S. Sherman Antitrust Act, Articles 81 and 82 of the Rome Treaty and other laws.

For example, U.S. antitrust case law on franchise tying arrangements is quite diverse. One decision treats the trademark license as a separate tying product and the requirement of the purchase by fast food franchisees of non-essential cooking equipment and paper products unlawful. Another case permits franchisors to require franchisees to purchase "core products" (e.g., chicken) subject to detailed specifications, or from a designated list of approved sources. Sometimes, the "core product" (e.g., ice cream) and the trademark license (e.g., Baskin-Robbins) are treated as a single product incapable of being tied in violation of the law. Still another leading case involving McDonald's suggests that anything comprising the franchisor's "formula for success" may possibly be tied in the franchise contract. This may be especially lawful if there was full pre-contract disclosure by the franchisor.

INTERNATIONAL PATENT AND KNOWHOW LICENSING

This section concerns the most common form of lawful international technology transfer-patent and knowhow licensing. Before any patent licensing can take place, patents must be acquired in all countries in which the owner hopes there will be persons interested in purchasing the technology. Even in countries where the owner has no such hope, patent rights may still be obtained so as to foreclose future unlicensed competitors. Licensing is a middle ground alternative to exporting from the owner's home country and direct investment in host markets. It can often produce, with relatively little cost, immediate positive cash flows.

International patent and knowhow licensing is the most critical form of technology transfer to third world development. From the owner's standpoint, it presents an alternative to and sometimes a first step towards foreign investment. Such licensing involves a transfer of patent rights or knowhow (commercially valuable knowledge, often falling short of a patentable invention) in return for payments, usually termed royalties. Unlike foreign investment, licensing does not have to involve a capital investment in a host jurisdiction. However, licensing of patents and knowhow is not without legal risks.

From the licensee's standpoint, and the perspective of its government, there is the risk that the licensed technology may be old or obsolete, not "state of the art." Goods produced under old technology will be hard to export and convey a certain "second class" status. On the other hand, older more labor intensive technologies may actually be sought (as sometimes done by the PRC) in the early stages of development. Excessive royalties may threaten the economic viability of the licensee and drain hard currencies from the country. The licensee typically is not in a sufficiently powerful position to bargain away restrictive features of standard international licenses. For all these reasons, and more, third world countries frequently regulate patent and knowhow licensing agreements. Such law is found in the Brazilian Normative Act No. 17 (1976) and the Mexican Technology Transfer Law (1982) (repealed 1991), among others. Royalty levels will be limited, certain clauses prohibited (e.g., export restraints, resale price maintenance, mandatory grantbacks to the licensor of improvements), and the desirability of the technology evaluated.

Regulation of patent and knowhow licensing agreements is hardly limited to the third world. The Common Market, for example, after several test cases before the European Court of Justice, issued a "block exemption" controlling patent licensing agreements. Many of the licensing agreement clauses controlled by this 1984 Regulation were the same as those covered by third world technology transfer legislation. Its successors, Regulations 240 of 1996 and 772 of 2004, broadly cover technology transfer agreements (including, since 2004, software copyright licensing). EU regulation prohibits production restraints, forbids the fixing of retail prices for the licensed product by the licensor, limits the licensor's power to select to whom the licensee may sell, controls the "grant back" of product improvements and determines the licensee's right to challenge the validity of intellectual property. It also affects exclusive licensing arrangements, the allocation of geographic territories among licensees, trademark usage, tying arrangements, fields of use, the duration of the license, quality controls, and discrimination between licensees by the licensor. Regulation of patent, knowhow and software copyright licensing in the United States is less direct and predominantly the concern of patent and antitrust law (e.g., tying practices).

The licensor also faces legal risks. The flow of royalty payments may be stopped, suspended or reduced by currency exchange regulations. The taxation of the royalties, if not governed by double taxation treaties, may be confiscatory. The licensee may produce "gray market" goods (*infra*) which eventually compete for sales in markets exclusively intended for the licensor. In the end, patents expire and become part of the world domain. At that point, the licensee has effectively purchased the technology and becomes an independent competitor (though not necessarily an effective competitor if the licensor has made new technological advances).

Licensing is a kind of partnership. If the licensee succeeds, the licensor's royalties (often based on sales volumes) will increase and a continuing partnership through succeeding generations of technology may evolve. If not, the dispute settlement provisions of the agreement may be called upon as either party withdraws from the partnership. Licensing of patents and knowhow often is combined with, indeed essential to, foreign investments. A foreign subsidiary or joint venture will need technical assistance and knowhow to commence operations. When this occurs, the licensing terms are usually a part of the basic joint venture or investment agreement. Licensing may also be combined with a trade agreement, as where the licensor ships necessary supplies to the licensee, joint venturer, or subsidiary. Such supply agreements have sometimes been used to overcome royalty limitations through a form of "transfer pricing," the practice of marking up or down the price of goods so as to allocate revenues to preferred parties and jurisdictions (e.g., tax havens).

PROTECTION FROM PIRACY

Theft of intellectual property and use of counterfeit goods are rapidly increasing in developing and developed countries. Such theft is not limited to consumer goods (Pierre Cardin clothing, Rolex watches). Industrial products and parts (e.g., automotive brake pads) are now being counterfeited. Some developing countries see illegal technology transfers as part of their economic development. They encourage piracy or choose not to oppose it. Since unlicensed producers pay no royalties, they often have lower production costs than the original source. This practice fuels the fires of intellectual property piracy. Unlicensed low cost reproduction of entire copyrighted books (may it not happen to this book) is said to be rampant in such diverse areas as Nigeria, Saudi Arabia, and China. Apple computers have been inexpensively counterfeited in Hong Kong. General Motors estimates that about 40 percent of its auto parts are counterfeited in the Middle East. Recordings and tapes are duplicated almost everywhere without license or fee. And the list goes on.

Legal protection against intellectual property theft and counterfeit goods is not very effective. In the United States, trademark and copyright holders may register with the Customs Service and seek the blockade of pirated items made abroad. Such exclusions are authorized in the Lanham Trademark Act of 1946 and the Copyright Act of 1976. Patent piracy is most often challenged in proceedings against unfair import practices under Section 337 of the Tariff Act of 1930. Section 337 proceedings traditionally involve some rather complicated provisions in Section 1337 of the Tariff Act of 1930. Prior to 1988, the basic prohibition was against: (1) unfair methods of competition and unfair acts in the importation of goods, (2) the effect or tendency of which is to destroy or substantially injure (3) an industry efficiently and economically operated in the United States Such importation was also prohibited when it prevented the establishment of an industry, or restrained or monopolized trade and commerce in the United States.

The Omnibus Trade and Competitiveness Act of 1988 revised Section 337. The requirement that the U.S. industry be efficiently and economically operated was dropped. The importation of articles infringing U.S. patents, copyrights, trademarks or semiconductor chip mask works is specifically prohibited provided a U.S. industry relating to such articles exists or is in the process of being established. Proof of injury to a domestic industry is not required in intellectual property infringement cases. Such an industry exists if there is significant plant and equipment investment, significant employment of labor or capital, or substantial investment in exploitation (including research and development or licensing).

Determination of violations and the recommendation of remedies to the President under Section 337 are the exclusive province of the International Trade Commission (ITC). Most of the case law under Section 337 concerns the infringement of patents. While not quite a per se rule, it is nearly axiomatic that any infringement of United States patent rights amounts to an unfair import practice for purposes of Section 337. Section 337 proceedings result in general exclusion orders permitting seizure of patent counterfeits at any U.S. point of entry. However, the Customs Service finds it extremely difficult when inspecting invoices and occasionally opening boxes to ascertain which goods are counterfeit or infringing. Many counterfeits do look like "the real thing."

For most seizure remedies to work, the holder must notify the customs service of an incoming shipment of offending goods. Use of private detectives can help and is increasing, but such advance notice is hard to obtain. Nevertheless, the Customs Service seizes millions of counterfeit goods each year. Counterfeit toys, for example, are commonly seized.

Infringement and treble damages actions may be commenced in United States courts against importers and distributors of counterfeit goods, but service of process and jurisdictional barriers often preclude effective relief against foreign pirates. Even if such relief is obtained, counterfeiters and the sellers of counterfeit goods have proven adept at the "shell game," moving across the road or to another country to resume operations. Moreover, the mobility and economic incentives of counterfeiters have rendered the criminal sanctions of the Trademark

Counterfeiting Act of 1984 largely a Pyrrhic victory. Ex parte seizure orders are also available under the 1984 Act and the Lanham Trademark Act when counterfeit goods can be located in the United States. Goods so seized can be destroyed upon court order.

International solutions have been no less elusive. The WTO agreement on TRIPs addresses these problems by mandating certain national remedies, but their effectiveness remains to be tested. Various United States statutes authorize the President to withhold trade benefits from or apply trade sanctions to nations inadequately protecting the intellectual property rights of U.S. citizens. This is true of the Caribbean Basin Economic Recovery Act of 1983, the Generalized System of Preferences Renewal Act of 1984, the Trade and Tariff Act of 1984 (amending Section 301 of the 1974 Trade Act), and Title IV of the 1974 Trade Act as it applies to most favored nation tariffs. Slowly this carrot and stick approach has borne fruit. Under these pressures for example, Singapore drafted a new copyright law, Korea new patent and copyright laws, and Taiwan a new copyright, patent, fair trade and an amended trademark law. Brazil introduced legislation intended to allow copyrights on computer programs. Though these changes have been made, there is some doubt as to the rigor with which the new laws will be enforced when local jobs and national revenues are lost.

GRAY MARKET GOODS

One of the most controversial areas of customs law concerns "gray market goods," goods produced abroad *with authorization* and payment but which are imported into *unauthorized* markets. Trade in gray market goods has dramatically increased in recent years, in part because fluctuating currency exchange rates create opportunities to import and sell such goods at a discount from local price levels. Licensors and their distributors suddenly find themselves competing in their home or other "reserved" markets with products made abroad by their own licensees. Or, in the reverse, startled licensees find their licensor's products intruding on their local market shares. In either case, third party importers and exporters are often the immediate source of the gray market goods, and they have little respect for who agreed to what in the licensing agreement. When pressed, such third parties will undoubtedly argue that any attempt through licensing at allocating markets or customers is an antitrust or competition law violation.

In the early part of the century, gray market litigation provoked a Supreme Court decision in *A. Bourjois & Co. v. Katzel*, 260 U.S. 689 (1923) blocking French cosmetics from entering the United States. A U.S. firm was assigned the U.S. trademark rights for French cosmetics as part of the sale of the American business interests of the French producer. The assignee successfully obtained infringement relief against Katzel, an importer of the

French product benefitting from exchange rate fluctuations. The Supreme Court reversed a Second Circuit holding which followed a line of cases allowing "genuine goods" to enter the American market in competition with established sources. The Supreme Court emphasized the trademark ownership (not license) and independent public good will of the assignee as reasons for its reversal.

Congress, before the Supreme Court reversal, passed the Genuine Goods Exclusion Act, now appearing as Section 526 of the Tariff Act of 1930. This Act bars *unauthorized importation* of goods bearing trademarks of U.S. citizens. Registration of such marks with the Customs Service can result in the seizure of unauthorized imports. Persons dealing in such imports may be enjoined, required to export the goods, destroy them or obliterate the offending mark, as well as pay damages. The Act has had a checkered history in the courts and Customs Service. The Customs Service view (influenced by antitrust policy) was that genuine (gray market) goods may be excluded only when the foreign and U.S. trademark rights are not under common ownership, or those rights have been used without authorization. The practical effect of this position was to admit most gray market goods into the United States, thereby providing substantial price competition, but uncertain coverage under manufacturers' warranty, service and rebate programs. Some firms, like K Mart, excel at gray market importing and may provide independent warranty and repair service contracts. Since 1986, New York and California require disclosure by sellers of gray market goods that manufacturers' programs may not apply.

A split in the federal courts of appeal as to the legitimacy in light of the Genuine Goods Exclusion Act of the Customs Service position on gray market imports resulted in a U.S. Supreme Court ruling. In an extremely technical, not very policy oriented decision, the Supreme Court in *K Mart Corp. v. Cartier, Inc.*, 486 U.S. 281 (1988) arrived at a compromise. The Customs Service can continue to permit entry of genuine goods when common ownership of the trademarks exists. The Service must seize such goods only when they were authorized (licensed), but the marks are not subject to common ownership. Many believe that the bulk of U.S. imports of gray market goods have continued under this ruling.

An attempt in 1985 by Duracell to exclude gray market batteries under Section 337 of the Tariff Act of 1930 as an unfair import practice was upheld by the U.S. International Trade Commission, but denied relief by President Reagan in deference to the Customs Service position.

Injunctive relief under trademark or copyright law is sometimes available against gray market importers and distributors. In *Quality King Distributors, Inc. v. L'anza Research Intern., Inc.*, 523 U.S. 135 (1998), however, the U.S. Supreme Court held that the "first sale doctrine" bars injunctive relief under the Copyright Act against gray market re-importation of U.S. exports. In *Lever Bros.*, the D.C. Circuit allowed Trademark Act injunctive relief against materially different gray market goods where those differences had not been disclosed in labeling. When available, injunctive relief applies only to the parties and does not prohibit gray market imports or sales by others. This remedy is thus useful, but normally insufficient.

Most foreign jurisdictions permit entry of gray market goods. The use of intellectual property rights to block trade in gray market ("parallel") goods within the Common Market has been repeatedly denied by the European Court of Justice in its competition and customs law rulings. Once authorized goods reach the market and title has passed to others, intellectual property rights in them are said as a matter of European law to be "exhausted." But under the *Silhouette v. Hartlauer,* opinion of the European Court of Justice intellectual property rights can be used to block the importation of gray market goods from outside the Common Market. In other words, the exhaustion doctrine does not apply externally. Levi Strauss, for example, has seized upon this distinction to actively pursue EU importers of blue jeans from non-EU sources.

TRANSBORDER DATA FLOWS

Because information transfers are linked with employment and trade patterns, many countries have taken a keen interest in regulating transborder data flows (TBDFs). Technical strides in satellite communications and the digital age make regulation a challenge. In 1981, the OECD approved fourteen principles as Guidelines on the Protection of Privacy and TransBorder Flow of Personal Data. In 1998, Europe finalized a data privacy directive that is noticeably more protective of individual privacy than U.S. law. Any information relating to natural persons must be secure, current, relevant and not excessive in content. In most cases, personal data may be processed only with individual consent. Individuals have broad rights of disclosure, access, correction and erasure of data, particularly before it is used in direct marketing.

Transfers of data to non-EU countries are prohibited unless the recipient jurisdiction provides an "adequate level of protection." Whether the United States does so is hotly debated. To remove risks of liability under the European law, "safe harbors" have been created by EU-USA agreement for firms willing to abide by the EU rules on data privacy. The primary safe harbor involves participation in self-regulating privacy groups (e.g., BBB Online) supervised by the U.S. Federal Trade Commission. EU law on data privacy has thus become a global industry standard.

SPECIAL 301 PROCEDURES

Extensive negotiations were conducted within the GATT under the Uruguay Round on trade-related intellectual property rights (TRIPs). The developed nations sought an Anti-Counterfeiting Code and greater patent, copyright and trademark protection in the third world. The developing nations resisted on nearly all fronts. The TRIPs negotiations failed to reach a conclusion as scheduled in December of 1990. Meanwhile, faced with massive technology transfer losses, "Special 301" procedures were established unilaterally by the United States in the 1988 Omnibus Trade and Competitiveness Act. These procedures are located in Section 182 of the Trade Act of 1974. They can lead to initiation of Section 301 proceedings under that Act. Section 301 proceedings are generally used to obtain market access for U.S. exporters of goods and services, but are also capable of being used to pressure and perhaps sanction other nations whose intellectual property policies diverge from U.S. standards.

Special 301 requires the U.S. Trade Representative (USTR) to identify those countries that deny "adequate and effective protection of intellectual property rights" or deny "fair and equitable market access to U.S. persons who rely upon intellectual property protection." The USTR must also identify "priority foreign countries" whose practices are the most "onerous or egregious" and have the greatest adverse impact on the United States, and who are not entering into good faith negotiations or making significant progress in negotiations towards provision of adequate and effective protection of intellectual property rights.

The USTR developed "watch lists" and "priority watch lists" under Special 301 while pursuing negotiations with the many nations on those lists. These negotiations had some success. Argentina agreed, as a result of Special 301 negotiations, to modify registration procedures for and improve protection of pharmaceuticals under its patent law. Mexico was removed from priority status on the Special 301 watch list after it announced new patent legislation. This legislation increased the term of Mexican patents to 20 years, offered protection for chemical and pharmaceutical products as well as biotechnology processes, restricted use of compulsory licenses and made improvements to the Mexican law of trademarks and trade secrets. Intellectual property reforms in Korea, Taiwan and Saudi Arabia also removed them from the USTR's priority watch list.

India, Thailand and the People's Republic of China were formally named the first priority Special 301 countries. Naming any country under Special 301 triggers the possibility of unilateral U.S. trade sanctions under Section 301 of the Trade Act of 1974. Early in 1992, the United States and the PRC reached a last minute agreement on intellectual reforms in the PRC. This agreement avoided trade sanctions. In 2008, China and Russia were priority watch listed, again with a focus on protection of intellectual property rights.

To a large degree, the potential for Special 301 trade sanctions has been diluted by U.S. participation in the World Trade Organization Agreement on TRIPs. Since 1995, nearly all U.S. intellectual property complaints have gone to WTO dispute settlement, a subject covered in our *International Trade and Economic Relations* Nutshell. The Special 301 "naming" and "watching" process, however, continues in full force. This is of particular significance to 'Russia, not yet a WTO member.

CHAPTER FOUR

FOREIGN INVESTMENT TRANSACTIONS

DEFINING THE FOREIGN INVESTMENT

Investment commonly involves the *ownership* of some of the equity in a business. It may also involve *control*. Ownership and control issues are often complex, especially in cross-border situations, as for example, when a corporation chartered in one nation has its center of management in a second nation and its owners (shareholders) are citizens of a third nation. While identifying the nation of the corporation's articles of incorporation (charter) is usually easy, it may not be easy to determine who owns or controls the entity, or even where that control occurs. Where the investor owns all the equity in the foreign investment, there is usually little question regarding who has ownership and control. But as the equity percentage owned by the foreign investor diminishes, the question of who has control arises. Ownership of a majority of the voting equity of the foreign entity usually means the entity is a subsidiary under the control of the investor.

If the investor from abroad has half the equity, who has control may be quite uncertain. No one

212

has control solely by virtue of ownership of 50 percent, but one of the 50 percent owners may be able to exert control. It may depend on the ability to control proxies, if such method of voting is permitted. Where the ownership is less than 50 percent, often true of a joint venture where the foreign owner is limited to 49 percent equity, control is quite likely to be the result less of the equity split, than some form of management agreement. Few multinational corporations with foreign investments in many nations are willing to hold 49 percent equity without very substantial participation in management, if not assurance of absolute control.

Restrictions on control and ownership are most likely to be part of the foreign investment legal and policy framework of developing and nonmarket economy nations. As developing and transitional nations join international trade organizations and regional economic groups, such as the WTO, EU or NAFTA, they are required to reduce or abolish restrictions on foreign investment. But often they are permitted to retain reservations that allow mandated reduction or abolition to occur over long periods of time, or even allowed to permanently retain limited restrictions.

BEYOND OWNERSHIP AND CONTROL

Ownership and control may define investment whether it is domestic or foreign. *Foreign* investment usually involves the ownership and control of some form of service or manufacturing industry that is located in another country. That country may be close and similar in many ways, such as Canada, or far away and different in many ways, such as Indonesia. The foreign investment confronts many new methods of living and working. Different legal systems may be involved, as may different languages, currencies, cultures, forms of doing business, concepts of legal practice, forms of labor participation and workers' rights, levels and forms of officer compensation, risks of expropriation, intrusiveness of government participation, attitudes towards democracy and socialism, standards of business dress and decorum, methods of finance and rules governing discrimination in the workplace. These differences, rather than the concepts of ownership and control, are what must be understood and dealt with for the foreign investment to succeed. A successful international business lawyer knows how to give advice on more than the different legal systems; non-legal advice may extend to any of the above areas, and more.

REASONS FOR ESTABLISHING
A FOREIGN INVESTMENT

Foreign investments are initiated for many different reasons. Sometimes it is the natural succession to a successful period of increasing export sales to a foreign nation, when the company believes the foreign market is sufficiently large to justify foreign production. Local, foreign production will reduce transportation costs of finished products sold in the domestic market of the foreign nation, and will allow the use of local resources available at lower cost, especially labor.   Foreign investment may follow immediately after a successful period of export sales, or follow a period of foreign production not by means of a direct equity investment, but by licensing the technology for foreign production to a domestic firm in the foreign nation.   An example is the aircraft manufacturing industry.   In order to assure participation in sales in the increasing Asian market, especially China, United States and European aircraft manufacturing companies have moved the manufacture of some parts to Asia, both by licensing and by new direct foreign investment.

The multinational company may dislike transferring technology to a company owned by a host nation party, whether due to a fear of loss of that technology, or an inability to control production quality.   The fear of loss of the technology is of special concern when the technology consists of knowhow, which often lacks the more specific protection provided patents, trademarks and copyrights.   Such fear is particularly well founded with respect to nations which do not afford very strong protection to intellectual property rights.   Even if a transfer of technology license to an unrelated company in another nation has resulted in a profitable relationship, the technology owning multinational may prefer to establish a wholly or majority owned subsidiary to take over the production of the goods or services.   The multinational may not wish to share in the profits with the licensee when it could do the production itself, and keep better control over production quality.

The foreign investment that follows export sales or a transfer of technology tends to be *voluntary* in the sense that the company makes the decision for business reasons, not because the framework of laws and policies of the foreign government require local production. In some cases, however, especially in developing nations with balance of payments problems, the government may make it very difficult, if not impossible, for other nations' businesses to export to the country. Tariffs, quotas and other nontariff barriers may be used both to reduce imports and the consequent demand for scarce foreign currency to pay for the imports, and also to offer considerable protection to domestic industries. The answer may be to establish a direct foreign investment. This would be to some degree an *involuntary* investment, in that it is not one of several alternatives available, but the only allowable form of doing business.

WHERE TO ESTABLISH THE FOREIGN INVESTMENT

Lawyers are not usually asked this question, but they may be asked to do a risk analysis of investing in several possible foreign locations. The legal climate may be the deciding factor in location. For example, a company may be interested in starting an investment in the European Union. One of the newer members may have attractive incentives such as lower labor costs. But what is the legal climate in such nations? Are there vestiges of the old socialism that will be hard to deal with? Are incentives likely to short-lived? Might the nation return to socialism? If the investment is proposed for a market economy, will the nation remain that form? Can you predict the future for Venezuela better than for Hungary? Is there an unwritten law, or "operational code", that governs investment and differs from the written law? If so, does it differ very much, and is it more or less restrictive?

WHO GOVERNS FOREIGN INVESTMENT?

The expected source of governance is by the host nation where the affiliate or subsidiary is located. There may or may not be an express foreign investment law, but there will be many rules of governance such as the corporation or company law, labor law, environmental rules, bankruptcy laws and perhaps investment incentive programs. There are other sources of governance. The home nation may govern its multinationals' activities abroad, in such areas as antitrust, securities regulation, prohibitions of payments to foreign officials, export restrictions, and boycott or antiboycott rules. Additional regulation may be by multi-nation organizations, such as the United Nations, the EU, the NAFTA or the WTO, and also by international law. Foreign investment thus differs from domestic investment by the broader scope of sources of governance, as well as the diversity of approaches to different rules (e.g., mandatory joint ventures), and the uncertain status of alleged customary rules of international law (e.g., standards of compensation for expropriation).

RESTRICTIONS ON FOREIGN INVESTMENT AT VARIOUS STAGES

Some nations place numerous obstacles for approval of the establishment of a foreign investment. They occur at the stage of formation, during the operation of the business, and or during withdrawal. Restrictions may include mandatory joint ventures, export mandates, import substitution, use of a subsidiary rather than a branch, limits on the number of foreign employees or directors, and many other areas. Often once established there is little further restriction either during the operation or withdrawal of the investment that would not be expected of a domestic investment in the United States. But some nations make it easy to establish an investment but not easy to operate. Currency controls, increasingly shorter work weeks, workers' participation in management, and limits on profit transfers and payment for technology may reduce profit expectations. Finally, there may be severe restrictions on withdrawal, from inability to repatriate capital to difficult insolvency laws. Many of the "laws" may actually be unwritten policies that are difficult to know about in advance of actual operation. Such issues are merely further examples of the challenges and risks of a foreign investment.

RESTRICTIONS ON FOREIGN INVESTMENT—DEVELOPING NATIONS

Until the early 1970s, there were comparatively few restrictions on foreign ownership in market economy developing nations. During the 1960s, many large multinationals expanded abroad by opening new plants or by acquiring locally owned enterprises. The acquisition of existing enterprises in developing nations generated concern and often hostility, and led to the adoption of laws in many developing nations regulating foreign investment. Those laws tended to have fairly common approaches to foreign investment. First, the acquisition of host nation enterprises was either limited or prohibited. Second, new investment was required to allow certain percentages of local equity participation. Some areas of investment, such as export oriented extractive industries, communications, transportation, banking, insurance and electricity, often were reserved for either exclusively state owned enterprises, or enterprises owned by nationals to the exclusion of all foreign participation. Other areas of business, those not expressly designated for the above limits, could have specific levels of participation by foreign investors. As in the case of the transfer of technology, a government agency had to approve acquisitions or new investment. The agency usually was allowed discretion in granting exceptions, and frequently the statute provided a list of criteria for approving or disapproving the proposed investment. Common criteria, whether in those lists or in the unwritten policy of the approving agency, would include (1) assisting in generating economic development, (2) agreeing on the number of workers to be employed, (3) considering the effect on existing national businesses, (4) considering the effect on balance of payments, (5) mandating the use of domestic materials and parts, (6) requiring financing be obtained from abroad, (7) contributing to host nation acquisition of advanced technology, (8) locating the plant in designated development zones, and (9) establishing research and development facilities in the nation.

Investment laws were often supplemented by regulations, guidelines and decisions of foreign investment registration and review agencies. Frequently the decisions of review agencies were not made available to the public. But attorneys occasionally gained access to these decisions through personal contacts in the government, and counsel with such access were better able to assist in predicting how the agencies were likely to respond to applications for exceptions to the restrictive investment laws. What thus confronted potential investors in developing nations were not only the restrictive investment laws on the books, but written and unwritten guidelines and policies that generally moderated many of the restrictions.

Developing nation joint venture laws were quite different from joint venture laws in nonmarket economy nations. The latter were passed by nations which had long prohibited any foreign investment; new investment laws were intended to "attract" foreign investment, but initially only to a maximum level of 49 percent foreign ownership. Foreign equity was sometimes limited by constitutional provisions that placed the ownership of the means of production and distribution in the state. Developing nation joint venture laws, contrastingly, were intended to "restrict" new investment, and also to encourage, or coerce, existing wholly foreign owned investment to sell majority ownership to local individuals or entities owned by local investors or the state.

The laws were rarely retroactive by their terms, but they often contained features that made them retroactive in application. Sometimes the foreign investment law did not apply to existing companies, but a company could neither expand into new lines of products nor open new locations without converting the entire company to a joint venture. That meant reducing the foreign equity to no more than 49 percent. Devices were created by the foreign investors to avoid this impact, such as fragmenting the manufacturing of products, by adopting the joint venture for new subsidiaries producing new products, but keeping the old enterprise wholly foreign owned.

Accompanying the mandates for local ownership were similar requirements for local management. Where foreign equity was limited to 49 percent, that same percentage would apply to the number of foreigners allowed on the board. But a minority in *numbers* did not necessarily mean a minority in *influence*, and the local board members usually were motivated by the same profit goals as the foreign parent appointees. Nationalism might arise among the board members, however, if the parent wanted the foreign affiliate to shift production to another nation, or take any action that appeared to benefit the company's activities in another nation at the expense of the entity in the host nation.

Some developing countries, after several years of reasonable compliance with the host nation's restrictive rules by multinational enterprises, began to wonder why their nations had not increased their rates of development. No one gave much thought to the fact that developing nation private shareholders had the same aspirations of profit as developed nation shareholders, and developing nation directors acted in the same way as their counterparts in developed nations. Shifting ownership from foreign to domestic was no guarantee of economic development in the nation as a whole. To encourage more investment, many nations with restrictive laws began to allow total foreign ownership under written or unwritten "exception" provisions. The foreign investor was allowed to retain total ownership if it transferred its most modern technology to the host nation, or located the proposed plant in an area of high unemployment or a zone designated for economic development, or exported a high percentage of its output, or located research and development facilities in the nation.

The IBM company is a good example of a pragmatic approach to investment but with a firm *no equity joint venture* policy. In Mexico, IBM expanded production considerably even after the enactment of the strict investment law in 1973, by agreeing to produce the most recent models and by exporting a high percentage of production. Contrastingly, when uncompromisingly told by the Indian government in the 1980s that it had to alter its Indian investment structure to an equity joint venture, with a majority Indian owned, IBM withdrew its investment. It later returned when the Indian rules were altered.

After (1) the debt crisis in the early 1980s, (2) the opening to investment by many *non*market economies in transition to market economies, and (3) the election of less "populist" governments in many developing nations, the rules of the game began to change dramatically in the 1980s and 1990s. Developing nations as well as nonmarket economies pushed aside the "myth of privatization" and began to take it seriously, selling off many state owned industries. Restrictive investment laws were interpreted in favor of foreign investors' wishes, and subsequently replaced by laws more encouraging than restrictive of investment. Even India seems determined to attract more foreign investment by relaxing its restrictions as the new century unfolds.

Foreign investment laws adopted since the 1980s usually allow total foreign ownership, but often restrict some areas for continued state ownership. Joint ventures are still encouraged, but when formed they tend to be more voluntary than involuntary. Sometimes continuing restrictions on foreign ownership of land induces a joint venture, as might risk analysis which suggests limiting equity participation, even though market studies encourage entering the market.

The ability under local law to form a foreign investment is now less the issue than the method chosen. For the host nation, the initiation of a new investment ("greenfields" investing) may be preferred over the acquisition of an existing one, and a joint venture preferred over total foreign ownership, but the foreign investor often is the one making the final choice. Many nations, including some developed nations, have some method of reviewing acquisitions, for such various reasons as national security or national economic interests.

Most developing nations encourage foreign investment to a greater degree than three-four decades ago, especially during the often hostile North-South dialogue era of the late 1960s and 1970s. A few nations have returned to restrictive policies, including Venezuela and Bolivia, resulting in a lessening of foreign investment. Most nations formerly hostile to foreign investment have become more receptive to investment than during that earlier troubled era. Essential to understand is that there is a *dynamic* process to investment attitudes among nations. The laws of a host nation in place at one time ought not to be viewed as representative of the legal framework likely to exist a decade or two in the future. Investors must be prophets *not* in their own land, and be aware than the dynamic process of economic and political development and change is the engine that pulls the train of rules on trade and investment.

RESTRICTIONS ON FOREIGN INVEST-MENT—NONMARKET AND TRAN-SITION ECONOMY NATIONS

Nonmarket economy nations in many cases have also been developing nations. Thus nonmarket economy nations often have imposed limitations on the initiation of foreign investment that parallel those in developing nations. But there are differences in the restrictions due to the nature of a nonmarket economy. The restrictive rules on foreign investment were part of the political-economic Marxist philosophy adopted by most nonmarket economies, and expressed by the term *nonmarket economy*. But as these nations failed to achieve the levels of growth occurring in market economies, and failed to produce internally or acquire from abroad advanced technology, they began to trade with and then admit some limited foreign investment. When the wall between the market and nonmarket economies came down in the late 1980s, the rush to become market economies began in earnest.

Earlier, many nonmarket economies had attempted to obtain technology through transfers to local, state owned productive facilities. But they failed, usually because of inadequate legal protection of intellectual property. The lack of adequate protection was sometimes due to a stated belief that intellectual property was not subject to private own-

ership, but was the patrimony of mankind. Philosophical differences about ownership of the means
of production and distribution persist even as nonmarket economies enter the transition to market
economies. Often there are poor links of communication between foreign investors and the newly
developing local business community. Labor has
been vocal and sometimes well organized, and government ministries sometimes continue to be the
negotiators or lobbyists for local, private business.
Political interference is a continuing characteristic
of investment in nonmarket economies. But it is a
frustrating and elusive interference—the one who
has the final say in the government is often "everyone and no-one".

Market economy nation companies do not wish to
risk valuable technology and other intellectual property to Marxist principles of the patrimony of mankind. They would thus license technology only to
wholly or majority owned subsidiaries, which local
law often did not permit. Consequently, nonmarket economies were unable to gain access to very
much advanced technology, because of their refusal
to admit direct foreign equity investments, or provide protection to licensed technology. In the early
1970s, however, the desire for better technology
pushed some of the rigid Marxist theory to the back
burner in an ever increasing number of nonmarket
economy nations.

Poland, Yugoslavia, Hungary and Romania each
adopted joint venture laws, nevertheless limiting
the foreign equity participation to 49 percent.

Since the nonmarket economies did not have equity share corporations, nor corporation or company laws governing the formation and operation of such entities, the two principal incidents of share ownership, management participation and profits, necessarily had to be creations of the joint venture *contract* rather than share certificates.   Profits often would be taken in the form of some percentage of the production, to be sold in Western markets. Called *compensation* or *buy-back* agreements, they are included under the umbrella of *countertrade.* These arrangements were not without difficulties, however, as the quality of nonmarket economy production was often poor, with high percentages of returns of unacceptable products.   Furthermore, unless the parent company expanded its markets in the West, the nonmarket economy entity production taken as profit and sold in the West, would necessarily displace some Western production.   What goodwill may have been created in the nonmarket economy could be lost in the Western nation affected by a loss of its production.

The second element of direct investment, participation in *control,* creates more philosophical problems than the problems of profit sharing, which are often related to currency shortages.   In the nonmarket economies, management was in the hands of the state or, as in Yugoslavia under "workers' social property" theory, directly in the hands of a plant's workers.   Joint venture contracts sometimes provided for sharing major management decisions, but did not allow management to be dominated in numbers by foreign participants. A minority of a managing board, however, might be accepted by the majority as the influential management group. The participation of workers in ownership and control has influenced the role of unions as nonmarket nations have entered the transition phase. Governments often are not certain how to deal with their work force, but have tended to attempt to allow them to participate in ownership, and sometimes management representation, when state owned entities are privatized, and to allow them to organize in what in some countries are very strong unions. But these unions often lack direction.

Joint venture laws varied significantly throughout the nonmarket economy world. The Eastern European laws developed over nearly two decades of experience, and were occasionally amended to accommodate new problems. China enacted a joint venture law in 1979, which was brief and unclear, but underwent modifications in fact and in interpretation as the Chinese economy moved to adopt more market economy characteristics. By 1986, the Chinese were even allowing wholly owned subsidiaries. Contrastingly, the 1982 Cuban joint venture law generated little response from foreign investors (U.S. investors are not been permitted to invest in Cuba), for reasons that were obvious to all but the Cuban government. The 1982 law was outmoded when it was enacted in comparison to the amendments occurring in Eastern European joint venture laws. Cuba wanted the benefits of foreign investment, without assuming any obligations of a host nation.   In 1995 a new law replaced the old, offering new concessions, but still a decade or more behind developments in those nations already well into the period of transition towards market economies.   When a nation's investment law is as unrealistic as that of Cuba, new foreign investment usually focuses on a contract with the government that often ignores some of the restrictive rules of the investment law.

If any label is merited by the nonmarket economies regarding the acceptance of foreign investment, it is that of "pragmatic accommodation." The most significant changes in the rules regarding foreign investment have occurred in those NME nations where there have been similarly meaningful changes in allowing free market elements to penetrate domestic trade.   These changes are usually frustratingly slow and sometimes subject to periodic suspension, but they represent extraordinary alterations in the fundamental economic structures and attitudes of nations long satisfied with a place in the obscure recesses of the international trading community.   Many of the nations in transition have moved well into the next phase, ridding the state of significant involvement of ownership of the nation's means of production and distribution.   It is the era of privatization.

PRIVATIZATION: THE FOCUS OF THE 1990s

The lessening of state ownership of the means of production and distribution has been carried out principally by the process of privatization. While such conversion is a critical aspect of the transition of nonmarket economies to market economies, privatization is also occurring with vigor in many developing, *market* economy nations. The reason is partly shared by both forms of economy. State ownership of the means of production and distribution of goods and services is increasingly viewed as philosophically inappropriate as an activity for the government. More practically, most state enterprises have been unable to operate at a profit, causing a drain on state resources. Privatization is viewed as a means of reducing the drain on national revenue used to subsidize state owned enterprises, a way to raise revenue to improve national infrastructure, and a possible future source of revenue if private ownership means improving the efficiency of manufacture to the point of competing in world markets and increasing export revenue.

Additionally, privatization is thought to be a better way to provide goods and services demanded by a nation's population. This view extends to the largest developed nations. Britain, Italy, France and Germany have all privatized large state owned industries. U.S. privatization ideology has extended to highways, ports, waste-water facilities, gas utilities, and many local government services such as parking garages, and even such recreational facilities as golf courses.

Not all enterprises have been placed on the market, but the NMEs often express a willingness to sell more large companies than some market economy developing nations in their own process of privatization. For example, Hungary sold the telecommunications company, MATAV, the airline MALEV, and a large lighting products company, Tungsram. But developing market economy nations were not been far behind. Argentina sold 45% of the oil and gas company YPF, its airlines Aerolineas Argentinas, and the Telecom company. Some national companies are referred to as "untouchables". But even they are having parts sold. Mexico's previously untouchable oil enterprise, PEMEX, has sold retail outlets, and its petrochemical production. Foreign investment is now allowed in gas production. Only oil production remains for the time-being "untouchable". Mexico's privatization of parts of PEMEX has not been without challenge and criticism, however, the process of privatization was at one time so sensitive in Mexico that it was referred to as "disincorporation."

As a comparatively new phenomenon, privatization has raised new issues for foreign investors. Privatization has become a process based on a mix of law and policy. The policy may be very pro-privatization, but backed by weak laws that do not answer many important questions. Most NMEs have adopted privatization laws that are periodically amended to govern such major issues as determining what to sell, the role of workers in approving the sale, the value of the business, the level of foreign participation allowed in a sale, rights of nationals and/or employees to ownership preferences, method of financing, and the creation of an adequate legal infrastructure (corporation laws, securities laws, bankruptcy laws, etc.) to support the process. In many cases these questions are not resolved in the written privatization laws of the nations. They must be dealt with in negotiations with the government.

One of the most difficult issue in privatization is how to value the business. Many nonmarket economy enterprises possess little of value for the new owner except the right to function as the business. Obsolete equipment must be replaced. New markets must be sought. Modern technology must be introduced. Work forces often must be reduced and the remaining workers trained in more efficient methods of production and the use of new technology. Accounting methods of the NMEs gave little attention to market economy concepts, and thus book value is generally useless. Since there was no share ownership there was no market value of ownership interests. The value issue in a privatization usually must be negotiated.

Even when a value has been established which seems generally acceptable, the absence of savings in the nonmarket economies probably means that foreign capital will be necessary to carry out the privatization. But there may be reservations about selling majority ownership and control to foreign investors. Additionally, the NMEs may offer their own nationals some preference in the way of certificates that may be exchanged for shares in privatized companies. This means that a foreign purchaser may obtain 80 percent of the equity of the enterprise, but be expected to pay for 100 percent of its value. At the head of the line of nationals seeking preferential treatment may be workers in the enterprise to be sold, holding some form of scrip exchangeable for shares.

The process of privatization is only partly completed. It is a necessary concomitant to becoming a market economy, and has continued into the new century. If there is any doubt about the seriousness of nations to privatize, the figures speak loudly. The IFC of the World Bank reported that some 2,700 state owned enterprises were privatized between 1988 and 1993 in more than 95 countries, raising about $271 billion in revenue.

POLICY VERSUS LAW: DEALING WITH THE OPERATIONAL CODE OR THE WAY THINGS WORK

The written laws of the developing nations are the principal framework for regulating the foreign investor. Many developing and nonmarket economies have specific laws governing foreign investment. These laws are what the public (and too often the foreign investor) believes comprise the *exclusive* framework for investment. But each nation has another level of law, that which is unwritten. It is the "way things work," an operational code. It consists of unpublished regulations and rulings that are applied in some cases, but not even mentioned in others. The Brazilians call them "drawer regulations." Investors in China are sometimes confronted with laws they have never heard of, and which they are told may not even be read by foreigners. This operational code allows the government to give different treatment to different investors. Fortunately, many local attorneys know what they are and how to use them. They are a reason for choosing local counsel wisely.

RESTRICTIONS ON FOREIGN INVEST-MENT IN DEVELOPED, MARKET ECONOMY NATIONS

The enactment of laws affecting foreign investment is not limited to the developing nations and nonmarket economy nations. Investors attempting to establish equity investments in Japan confront numerous obstacles, although no written, restrictive foreign investment law exists. Many new foreign investors began to establish a base in the European Union for fear that a "Fortress Europe" would develop (the consequence of the achievement of a "Europe Without *Internal* Frontiers") that would restrict foreign investment. Canada adopted a fairly restrictive foreign investment law in 1973, but following much criticism from abroad and debate within, the law was replaced with the far less restrictive Investment Canada Act in 1985. The 1985 law, which required review of large proposed investments, was incorporated into the 1989 Canada-United States Free Trade Agreement (CFTA), but with major exceptions for U.S. investors. The North American Free Trade Agreement (NAFTA) Chapter 11 establishes investment rules, reflecting to some extent the provisions in the earlier CFTA. France, Korea and other developed nations additionally review some foreign investment on national interest grounds. One ought not assume that control of foreign investment is limited to developing and nonmarket economy nations. Or assume that the United States does not control foreign investment in the United States.

The United States has long promoted an image of an investment encouraging nation, where only a few areas are subject to ownership and control limitations, such as national defense, nuclear energy and domestic air transportation. Upon occasion (e.g., fear of Japanese trade domination in the 1980s) proposals have been introduced in the Congress to require some level of registration of foreign investment, but invariably they have been defeated as restrictive and discouraging of desirable job-creating foreign investment. A Committee on Foreign Investment in the United States (CFIUS), was created in 1975 to monitor foreign investment (www.treas.gov/oii). CFIUS became the presidential designee to monitor and review foreign investment when Congress in 1988 enacted the Exon-Florio Amendment of the Defense Production Act (DPA), as part of the Omnibus Trade and Competitiveness Act. The Exon-Florio law was partly the response to the proposed acquisition of Fairchild Semiconductor Corporation by the Japanese company Fujitsu, Ltd. Fairchild was engaged in defense manufacturing. CFIUS had reviewed this proposed acquisition (before the enactment of Exon-Florio) and determined that national security interests were at risk, but CFIUS had no authority to stop the acquisition. Fujitsu nevertheless terminated its proposed acquisition in the face of government pressure.

The first major amendment to Exxon-Florio came in 1992, after Congressional dissatisfaction with the way the President and CFIUS handled the proposed takeover of part of LTV by Thomson-CSF, a conglomerate with majority ownership by the French government. The expected purchase by Thomson of LTV's missile division was terminated by Thomson when it believed it could not expect to gain approval under Exon-Florio from the Department of Defense. Congress had intervened because members were upset with the failure of the administration to act more strictly. Thomson's withdrawal led to litigation as well as to the 1992 amendments.

The Foreign Investment and National Security Act (FINSA) of 2007 reformed and codified the responsibilities of the CFIUS. As in the case of both the original CIFUS and the 1992 amendments, proposed investment in the United States drove the changes. This time it was the 2006 proposed sale to Dubai Ports World International of a British company that held leases to operate six major U.S. ports. Of additional concern was the 2005 proposal by China National Offshore Oil Corporation to purchase shares of Unocal, outbidding Chevron. These two experiences caused CFIUS review filings to increase some 75%.

The FINSA continues Presidential authority (essentially exercised by his designee—the CFIUS) to investigate effects on national security from mergers, acquisitions and takeovers which might result in foreign control. If national security is threatened, the President may prohibit the action. The review, which is essentially voluntary by parties filing a notification with CFIUS, allows a safe harbor for the transaction if it receives CFIUS approval. Review *must* occur if the purchasing foreigner is controlled by or acting on behalf of a foreign government. The law additionally prohibits the sale of some U.S. companies to certain foreign investors, principally those entities involved with foreign governments. FINSA will cause a significant increase in the proposed transactions subject to review. The Department of Homeland Security is now an important player within CFIUS. It may be tempted to use CFIUS to gain control over actions of the parties, regardless of the presence or absence of any serious national security link, especially in the area of cyber security.

Exon-Florio gives the President authority to block an acquisition within statutory guidelines. He must find (1) "credible evidence" that foreign "control" might "impair the national security," and (2) that U.S. law (other than Exon-Florio and the IEEPA) does not provide adequate and appropriate authority for the President to protect national security. It is unclear what industries affect national security, although the law suggests (1) "domestic production needed for projected national defense requirements," (2) "capability and capacity of domestic industries to meet national defense requirements," and (3) "control ... by foreign citizens as it affects the capability and capacity of the United States to meet the requirements of national security." Certainly the defense industry, to the extent it may be defined, is included. Also included are nondefense industries which manufacture products which have strategic significance, particularly when they have a large share of the U.S. market and there are no easily located substitutes. What action the President may take is not included in the statute, which refers to "appropriate relief." The presidential findings are not reviewable. Important language added by the FINSA, and yet undefined, is when a transaction would result in foreign control of "critical infrastructure." Other issues to be resolved include the determination of which energy assets are "major," and which technologies are "critical."

Of the almost one thousand notifications presented to the executive under the voluntary reporting system, only a little more than a dozen have proceeded to a formal investigation, causing critics to charge that the law is not being used to block investment as allegedly intended. European owned companies have not considered Exon-Florio to be a block to investment in the United States, but more an administrative annoyance. The Department of Defense, as might be expected, has become a major participant in requesting investigations. One example is where Defense joined the Departments of

Energy, Treasury and Commerce to challenge the proposed acquisition of General Ceramics by the Japanese company, Tokuyama Soda Co., Ltd. General Ceramics manufactured ceramics used in nuclear weapon electronic circuits. There was evidence that Japan was urging its businesses to manipulate their acquisitions to avoid Exon-Florio challenges. It appeared likely that the acquisition would be blocked, and General Ceramics sold its defense related business to another company, leading CFIUS to find no objection to the acquisition.

The one case where a proposed acquisition led to a presidential order blocking the acquisition involved China's National Aero-Technology Import and Export Corp.'s (CATIC) proposed acquisition of MAMCO Mfg, a Seattle aircraft parts manufacturer. The investigation disclosed that the buyer CATIC had previously violated U.S. export control laws in purchases of General Electric aircraft engines. There were also concerns about CATIC's attempts to gain technology to build jet fighters able to refuel during flight, and carrying on some covert operations in the United States for the Chinese government. The Executive Order calling for divestment referred only to the threat to national security, providing no detailed supporting reasons.

Exon-Florio has been used by U.S. target corporations whose management is hostile to a proposed takeover. It was an unanticipated consequence of the enactment of Exon-Florio. The target company may use the post-notification review period to try to delay the takeover, even to the extent of providing misleading information to CFIUS. The intention would be to cause CFIUS to undertake an investigation. Such delay may be enough to discourage the foreign would-be acquirer, even though there are no legitimate national security grounds to expect an ultimate presidential blockage. There are no clear sanctions for use of Exon-Florio to block a hostile takeover, but providing false or misleading information to CFIUS would seem to violate federal criminal statutes. If the U.S. government intends to be receptive to foreign investment, including investment by way of acquisition, the misuse of Exon-Florio is counterproductive to that policy of openness.

Exon-Florio is viewed by many in Congress as the means by which Congress might increase control over foreign investment. The 1992 amendments and the 2007 FINSA did not solve all Congressional concerns. Remaining open to further consideration, in addition to clearer definitions and a time limit for filing notifications as noted above, are coverage of the acquisition of "critical" technologies with the test constituting the effect on "economic" versus "national" security; consideration of the concentration in the industry (it can be under antitrust laws), including as a factor whether the target company has received U.S. government funds; and transferring the chairmanship of CFIUS from Treasury to Commerce.

FINANCING THE FOREIGN INVESTMENT

Some investment is done using the parent corporation's retained earnings. Or using its traditional borrowing sources for investments in the United States. The foreign investment opens new possible sources, including the same kind of lending institutions in the foreign host nation as are used in the United States. But additional possible sources exist, such as international development banks and agencies, including the World Bank's International Finance Corporation (IFC), or the U.S. Overseas Private Investment Corporation (OPIC). Some international lending authorities invest primarily in infrastructure, which may not benefit many production companies but may be of interest to a U.S. construction business.

THE AFFECT OF A DIFFERENT CURRENCY ON THE FOREIGN INVESTMENT

Imagine that every state within the United States had a different currency. A New York corporation wishing to open a subsidiary in New Mexico might encounter currency controls in New Mexico, or a currency artificially fixed to that of another state, perhaps Texas. This is partly why most of the members of the European Union have abandoned centuries old currencies for adoption of a common EU currency, the Euro. When a business invests in a nation with a different currency, many issues arise. Can or may the foreign currency be readily converted into dollars? What foreign hotel investment in Havana wants its earnings restricted to Cuban pesos? They are not convertible in any other nation. What happens when a convertible currency in, for example, Mexico, suddenly collapses just before the foreign investor planned to convert and repatriate it to the U.S. parent? How much local currency should be retained for business needs? The investor must learn about hedging, buying contracts that assure later conversion at a determined rate. All of this attention to a different currency costs money, and that usually means transferring such costs on to the ultimate consumer.

TRANSFER PRICING

If the U.S. investment in another nation faces restrictions on repatriating profits to the parent, but allows transfers to pay for technology, perhaps the parent will simply raise the price charged the foreign subsidiary for technology and thus operate without showing any profits that if existed would be frozen in the non-transferrable foreign currency. That would also mean no taxes because there were no profits, even though there were actually disguised profits. Transfer pricing is used for many reasons, usually to avoid what are considered onerous and unfair rule changes in the host nation. They obviously are disliked by the host government that may lose needed tax revenue. And they may be very much disliked by any host nation joint venture equity partners that lose dividends because the profits (in which they would share) were re-named technology payments (in which they do not share).   Transfer pricing is not only a problem for developing nations, any nation that is host to for-eign investment worries about and tries to prevent such transfer pricing.   California was concerned that some foreign investors in California were not paying proper California state income taxes and in the 1990s adopted a unitary tax.   It required tax-able profits to be roughly equal to the percent of the company's assets, employees and sales existing in California.

THE ROLE OF BILATERAL INVESTMENT TREATIES

International law has been slow to establish stan-dards regarding how nations ought to treat foreign investment.   The United Nations' efforts in the 1970s to draft a code of conduct for multinational enterprises did not include provisions regulating the conduct of host nations.   The one-sided efforts of the UN were thus quite unsatisfactory to foreign investors, who sought assistance from their home nations.   Bilateral investment treaties (BITs) have provided some help.   To promote national treat-ment and protect U.S. investors abroad, the United States embarked on the BIT program in the early 1980s.   The BIT program followed earlier extensive use of Friendship, Commerce, and Navigation (FCN) treaties.   Unlike the FCNs, the model BIT focuses more exclusively on investment related issues, such as employment of one's nationals in a foreign subsidiary. As a result of a 1982 U.S. Supreme Court ruling, the earlier used FCN treaty afforded no protection to a foreign company wanting to nearly exclusively hire its own nationals. Under the typical BIT, explicit freedom to hire foreign nationals exists in a narrow range of management provisions. But investment screening mechanisms and key sectors often remain exempt from BIT protection, typically listed in a BIT Annex. While elimination of foreign investment screening and imposition of performance requirements has been an object of the BIT program, these provisions of the model BIT have been weakened in the treaties currently in force.

It is not only the United States which has emphasized the BIT, they are common features of most developed nations in their relations with host nations for foreign investment. For example, China has investment protection agreements with such nations as Australia, Austria, Belgium-Luxembourg, Denmark, France, Germany, Japan, the Netherlands, and the United Kingdom. A benefit of such an agreement is that its provisions prevail over domestic law, although the agreements usually allow for exceptions to investment protection when in the interests of national security.

The United States has entered into a number of bilateral *investment* treaties, as well as a number of less formal bilateral *trade* agreements. But many of the earlier trade agreements merely referred to investment as an area for further discussion, tending to deal only with tariff and nontariff barriers to trade.   The bilateral *investment* treaties by their nature do address investment issues.   They generally replace earlier FCN treaties, to the extent that they apply to investments.   Most of the BITs negotiated by the United States have been with small developing countries, such as Albania, Latvia and Ruwanda, and Uruguay.   But the United States has signed BITs with such important trading nations as Argentina and Russia.   The Argentina-United States BIT follows the U.S. BIT prototype of addressing both investment protection and investor access to each other's markets.   The Russia agreement awaits Russian approval.   The provisions of the BITs are perhaps fairly compared to the investor protection contained in Chapter 11 of the NAFTA with Canada and Mexico.

The BITs do not prohibit nations from enacting investment laws, but provide that any such laws should not interfere with any rights in the treaty. The free access aspect of some BITs may not be perceived as a right.   Thus investment laws might be enacted that limit access to certain areas, but would not create a right of the other party to challenge the law under the BIT.

One important provision the United States seeks to include in its BITs is the "prompt, adequate and effective" concept (if not always the language) of compensation following expropriation.   Many of the nations which have recently agreed to this language disputed its appropriateness during the nationalistic

North-South dialogue years of the 1960s and 1970s. But as they began to promote rather than restrict investment, these nations had to accept the idea that expropriated investment should be compensated reasonably soon after the taking ("prompt"), based on a fair valuation ("adequate"), and in a realistic form ("effective"). The Argentina-United States BIT uses language referring to the "fair market value ... immediately before the expropriatory action."

Most BITs do not include provisions for consultations when differences arise in the interpretation of the treaty. The Argentina-United States BIT is one of a few exceptions. BITs do often provide for arbitration, sometimes with no necessary recourse to prior exhaustion of local remedies.

The BIT process is quite dynamic. Each successive agreement with a new country may include some new provisions. The United States has a prototype agreement, but it has been modified as host nations have sought new foreign investment and have been willing to sign a BIT to establish the most attractive conditions for that investment. It is certain that the BITs in existence today will not be identical to BITs executed in years ahead. BITs are an important contribution of the developed home nation to lessening the risk for their multinationals investing abroad. A BIT establishes some ground rules for investment on a bilateral, treaty basis which should not be unilaterally altered by the host nation to impose restrictions on the investments which are inconsistent with the BIT. Certainly, revolutionary governments have ignored similar agreements in the past and may in the future. But the BITs do provide some investment security, at least as long as the host governments remain relatively stable, and receptive to foreign investment. BITs have not disappeared following the creation of the WTO and its Agreement on Trade-Related Investment Measures (TRIMs). The GATT/WTO rules regarding investment are a step in the right direction, but remain less specific than agreements among smaller groups of nations (such as the NAFTA), or bilateral agreements.

FOREIGN INVESTMENT UNDER THE NORTH AMERICAN FREE TRADE AGREEMENT

U.S. foreign investors in Canada and Mexico benefit from the provisions of the North American Free Trade Agreement (NAFTA). Chapter 11 covers foreign investment. Section A includes provisions affecting Investment, while Section B addresses the Settlement of Disputes between a Party and an Investor of Another Party. The investment provisions in chapter 11 to some extent reflect provisions in the earlier Canada-United States FTA, but there are some provisions unique to the NAFTA. For example, provisions for local management and control were important provisions in the 1973 Mexican Investment Law. NAFTA, as well as the newer 1993 Mexican Investment Law, prohibit mandating the nationality of senior management. But NAFTA does allow for requirements that the majority of the board of an enterprise that is a foreign investment be of a particular nationality, or be resident in the territory, provided that such a requirement does not materially impair the investor's control over the investment. The provisions attempt to balance eliminating the distortions associated with mandating local management, with ensuring that host nation input is provided.

NAFTA investment rules are based on the concepts of national treatment and most-favored-nation status. Thus, each Party must grant investors of the other NAFTA Parties treatment no less favorable than is granted to domestic investors. Also, each Party must grant investors of the other Parties treatment no less favorable than it grants to any other nation outside NAFTA. Performance requirements are prohibited under NAFTA, under provisions that specifically list seven areas of prohibited performance requirements. But a nation may impose measures to protect life or health, safety, or the environmental. Incentives to invest may not be conditioned on most performance requirements, but may be conditioned on location, provision of services, training or employing workers, constructing or expanding facilities, or undertaking research.

NAFTA allows investors to freely transfer profits, dividends, interest, capital, royalties, management and technical advice fees, and other fees, as well as proceeds from the sale of the investment and various payments (such as loan repayments). But limitations on transfers may be made involving certain bankruptcy actions, securities dealings, criminal acts, issues involving property, reporting of transfers, and to ensure satisfaction of judgments.

Each of the member nations of NAFTA listed exceptions to the investment rules, thus deviating from the basic principle of national treatment. Some exceptions were mandated by the nation's constitution, others by federal law. Where a nation has made exceptions which disallow foreign participation, it may either reserve the area for national ownership or exclusively for private domestic ownership. But it may also allow some foreign participation. Thus, some of the restrictive nature of earlier investment laws is preserved, but in a considerably more limited form.

FOREIGN INVESTMENT UNDER THE GATT/WORLD TRADE ORGANIZATION

Previous to the Uruguay Round the GATT did not address issues of foreign investment. But the Uruguay Round produced rules on foreign investment, referred to as the Agreement on Trade-Related Investment Measures, (TRIMs). As must be expected with any large organization with divergent views, its negotiated provisions are not likely to be as comprehensive as those in smaller trade agreements, such as discussed above in the NAFTA. The WTO TRIMs provisions are considerably briefer than those in the NAFTA, and only one provision relates to dispute settlement. That article states that the provisions of the General Agreement relating to Consultation (XXII), and Nullification and Impairment (XXIII), and the Understanding on Rules and Procedures Governing the Settlement of Disputes under those articles, apply to consultations and dispute settlement under the TRIM provisions. Thus, there are no separate provisions directed to the uniqueness of investment disputes, as in the NAFTA Chapter 11. It will take time to determine how effective the WTO provisions are to resolving investment disputes. While the investment dispute provisions of the NAFTA have been extensively used to date, the WTO TRIMs have received little attention.

The WTO investment rules or TRIMs first set forth a national treatment principal. TRIMs which are considered inconsistent with WTO obligations are listed in an annex, and include such performance requirements as minimum domestic content, imports limited or linked to exports, restrictions on access to foreign exchange to limit imports for use in the investment, etc. Developing countries are allowed to "deviate temporarily" from the national treatment concept, thus diminishing in value the effectiveness of the WTO investment provisions, and obviously discouraging investment in nations which have a history of imposing investment restrictions, and making such agreements as the NAFTA all the more useful and likely to spread.

The essence of the TRIMs is to establish the same principle of national treatment for investments as has been in effect for trade. TRIMs are incorporated in the overall structure of the WTO, alongside trade measures, rather than being treated as a quite distinct area. Because all the deficiencies of the WTO with regard to trade measures may apply to TRIMs, it remains to be seen how effective these measures will be in governing foreign investment. Because the measures are much less certain than those included in bilateral investment treaties, and small area free trade agreements, it is likely that much of the regulation of foreign investment will develop in the context of the latter rather than within the WTO.

THE OECD AND THE MULTILATERAL AGREEMENT ON INVESTMENT

Bilateral investment treaties have been present for several decades, but have been quite limited in scope. Regional agreements such as the NAFTA and the WTO are both more recent and more extensive in addressing foreign investment issues. The next development was thought to be the adoption of the Multilateral Agreement on Investment (MAI) by the Organization for Economic Cooperation and Development (OECD). The nature of the OECD, dominated by developed nations, although less so than in its earlier years, means the MAI is more likely to focus on concerns of the multinational corporations of developed nations than the aspirations of the developing nations that host investment. But there were insurmountable disagreements in the negotiations, and hope for an early settlement of differences ended. Most of the OECD members wished to include limits on the extraterritorial application of laws, such as attempts to impose a nation's boycott on third nations, or govern the acts of foreign subsidiaries. The United States generally opposes such limitations on its use of extraterritorial application of laws. Conclusion of the MAI is now unlikely. At the very best it may be said to be on the "back burner."

THE SETTLEMENT OF INVESTMENT DISPUTES: GENERAL

Investment disputes often involve claims by the foreign investor that the host nation interfered with the investment to the degree that it constitutes a taking of property. A taking may violate international law, but that area is poorly defined in international law and the subject of continuing and vigorous disputed by different nations. The International Court of Justice has been a disappointment in establishing some rules for expropriation. Investors have thus sought other forums for investment dispute settlement. Host nation domestic law may include how investment disputes are to be resolved. Often the law provides for stages, beginning with a form of mediation, then arbitration, and if not satisfied through use of the courts. This may be unsatisfactory to the foreign investor if the membership of the mediation and arbitration panels, and the rules under which they operate, appear to favor the host nation.   A more neutral settlement process is usually preferred.

THE SETTLEMENT OF INVESTMENT DISPUTES: NAFTA

The NAFTA investment dispute scheme is extensive and complex.   It essentially provides a mechanism to settle investment disputes by arbitration where a party to NAFTA has breached an obligation under Section A of Chapter 11 provisions relating to investment, or under provisions in Chapter 15 governing monopolies and state enterprises, and damage or loss has occurred from the breach.   Investors of a party are allowed to submit the claim directly, the first such permission in a trade agreement. The process first requires consultation and negotiation.   If unsuccessful, it proceeds to arbitration. The rules to be applied are those of ICSID or UNCITRAL, depending upon NAFTA Party participation in the ICSID Convention.   The arbitrators are selected by the parties to the dispute and the arbitration is enforceable.   The process is to some degree a mini-ICSID procedure, with participation limited to disputants and arbitrators of the three NAFTA parties.

Two important reservations were made by Canada and Mexico to the NAFTA investment dispute resolution provisions.   A Canadian decision following a review under the Investment Canada Act regarding an acquisition is not subject to NAFTA dispute settlement provisions, nor is a Mexican National Commission on Foreign Investment decision on an acquisition subject to such provisions.

Dispute settlement activity under Chapter 11 has been extensive, and replete with some unexpected uses. Several Chapter 11 investment disputes have raised doubt about the intended scope of the use of Chapter 11 dispute procedures. Several U.S. challenges by private investors have been made challenging the application of regulations adopted in Canada and Mexico that have allegedly prevented U.S. foreign investment from functioning. There is debate regarding whether the challenged regulatory provisions constitute regulation or expropriation. When the regulation measures challenged have been environmental protection laws, the concern over the use of Chapter 11 has been more serious and vocal. But an even more contentious case, involving a Canadian funeral home chain subjected to a huge punitive damages decision in a Mississippi state court, and facing severe limitations on the ability to appeal the decision, has challenged the fairness of the state legal system itself, rather than traditional expropriatory measures. These decisions may lead to revisiting the Chapter 11 dispute procedure.

THE SETTLEMENT OF INVESTMENT DISPUTES: ICSID

Some 150 nations have become parties to the 1966 Convention on the Settlement of Investment Disputes Between States and Nationals of Other

States. The Convention provided for the creation of the International Centre for the Settlement of Investment Disputes (ICSID) as part of the World Bank. The Convention and Centre provide for the arbitration of investment disputes, offering an institutional framework for the proceedings. Jurisdiction under the Convention extends to "any legal dispute arising directly out of an investment, between a Contracting State or ... any subdivision ... and a national of another Contracting State." But the parties must consent in writing to the submission of the dispute to the Centre. Once given, the consent may not be withdrawn.

Disputes regarding jurisdiction may be decided by the arbitration panel and appealed to a committee (ad hoc) created from the Panel of Arbitrators by the Administrative Council of the ICSID. The jurisdiction of the tribunal, challenged in a U.S. court, may well lead to a refusal to uphold the decision. Concern regarding the jurisdictional limitations led to the creation of the Additional Facility, which may conduct conciliation and arbitration proceedings for what are rather special disputes. It was not created to deal with the ordinary investment dispute, but with disputes between parties with long-term special economic relationships involving substantial resource commitments. The Additional Facility may be used only with the blessing of the ICSID Secretary General.

CONCLUSION

The regulation of foreign investment is practiced by nearly every nation in the world, both market and nonmarket economies, and developed and developing nations. The motivation for regulation is nearly always the protection of some domestic interest, whether national security, national economic interests or simply national interests. Important to recognize is that such regulation is a dynamic process. The adoption of the joint venture as a mandatory vehicle for foreign investment by developing nations and nonmarket economies on the 1970s proved to be only one stage in the development process. Unfortunately it is not always acknowledged as merely a stage in an evolving process.

Some nations view what is a transitory stage in the development process as a permanent key to success. But the world has witnessed the development of foreign investment regulation move through stages of nationalizations and mandatory joint ventures, from import substitution promotion to export production promotion, an era of privatization, and currently into an era of offering incentives to encourage foreign investment. Those nations which use investment controls carefully and sparingly, such as the Asian Four Tigers or Four Dragons, have achieved greater rates of growth than those nations which have to their losses viewed strict foreign investment controls as a panacea for economic stagnation. Where the world is headed in investment regulation is always hard to predict.

But as the new century unfolds, investment protection appears to be gaining a new justification—the protection of a nation's culture. Whether it proves to be truly a protection of important elements of culture, or another means of protecting inefficient domestic industry, remains to be played out on the international trade stage in the coming years.

CHAPTER FIVE

PROPERTY TAKINGS AND REMEDIES

Investments in foreign nations create risks that the host governments may "take" property and refuse to provide "proper" compensation. What is a "taking" and what is "proper" compensation have long been debated. The right to take is difficult to challenge; most nations have some form of eminent domain allowing government taking for public purposes. Thus, the issue usually becomes proper compensation. It is likely to be viewed by the investor as improper unless it is (1) paid with sufficient promptness, (2) adequate in amount, and (3) paid in an effective form.

DEFINING THE TAKING

The terms most frequently used when referring to the taking of foreign property are often neither clear in meaning nor consistently applied. The least intrusive act is usually called an *intervention*. That assumes the taking is intended to be temporary, and that the investment will be returned when the problems that motivated the taking are corrected. If the property is not returned in a reasonable period of time, the taking becomes at least a *nationalization*. The words *nationalization* and *expropriation* are often used interchangeably. They are usually intended to mean a taking followed by some form of compensation. But if no payment or inadequate payment follows the taking, the act may merit the label *confiscation*. The more usual case of a taking occurs when there is a nationalization or expropriation followed by an offer of some payment, but disagreement arises about whether the payment standard should be "just", "appropriate", "prompt, adequate and effective," or paid under some other label. These payment terms have never been very clearly defined.

Government interference may alternatively involve a series of steps that amount to a disguised, constructive, defacto, or "creeping" expropriation. A taking may occur almost imperceptibly and often over a substantial period of time. It is nevertheless a taking. Reasonable taxes on an investment might be raised to become confiscatory; mandatory labor legislation might attempt to transfer the financial resources of an investment to nationals of the host country; remittances and repatriations might be blocked or delayed to where host country inflation effectively consumes them; necessary government approvals might prove unobtainable; and other regulations dealing with various aspects of the investment might become burdensome to the point of constituting an overwhelming justification for abandoning the investment.

Expropriations may take all property of all investors, or be *selective*, or *discriminatory*, or *retaliato-*

ry. Or all three. The action may be selective by taking only one industry, or be discriminatory by taking either the property of a particular foreign investor, or all the property of all the investors of a particular foreign nation, or be retaliatory by taking property in response to acts of the foreign investor or its government.

When governments take property of *foreign* investors it is difficult to challenge successfully the public purpose of the taking nation, even though many expropriations clearly appear to have been motivated by little more than revolutionary fervor and with no sound economic justification. National courts, however, are not anxious to rule on the validity of the taking nation's satisfaction of the public purpose mandate.

THE "IZATIONS" OF THE PAST CENTURY

Expropriation in the last century effectively began when Russia (after the 1917 revolution), and Eastern European nations (after World War II), eliminated private ownership of the means of production and distribution. Mexico expropriated oil in 1938. Indonesia nationalized most Dutch owned property in the 1950s. Egypt expropriated the Suez Canal Company in 1956. Expropriations were frequent in the 1960s, beginning with the extensive takings by Cuba of all foreign owned properties. The most recent extensive nationalizations were those by Iran in the late 1970s when the revolutionary government also seized the U.S. embassy and its staff. This led to the creation of the Iran-United States Claims Tribunal, a nine member arbitration entity which began hearing claims in 1982. Up to March 2008 some 600 awards had been made from the approximately 3,500 claims filed. (www.iusct. org). The more than 130 decisions filed add significantly to the development of expropriation law.

In the 1970s, the pace of nationalization slowed. Many developing nations turned to a new *"ization"* (*e.g.*, Mexicanization or Peruvianization) process, mandating the conversion of wholly foreign owned subsidiaries to joint ventures with majority local ownership. But that process began to diminish in the early 1980s, particularly after the debt shock in 1982 led many developing nations to encourage more foreign investment in the hope that exports would increase and generate hard currency earnings to help pay foreign debts. The next stage was *privatization*, the reduction of state ownership by the sale of state owned enterprises invariably operating with government subsidies. The most significant privatizations of the final decade of the century took place in the former nonmarket economy nations of Eastern Europe. As the new century began, some sporadic nationalizations occurred, such as in Venezuela and Bolivia, and the meaning of expropriation was being tested in actions brought under the North American Free Trade Agreement (NAFTA), as the concept of expropriation was seemingly being expanded to include *regulatory* practices which impeded a foreign investment.

Nationalization of property has not been limited to acts by socialist or third world nations. The United Kingdom nationalized coal, steel, airline service and production, and other industries after World War II. France nationalized nearly all banks in 1982. (Many of the U.K. and French nationalized properties were later returned to the private sector, through the process of privatization.) But in both the United Kingdom and France, the takings were of property owned nearly exclusively by nationals rather than by foreign investors. The United States is not without its government's hand in the ownership of business. Part of the nation's passenger railway service was transferred to government ownership. But that involved an industry in severe financial distress. National ownership was viewed as a means of saving a dying, vital service sector, rather than displacing ownership successfully operated by the private sector. Nationalizations as an alternative to bankruptcy are a special and separate classification of property takings.

Actions that lead a country to nationalize a foreign owned commercial enterprise are difficult to predict. A taking of property may follow a change in administration, whether that results from revolution (Cuba, Indonesia, Iran, USSR) or election (Chile, Venezuela, Bolivia). Or the taking may occur during a non-threatened administration (Mexico, Great Britain). Nationalism and a sense of exploitation by foreigners may generate a takeover. Or the taking may occur because other methods of ownership are viewed as economically unsound, or politically or socially inappropriate. Most nationalizations are politically motivated; few have occurred within a stable government where a thorough economic study was first undertaken that concluded that certain sectors of industry ought to be state owned, or at least owned by nationals rather than foreigners.

A particular investment's susceptibility to being nationalized increases to the extent that it engages in what are viewed as essential national industries, such as extractive, export oriented natural resources, banking, insurance, international transportation (airlines, shipping), communications, national defense or agriculture. The entity is also more susceptible if it involves the use of people or processes that can be duplicated easily domestically; or if it consumes supplies that can be obtained easily from sources other than the affected investors; or if it does not have an essential value dependent upon the investor's goodwill or good name in the marketing of goods or services produced by the investment, and it has enough overall value to outweigh any bad press or other offsetting loss following a takeover.

INTERNATIONAL LAW

A nationalization may appear to be legal under domestic law, but it may not pass scrutiny under international law. What constitutes the international law of expropriation, however, is not easy to discern, particularly since the Third World in the late 1960s began to demand participation in formulating rules of international law applying to a nation's taking of property. Nations differ about what constitutes a public purpose and what is required compensation. They also differ regarding the legitimacy of discriminatory nationalizations, when the property of only one nation is taken, especially when that one nation is the colonial power formerly ruling the newly independent nation. Furthermore, some nations have presented lists of deductions to be applied to a multinational's valuation of its property, such as the Chilean deduction for what Chile considered to be excess profits for many past years of operation by foreign copper companies. Finally, and quite importantly, taking nations often reject the notion that any law other than *domestic* law should apply to a sovereign act of taking property, whether the property belongs to their own nationals or to foreigners. Different attitudes are sometimes ascribed to differences in colonial/colonialist political postures over the last two centuries, recency and rapidity of the country's industrial development, and differing attitudes toward public/private economic enterprise.

The right of a sovereign nation to full and permanent sovereignty over its natural resources and economic activities and the right to take privately owned property are long accepted international legal norms. That is true whether the property belongs to the country's own nationals or to foreigners. Most constitutions express that right. But the taking must be for a public purpose or in the public interest. Sovereignty nevertheless sometimes becomes a shelter for many acts defined no more specifically than "for the social welfare or economic betterment of the nation." The concept persists that a taking is improper if it cannot be justified for some public purpose. The difficulty of measurement, as well as the doubt that such measurement may be undertaken outside the taking nation, have caused the public purpose element of expropriations to be relegated to obscurity in conflicts of the past half-dozen decades. The expropriation issues of importance have not included whether there was justification for the taking, but what is a taking and whether the question of compensation was properly addressed by the taking nation.

The U.S. government has repeatedly stated its position regarding the proper international law rule for compensation. The view stresses "prompt, adequate and effective" elements to justify a nationalization. However correctly "prompt, adequate and effective" may express what the Department of State believes ought to be the standard. It is a view with only minimal support from other governments, and from many jurists, arbitrators and international law scholars. The more commonly used terms are "just" or "appropriate" compensation. While the United States adherence to a "prompt, adequate and effective" standard may create obstacles in the settlement of an expropriation case, that standard is applied in determining whether certain benefits of U.S. laws may be extended to countries which carry out expropriations. Ironically, when either the "just" or "appropriate" standard is applied, the measurement seems to include elements of the "prompt, adequate and effective" standard.

The conflict regarding the proper standard of compensation, and the debate whether international law or domestic law applies to a taking, has its modern roots for the United States in the 1938 Mexican expropriation of foreign owned petroleum investments. The United States recognized Mexico's sovereign right to take foreign property, but only upon payment of prompt, adequate and effective compensation according to international law. The Mexican response refuted both that alleged "prompt, adequate and effective" standard, and even the fundamental premise that international law rather than domestic law was the proper source of the applicable law. Mexico said it would pay because the Mexican constitution required payment, and it would pay according to Mexican standards of compensation. A settlement was ultimately reached regarding payment, but no settlement was reached regarding the standard under which the payment ought to be made. The next large scale nationalization of U.S. property was by Cuba in 1960. Like Mexico, Cuba refuted the prompt, adequate and effective standard. But unlike Mexico, Cuba's continued isolation from the United States more than fifty years after the Castro led revolution has prevented any settlement.

Soon after the Cuban expropriations, the U.N. General Assembly passed the Resolution on Permanent Sovereignty Over Natural Resources, affirming the right of nations to exercise permanent sovereignty over their resources and mandating the payment of "appropriate" compensation "in accordance with the rules in force in the State taking such measures in the exercise of its sovereignty and in accordance with international law." Although a U.N. General Assembly Resolution does not create international law, this Resolution appeared to be expressive of the customary international law of the day. A dozen years later, during which time the United Nations had expanded with the addition of many newly independent nations, the General Assembly addressed the issue again in the Declaration on the Establishment of a New International Economic Order, passed but with reservations by Japan, West Germany, France, the United Kingdom and the United States. Their concern was the absence of any reference to the application of international law in the settlement of nationalization compensation issues. Later that same year, the General Assembly passed the Charter of Economic Rights and Duties of States, with most of the major developed nations opposed to the article that stated that nationalization compensation was a *domestic* law matter.

The view of the developing nations expressed in the U.N. resolutions was consistent with how they justified expropriations in practice. Chile expropriated the Kennecott Copper Company's holdings, offering to pay according to Chilean law, but only after deducting excess profits that Kennecott allegedly had withdrawn from its Chilean operation over a number of years. Similar refusals to compensate were expressed by other developing nations. Unfortunately, the International Court of Justice has produced no international standard. The narrow ruling in the *Barcelona Traction* decision did not reach the issue of expropriation. The ICJ's predecessor, the Permanent Court of International Justice, held in 1928 in the often quoted *Chorzów Factory Case*, that there was a duty of "payment of fair compensation", and the *Norwegian Shipowners' Claims* arbitration in 1922 adopted a "just" standard.

Several arbitration and national court rulings have helped determine the path of development of an international rule of compensation. The *TOPCO-Libyan* arbitral award of 1977, declared the state of customary law to require "appropriate compensation". The *Banco Nacional de Cuba v. Chase Manhattan Bank*, 658 F.2d 875 (2nd Cir. 1981) decision in the United States in 1981, suggested that the consensus of nations was "appropriate compensation." The 1982 *Aminoil-Kuwait* arbitral award also approved "appropriate" as the accepted international standard. But the United States continued to argue the standard to be prompt, adequate and effective. The American Law Institute rejected that as the standard in revising the Restatement on Foreign Relations Law, adopting in the Restatement (Third) a standard of "just" compensation. That standard is believed to avoid the possible inclusion of deductions under an "appropriate" standard, but has received little support.

The Iran–United States Claims Tribunal, meeting at the Hague for more than two decades, did not apply a "prompt, adequate and effective" compensation standard in fact. Claims approved by the Tribunal, nevertheless, for the most part have been paid "promptly" from the funds established for such payment, and they have been paid in dollars, thus meeting any "effectiveness" standard. With respect to the "adequacy" element the tribunal has used various measurements of valuation that seem to satisfy any reasonable "adequacy" standard. Although this experience may support the "prompt, adequate and effective" standard espoused by the U.S. government, the Iranian claims process is *sui generis* because of the vast funds that Iran owned on deposit in the United States at the time of the nationalizations. If any conclusions are to be made regarding current international law of compensation, it seems clear that it is not *called* prompt, adequate and effective, but something very close to those terms seems to be included in the definition of appropriate or just compensation.

If the issue of compensation is reached, the value of the expropriated property must be established. That value may be established by direct negotiations with the taking government. Alternatively, valuation might be decided by an arbitral panel, as in the case of the Iranian nationalizations. But if the taking state refuses to pay compensation, the issue of valuation may come before a court outside the taking state. That could be an international forum, or, more likely, a court either in the nation

of the expropriated investor or in a third nation
where the taking nation has assets. Because of
lack of standing in the International Court of Justice, or reasons associated with defenses either of
sovereign immunity or the act of state doctrine, of
even because of possible obstacles to collecting under an OPIC or MIGA insurance policy, satisfaction
of the claim may have to wait until the U.S. government has negotiated a lump sum settlement with
the taking nation. The wait may be long; the 1960
Cuban nationalizations remain unresolved as the
new century unfolds. Once payment is made to a
nation which has negotiated the claims on behalf of
its nationals, international law plays no role in how
that sum is divided among claimants.

UNITED STATES LAWS AFFECTING THE NATIONALIZATION PROCESS

The U.S. Congress enacted several laws disclosing
a national position that expropriation must be accompanied by compensation, or, if not, the United
States will use its powers to deny various benefits
the nationalizing country otherwise might receive
from the United States. Treaty commitments and
provisions of other international agreements between the United States and investor hosting nations may serve to narrow expropriation uncertainties, such as provisions in the earlier, frequently
negotiated Treaties of Friendship, Commerce and
Navigation, or their successor, Bilateral Investment
Treaties (BITs). But BITs have not been concluded

with many important Third World nations where there is much foreign investment by U.S. nationals (e.g., Mexico, India, Brazil).

In addition to provisions governing expropriation, Bilateral Investment Treaties have three significant provisions dealing with (1) nondiscrimination in establishing and operating investments; (2) rights regarding transfers of investments; and (3) mandatory dispute resolution methods. Where these treaties do exist there is always the threat that a successor government may reject them, however in violation of international law such action may be. They are important treaties, nevertheless, and investors do gain an added challenge if their property is taken by a nation which has signed such a bilateral treaty with the United States.

The North American Free Trade Agreement (NAFTA) has a detailed provision in Chapter 11 governing the taking of property of a foreign investor from a Party. The right to take property is acknowledged, but only where there is a public purpose, a non-discriminatory taking, due process of law and minimum standards of treatment as contained in the NAFTA, and the payment of compensation. The compensation provisions do not refer to the prompt, adequate and effective standard urged by the United States, but quite clearly meet that standard by more specific language. Chapter 11 cases are developing a NAFTA jurisprudence on taking of foreign property that has drawn much criticism from challenged NAFTA Parties and observers, especially environmental law groups.

Government regulations, often directed to environmental issues, have been ruled to constitute expropriation in the manner they have been implemented. While the NAFTA covers the compensation side of expropriation in considerable detail, it does not adequately define what constitutes an expropriation. This must be resolved if investment and investment expropriation is to be included in further trade agreements.

The WTO Agreement on Trade-Related Investment Measures (TRIMs) has provisions that are not as encompassing as those in the NAFTA, and do not include provisions governing the taking of investment property. Perhaps as the issues noted above with the NAFTA expropriation provisions are resolved, further revisions to the WTO TRIMs will include this important investment issue.

Other domestic laws of the United States apply to nations which have expropriated property of U.S. nationals and have failed to provide compensation or to illustrate a willingness to negotiate a compensation agreement. Subsequent to the Cuban nationalizations, the Hickenlooper Amendment to the Foreign Assistance Act was enacted and provides, in part, that the:

President shall suspend assistance to the government of any country to which assistance is provided under this chapter or any other Act when the government of such country.... (A) has nationalized or expropriated or seized ownership or control of property owned by any United

States citizen ... (C) has imposed or enforced discriminatory taxes or other exactions, or restrictive maintenance or operational conditions, or has taken other actions, which have the effect of nationalizing, expropriating, or otherwise seizing ownership or control of property so owned, and such country, government agency, or government sub-division fails within a reasonable time ... to take appropriate steps ... to discharge its obligations under international law toward such citizen ... including speedy compensation for such property in convertible foreign exchange, equivalent to the full value thereof, as required by international law, or fails to take steps designed to provide relief from such taxes, exactions, or conditions, as the case may be; and such suspension shall continue until the President is satisfied that appropriate steps are being taken.

The Sabbatino, or Second Hickenlooper, Amendment was passed by an angry Congress soon after the U.S. Supreme Court, in *Banco Nacional de Cuba v. Sabbatino*, 376 U.S. 398 (1964) held that the Act of State doctrine prevented U.S. courts from hearing cases of foreign expropriation, even where there were allegations of violations of international law. The Congressional response reversed the presumption of *Sabbatino*, allowing U.S. courts to proceed unless the President stated that such adjudication would embarrass the conduct of foreign relations. Additional acts prohibit the United States from casting votes in organizations such as the World Bank or InterAmerican Development

Bank (IADB) for loans to countries which have expropriated property of U.S. nationals and refused compensation.

The U.S. 1996 Cuban Liberty and Democratic Solidarity (Libertad) Act promoted what could become a massive challenge to U.S. courts to address the Cuban expropriations. Title III of this commonly called Helms-Burton Act provided for expropriation claims against those foreign parties "trafficking" in property once owned by U.S. nationals. But each president has deferred the implementation of that provision and the litigation has been thwarted.

INSURING AGAINST THE RISKS OF FOREIGN INVESTMENT LOSSES

Investments abroad often are subject to risks that are not significant concerns to a domestic investment. An investment in the United States is not at risk from military conflict, or uncompensated expropriation, or losses from a currency that becomes inconvertible. Because these risks are not present in most developed, democratic nations, and because they present extremely complex risk measurement problems for investors entering developing nations, the *domestic* insurance industries generally have not offered insurance to cover such potential losses for investments made in high risk nations. It is thus to individual government and multi-nation organization investment insurance programs that foreign investors often must turn to reduce the consequences of these risks.

INSURANCE FOR FOREIGN
INVESTORS—OPIC

National insurance programs, such as the U.S. Overseas Private Investment Corporation (OPIC), support government policies that encourage domestic industries to engage in investment abroad. But critics of government "backed" insurance of U.S. investment abroad argue that the program encourages and subsidizes the transfer of productive facilities abroad, at the cost of jobs in the United States. Although OPIC has been the preeminent U.S, insurer of foreign investment risks, many members of Congress believe its role should be assumed by the private sector. They reject the concept that the government should engage in private sector support activities, and worry about the potential burden on U.S. taxpayers. While OPIC is supposed to write insurance adhering to private insurance industry principles of risk management, and on a self-sustaining basis, it does not always or even regularly do so, perhaps because OPIC insurance is backed by the full faith and credit of the United States. Because of the absence of significant expropriations over the past few decades, at least since those by Iran, OPIC has been a financial success that has allowed it to build reserves in excess of $4 billion, while claims have been nearly non-existent. As long as insurance claims remain dormant, OPIC is likely to avoid serious criticism from Congress and others about the risk to the general public. OPIC's role is increasing in financing foreign investment, however important its insurance programs remain.

Until the 1969 creation of OPIC, AID was the primary organization through which the U.S. government issued risk insurance to U.S. investors in developing nations. OPIC was established to "mobilize and facilitate the participation of U.S. private capital and skills in the economic and social development of less developed countries and areas, and countries in transition from nonmarket to market economies."

Initially three principal risks were covered by OPIC—risk of loss due to (1) inconvertibility, (2) expropriation or confiscation, or (3) war, revolution, insurrection or civil strife, now referred to as political violence. Expropriation "includes, but is not limited to, any abrogation, repudiation, or impairment by a foreign government of its own contract with an investor with respect to a project, where such abrogation, repudiation, or impairment is not caused by the investor's own fault or misconduct, and materially adversely affects the continued operation of the project." OPIC contracts have followed a more specific and enumerative approach, because the law does not define more specifically what actions constitute expropriation. The third form of coverage, political violence, covers loss of assets or income due to war, revolution , insurrection or politically motivated civil strife, terrorism or sabotoge. The usual OPIC contract provides protection against injury to the "physical condition, destruction, disappearance or seizure and retention of covered property directly caused by war or by revolution or insurrection and includes injury to the physical condition, destruction, disappearance or seizure and retention of covered property as a direct result of actions taken in hindering, combating or defending against a pending or expected hostile act whether in war, revolution, or insurrection." With terrorism becoming the major focus in many parts of the world, this class of OPIC insurance may become the most important. But the terrorism has been in developed nations, not in the nations where the insurance is written.

The investor must exhaust remedies before OPIC becomes obligated to pay any claim. All reasonable action must be taken by the investor, including initiating administrative and judicial claims, to prevent or contest the challenged action by the host government. Prior to the receipt of payment of a claim, the investor usually will be required to transfer to OPIC all right, title and interest in the insured investment, including when the government expropriatory action consists of preventing the investor from exercising effective control over and withdrawing funds received from the foreign entity as dividends, interest or return of capital. The investor has an ongoing obligation to cooperate with the U.S. government in pressing claims against the host government.

Otherwise qualifying countries may be denied OPIC insurance if they do not extend internationally recognized workers' rights to domestic workers, or if they do not respect human rights, but presidential discretion may result in a waiver of this prohibition on national economic interest grounds.

INSURANCE FOR FOREIGN INVESTORS—MIGA

OPIC insurance is limited to U.S. investors. To encourage increased investment in the developing nations, similar insurance has been established on an international level by the World Bank's 1985 Multilateral Investment Guarantee Agency (MIGA). With the expected completion of Mexico's admission process, all the major nations are subscribers to MIGA.

Risks covered by MIGA include inconvertibility, deprivation of ownership or control by governmental actions, breach of contract by the government where there is no recourse to a judicial or arbitral forum, and loss from military action or civil disturbance. The insurance may cover equity investments or loans made or guaranteed by holders of equity (probably including service and management contracts), and also licensing, franchising and production sharing agreements.

Generally, investors must be from a member country, and only foreign investors qualify. There was considerable discussion regarding insuring only in those developing nations which adopted standards for protecting foreign investment, but the final Convention did not include any such conditions. Such standards may nevertheless be a factor in writing insurance, if any measure of risk management principles is to be followed. The highest percentage of MIGA coverage is in sub-Saharan Africa, followed by Asia, and then by Latin America and the Caribbean.

The viability of MIGA is dependent both on its care in selecting risks to insure, and its ability to negotiate settlements after paying claims. Unlike national programs, such as OPIC, MIGA has the backing of a large group of nations when it presses a claim. Only experience will disclose the extent to which politics will enter the claims procedures. The intention is to avoid political interference and consider solely legal issues. MIGA has yet to face claims experience. If over time the risks MIGA insures diminish, the use of such insurance will decrease. If on the other hand the risks become reality, the effectiveness of the claims procedures will become evident.

Creating MIGA within the World Bank structure offers benefits a separate international organization would lack. MIGA has access to World Bank data on nations' economic and social status, thus helping the assessment of risks. The World Bank has considerable credibility that favors MIGA, and encourages broad participation. It is not certain how MIGA will affect national programs, such as OPIC. A U.S. company, for example, might prefer dealing with OPIC because of greater confidence of claims being paid, of maintaining information confidentiality, and benefitting from legal processes established in bilateral investment treaties. MIGA acts to some degree as a gap filler for U.S. investors when OPIC insurance is not available or inadequate for the project. MIGA's success will likely be where it fills gaps rather than competes with established national insurance programs. Its real test will be when significant claims are made (only three have been paid and some fifty disputes have been re-solved)—the past two decades have not witnessed the expropriations that tested the viability of OPIC in the 1970s.

CHAPTER SIX

EU BUSINESS COMPETITION RULES [1]—EXTRATERRITORIAL ANTITRUST LAWS

The European Common Market has accomplished among other things, an institutionalization of competitive market doctrines. The role of the Court of Justice and Court of First Instance in interpreting Articles 81 and 82 (formerly Articles 85 and 86) of the EC Treaty is one example of the movement toward greater union. In that sense, these articles assume some of the function of the interstate commerce clause of the U.S. Constitution. Articles 81 and 82 have a mandatory effect upon any international trade or investment touched by their reach. The articles evidence the degree of rule-making complexity and detail achieved in one area of law. Recent Court of Justice and Court of First Instance rulings about their application to persons, things and events beyond the territorial limits of the Union serve to introduce the larger issue of extraterritorial laws and international business transactions.

In general, Article 81(1) aims to prohibit "arms length" competitors from agreeing between them-

1. For much more extensive coverage, see Folsom's *European Union Law in a Nutshell.*

selves to prevent, restrain or distort competition. Article 81(1) is roughly analogous to the prohibition against restraints of trade in Section 1 of the U.S. Sherman Antitrust Act. Broadly speaking, Article 82 prohibits dominant enterprises from abusing their position to the prejudice of competitors or consumers. This prohibition is more encompassing than monopolization as an offense under Section 2 of the Sherman Act.

Articles 81 and 82 are complicated and elastic. Although each article lists certain proscribed business practices, much of their specific, substantive content has been generated by Commission and Court interpretations. Numerous treatises (including several multi-volume works) are devoted to European competition law. A notable feature is their applicability to publicly owned enterprises (of which there are many). For example, the European Court affirmed the applicability of Article 82 to RAI, the Italian state broadcasting monopoly, provided that such application would not obstruct its tasks.

ENFORCEMENT

The terms of Articles 81 and 82 are enforced, in the first instance, by the Commission and since 2004 by member state competition law authorities and national courts. The Commission has the power to investigate, *sua sponte* or upon complaint by interested persons or member states, possible violations of Articles 81 and 82. The Commission may obtain information from national authorities as part of its investigatory process and it may require those authorities to conduct investigations for it. The Commission may require enterprises to produce records or documents necessary to its investigation. When there is a failure or refusal to comply with a Commission investigation or enforcement decision, the Commission may seek a compliance order from the Court. Several procedural requirements for Commission investigations and hearings have been discussed by the Court of Justice. One notable decision upheld the authority of the Commission to conduct searches of corporate offices *without* notice or warrant when it has reason to believe that pertinent evidence may be lost. Another notable decision permitted a Swiss "whistle blower" who once worked for Hoffman-La Roche (a defendant in competition law proceedings) to sue in tort for disclosure of his identity as an informant.

The subject matter of Articles 81 and 82 is commerce, yet their impact is as political as commercial. Astute observers have noted that a significant number of the leading "test cases" have involved defendants from Japan, the United States, Switzerland and other non-members. It is, of course, politically much more acceptable when Articles 81 and 82 are applied to foreign firms. But they have also been applied extensively to European enterprises. The quantity and significance of competition law is sufficient to have generated a growing number of lawyers who specialize in giving advice about the effects of Articles 81 and 82 on transactions in the Common Market.

A person who ignores the reach of Articles 81 and 82 may experience severe consequences, but nothing comparable to the felony criminal sanctions and private treble damages actions found in U.S. antitrust law. Article 81(2) renders offending business agreements null and void. Nullity is most often raised as a defense to enforcement of contracts, licenses and joint ventures in national legal proceedings. Fines may be levied by the Commission for supplying false or misleading information or for holding back information in connection with inquiries about the applicability of the articles, and further fines may be levied if persons or activities are found to have contravened Article 81 or 82.

For example, the Belgian and French subsidiary enterprises of the Japanese electrical and electronic group, Matsushita, were fined by the Commission for supplying it with false information about whether Matsushita recommended retail prices for its products. Furthermore, offending activity may be penalized per day until there is compliance with a Commission order. All Commission decisions imposing fines or penalties under competition law are subject to judicial review by the Court of First Instance. In early years the Court tended to reduce the amounts involved because of the developmental state of Article 81 and 82 law. In more recent decisions, the Court has upheld substantial fines and penalties imposed by the Commission in competition law proceedings.

Written communications with external EU-licensed lawyers undertaken for defense purposes are confidential and need not be disclosed. Written communications with in-house lawyers are not exempt from disclosure, nor are communications with external non-EU counsel. Thus communications with North American attorneys (who are not also EU-licensed attorneys) are generally discoverable. For example, the Commission obtained in-house counsel documents from John Deere, Inc., a Belgian subsidiary of the U.S. multinational. These documents were drafted as advice to management on how to avoid competition law liability for export prohibition restraints. They were used by the Commission to justify the finding of an intentional Article 81 violation and a fine of 2 million EUROS. U.S. attorneys have followed these developments with amazement and trepidation. Disclaimers of possible nonconfidentiality are one option to consider in dealing with clients. At a minimum, U.S. attorneys ought to advise their clients that the usual rules on attorney-client privilege may not apply.

Article 81 and 82 fines are reducible to judgment in the courts of any member state. Because regional law supercedes only inconsistent laws in any of the members states, violating Article 81 or 82 may not preclude additional sanctions for breach of a member state's business competition laws (e.g., laws which may authorize an aggrieved person to receive damages). Indeed it is possible, as several examples suggest, that multiple liability under British or German competition law (the most vigorous in the Common Market), European Union law and

U.S. antitrust law can simultaneously occur. With such a high level of risk, law in this area is ignored only at great peril to international business.

ARTICLE 81—EXEMPTIONS

Not all anticompetitive agreements violate Article 81(1). By operation of Article 81(3), Article 81(1) may not apply to an agreement, decision or concerted practice which contributes to an improvement of production or distribution of goods, or which promotes technical or economic progress (while allowing consumers a fair share of the resulting benefit), *provided* the agreement or concerted practice does not serve to eliminate competition in a substantial part of the products in question. Since 2004, the Commission, member state competition law authorities, and member state courts share decisionmaking power concerning individual exemptions under Article 81(3). Various procedural rules and Guidelines ensure that the Commission can have the final say on individual exemptions should it wish to do so.

Council and Commission regulations operate to exclude from Article 81(1) certain vertical purchasing, distribution and franchise agreements, categories of research and development agreements, specified agreements in the technology transfer area, and horizontal agreements among smaller firms for product specialization. Also exempted by regulation are certain motor vehicle distribution and servicing agreements. These regulations are known as "block exemptions" since they are based upon the legal criteria of Article 81(3). They have the practical effect of dramatically reducing the Commission's workload because it is not necessary to apply for a block exemption. Parties need only conform their conduct to the terms of these regulations, which often detail permitted, permissible and prohibited contract clauses.

Lawyers representing clients doing business in Europe usually prefer to structure contracts and other arrangements in accordance with block exemptions since this preserves confidentiality. Voluntary adherence to block exemptions has become a successful, cost-effective way of implementing Article 81. The meaning of the regulations is better understood by a review of the leading cases previously brought by the Commission to test its authority in each of these fields. Lines drawn in the block exemptions may later be reviewed in private litigation or public enforcement proceedings.

Such agreements and concerted practices are only a partial list of Council, Commission and Court regulatory concerns under Articles 81 and 82. In 1987 the Court of Justice ruled that Article 81 applies to mergers and acquisitions, activities previously thought to fall only under Article 82. This decision is yet another indication of the significance of competition law to those drafting distribution contracts, licensing agreements, joint ventures and other business arrangements. Counsel should be especially circumspect about any contractual or licensing term that may tend to divide up the Common Market by allocating territories or customers. Since great effort has been made to create the Common Market, private market division arrangements inhibiting competition in goods or services are practically "per se" offenses under Articles 81 and 82. This is sometimes true even of intrabrand vertical market division restraints, which are now frequently permitted under the Rule of Reason approach to U.S. restraint of trade law.

COMMISSION REGULATION OF MERGERS

In 1989, the Council of Ministers unanimously adopted a Regulation on the Control of Concentrations Between Undertakings ("Mergers Regulation"). This regulation became effective in 1990 and was significantly amended late in 2003. It vests in the Commission the power to oppose large-scale mergers and acquisitions of competitive consequence to the Common Market. The control process established by the Mergers Regulation commences when a concentration must be notified to the Commission. The duty to notify is triggered only when the concentration involves enterprises with a combined worldwide turnover of at least 5 billion EUROS *and* two of them have an aggregate region-wide turnover of 250 million EUROS.

As a general rule, concentrations meeting these criteria cannot be put into effect and fall exclusively within the Commission's domain. The effort here is to create a "one-stop" regulatory system. However, certain exceptions apply so as to allow national authorities to challenge some mergers. For example, this may occur under national law when two-thirds of the activities of each of the companies involved take place in the same member state. The member states can also oppose mergers when their public security is at stake, to preserve plurality in media ownership, when financial institutions are involved or other legitimate interests are at risk. If the threshold criteria of the Mergers Regulation are not met, member states can ask the Commission to investigate mergers that create or strengthen a dominant position in that state. States that lack national merger controls seem likely to do this. Since 2004, parties to a merger that is subject to notification in three or more member states may request "one-stop" review by the Commission, which will occur provided no member state objects.

Once a concentration is notified to the Commission, it has one month to decide to investigate the merger. If a formal investigation is commenced, the Commission ordinarily then has four months to challenge or approve the merger. During these months, in most cases, the concentration cannot be put into effect. It is on hold.

The Commission evaluates mergers in terms of their "compatibility" with the Common Market. The 1990 Mergers Regulation stated that if the concentration created or strengthened a dominant position such that competition was "significantly impeded," it was incompatible. Effective 2004, this test was replaced by a prohibition against mergers that "significantly impede effective competition" by creating or strengthening dominant positions. Thus the new test focuses on effects not dominance. A set of Guidelines on Horizontal Mergers issued by the Commission in 2004 elaborate upon this approach. It is thought that this change will bring EU and U.S. mergers law closer together (the U.S. test is "substantial lessening of competition").

During a mergers investigation, the Commission can obtain information and records from the parties, and request member states to help with the investigation. Fines and penalties back up the Commission's powers to obtain what it needs from the parties. If the concentration has already taken effect, the Commission can issue a "hold-separate" order. This requires the corporations or assets acquired to be separated and not, operationally speaking, merged. Approval of the merger may involve modifications of its terms or promises by the parties aimed at diminishing its anticompetitive potential. Negotiations with the Commission to obtain such clearances may follow. If the Commission ultimately decides to oppose the merger in a timely manner, it can order its termination by whatever means are appropriate to restore conditions of effective competition. Such decisions can be appealed to the Court of First Instance.

The first merger actually blocked by the Commission on competition law grounds was the attempted acquisition of a Canadian aircraft manufacturer (DeHaviland—owned by Boeing) by two European companies (Aerospatiale SNI of France and Alenia e Selenia Spa of Italy). Prior to this rejection in late

1991, the Commission had approved over 50 mergers, obtaining modifications in a few instances. The Commission, in the DeHaviland case, took the position that the merger would have created an unassailable dominant position in the world and European market for turbo prop or commuter aircraft. If completed, the merged entity would have had 50 percent of the world and 67 percent of the European market for such aircraft.

In 1997, the Commission dramatically demonstrated its extraterritorial jurisdiction over the Boeing-McDonnell Douglas merger. This merger had already been cleared by the U.S. Federal Trade Commission. The European Commission, however, demanded and got (at the risk of a trade war) important concessions from Boeing. These included abandonment of exclusive supply contracts with three U.S. airlines and licensing of technology derived from McDonnell Douglas' military programs at reasonable royalty rates. The Commission's success in this case was widely perceived in the United States as pro-Airbus.

The Commission blocked the MC Worldcom/Sprint merger in 2001, as did the U.S. Dept. of Justice. Both authorities were worried about the merger's adverse effects on Internet access. For the Commission, this was the first block of a merger taking place outside the EU between two firms established outside the EU. Much more controversy arose when in 2001 the Commission blocked the GE/Honeywell merger after it had been approved by U.S. authorities. The Commission was particularly concerned about the potential for bundling engines with avionics and non-avionics to the disadvantage of rivals. Appeal of this decision is pending. The United States and the EU in the wake of GE/Honeywell, have agreed to follow a set of "Best Practices" on coordinated timing, evidence gathering, communication and consistency of remedies.

THE EXTRATERRITORIAL REACH OF ARTICLES 81 AND 82

There is a question about the extent to which the competition rules extend to activity anywhere in the world, including activity occurring entirely or in part within the territorial limits of the United States. Decisions by the Commission and the Court of Justice suggest that the territorial reach of Articles 81 and 82 is expanding and may well extend to an international business transaction occurring within the United States.

For an agreement to be incompatible with the Common Market and prohibited under Article 81(1), it must be "likely to affect trade between member states" and have "the object or effect" of impairing "competition within the Common Market". The Court has repeatedly held that the fact that one of the parties to an agreement is domiciled in a third country does not preclude the applicability of Article 81(1) if the agreement is effective in the territory of the Common Market. Swiss and British companies, for example, argued that the Commission was not competent to impose competition law fines for acts committed in Switzerland and Britain (before joining the EU) by enterprises domiciled outside the Union solely because the acts had effects within the Common Market. Nevertheless, the Court held those companies in violation of Article 81 because they owned subsidiary companies within the Union and controlled their behavior. The foreign parent and its subsidiaries were treated as a "single enterprise" for purposes of service of process, judgment and collection of fines and penalties. In doing so, the Court observed that the fact that a subsidiary company has its own legal personality does not rule out the possibility that its conduct is attributable to the parent company.

The Court has extended its reasoning to the extraterritorial application of Article 82. A U.S. parent company, for example, was held potentially liable for acquisitions by its Italian subsidiary which affected market conditions within Europe. In another case, the Court held that a Maryland company's refusal to sell its product to a competitor of its affiliate company within the Union was a result of united "single enterprise" action. It proceeded to state that extraterritorial conduct merely having "repercussions on competitive structures" in the Common Market fell within the parameters of Article 82. The Court ordered the U.S. company, through its Italian affiliate, to supply the competitor at reasonable prices.

In 1988, the Court of Justice widened the extraterritorial reach of Article 81 in the *Woodpulp* case where pulp producers from the United States, Canada, Sweden and Finland were fined for price fixing activities affecting Common Market trade and competition. These firms did not have substantial operations within the EC. They were primarily exporters to the Common Market. This decision's reliance upon a "place of implementation" effects test is similar to that used under the Sherman Act.

THE EFFECTS TEST IN UNITED STATES AND EUROPEAN LAW

It may be a substantial jump to predict that Articles 81 and 82 bear upon a business transaction done in the United States or another non-EC country which merely inures to the competitive disadvantage of a company located within the Common Market. Yet in one of the *Dyestuffs* cases as early as 1969 the Commission took the position that:

> The rules of competition of the Treaty are therefore applicable to all restrictions on competition that produce within the Common Market effects to which Article 81, paragraph 1, applies. There is therefore no need to examine whether the enterprises that originated such restraints of competition have their head office within or outside of the Community. *Commission v. I.C.I.*, 8 Common Mkt.L.Rep. 494 (1969).

Although the Court's disposition of the *Dyestuffs* cases did not endorse such reasoning, the Commission has reasserted its "effects test" in subsequent arguments. The Commission's approach merits close consideration if only because the initiation of an Article 81 or 82 inquiry can generate local overhead costs for those involved in European business transactions. That courts in the United States have also used an "effects test" in connection with the question of the extraterritoriality of U.S. antitrust laws increases the potential for uncertainty and costs in international transactions.

U.S. courts have long asserted the right to apply the Sherman Antitrust Act to foreign commerce intended to or affecting the U.S. market. In some cases, this approach has been tempered to allow consideration of the interests of comity and foreign countries in the outcome. Some limits on the extraterritorial reach of the Sherman Act are created by the act of state doctrine and the Foreign Sovereign Immunities Act. But in the main, U.S. antitrust law has been applied to foreigners and overseas activities with a zeal sometimes approaching religious fervor. This fervor has carried over into other areas, such as the failed attempt of the Reagan administration to apply U.S. export control laws to European enterprises involved in the construction of the Soviet-era natural gas pipeline from Siberia to Western Europe.

Amendments to the Sherman Act in 1984 stress the "direct, substantial and reasonably foreseeable" nature of effects on U.S. foreign commerce as a prerequisite to antitrust jurisdiction. Nevertheless, the potential for conflict in this field is enormous. For example, a multinational enterprise headquartered in the United States but doing business in England could be constrained by U.S. antitrust law from fixing prices, yet permitted by European competition law under Article 81(3) to do exactly that. Assuming that the price fixing in question has effects in both markets, what course of action is to be followed? There is no easy answer. When the firm is located within a country other than one of the member states of the EU or the United States, but engages in activity having effects within those markets, the problem potential of extraterritoriality may be even more acute. Reconciling a conflict of antitrust laws applied extraterritorially by these two jurisdictions could become a flashpoint in international business.

EXTRATERRITORIAL ANTITRUST LAWS, BLOCKING STATUTES AND INTERNATIONAL SOLUTIONS

Business operations that transcend a nation's borders have focused concern about the extent to which the applicability of a nation's laws must stop at its territorial borders. Absent a controlling and readily enforceable international law, it is at least a fair question to ask whether national laws are needed to regulate extraterritorial business enterprises.

Reasons advanced to support an extraterritorial application of U.S. antitrust laws are founded on the idea that some extraterritorial extension is necessary to prevent their circumvention by multinational corporations which have the business sagacity to ensure that anticompetitive transactions are consummated beyond the territorial borders of the United States. An extraterritorial extension of antitrust laws can help to protect the export opportunities of domestic firms. Extraterritorial application of the antitrust laws can also help to ensure that the American consumer receives the benefit of competing imports, which in turn may spur complacent domestic industries. The effect of foreign auto imports on the car manufacturers in the United States may be cited as an example. In an increasingly internationalized world, extraterritorial antitrust may merely reflect economic reality.

On the other hand, the British argue that extraterritoriality permits the United States to unjustifiably "mold the international economic and trading world to its own image." In particular, the U.S. "effects" doctrine creates legal uncertainty for international traders, and U.S. courts pay little attention to the competing policies (interests) of other concerned governments. As the House of Lords stated in *Rio Tinto Zinc*: "It is axiomatic that in anti-trust matters the policy of one state may be to defend what it is the policy of another state to attack."

The British also argue, not without some support, that customary international law does not permit extraterritorial application of national laws. In making this argument, the British have a convenient way of forgetting about the extraterritorial scope of Articles 81 and 82, which are now part of their law. Moreover, in a curious reversal of roles illustrating the extremes of the debate, the British government applied the Protection of Trading Interests Act to block the pursuit of treble damages in *United States* courts by the liquidator of Laker Airways against British Airways and other defendants. A House of Lords decision reversed this ban but retained government restrictions on discovery related to the case.

Extraterritoriality is a matter of balance. The Executive, Legislative, and Judicial branches of government in the United States have reached out extraterritorially in the law of admiralty, antitrust, crime, labor, securities regulation, taxation, torts, trademarks and wildlife management. A balance drawn wrongly by one nation invites retaliatory action by others. In the case of antitrust judgments emanating from courts in the United States, most notably the "Uranium Cartel" treble damages litigation of the late 1970s, many nations consider that the balance has been wrongly drawn. Many nations have taken retaliatory action by enacting "blocking statutes."

Blocking Statutes

The United Kingdom blocking statute is the Protection of Trading Interests Act of 1980. This Act (without specifying U.S. antitrust law) makes it difficult to depose witnesses, obtain documents or enforce multiple liability judgments extraterritorially in the U.K. Violation of the 1980 Act may result in criminal penalties. Furthermore, under the "clawback" provision of the Act, parties with outstanding multiple liabilities in foreign jurisdictions (*e.g.*, U.S. treble damages defendants) may recoup the punitive element of such awards in Britain against assets of the successful plaintiff. The British Act invites other nations to adopt clawback provisions by offering clawback reciprocity. U.S. attorneys confronted with a blocking statute need to understand that multiple liability judgments combined with contingency fee arrangements are virtually unknown elsewhere.

The extensive array of pre-trial discovery mechanisms allowed in U.S. civil litigation rarely, if ever, have a counterpart in foreign law. Discovery subpoenas originating in U.S. litigation are often "shocking" to many foreign defendants. And the U.S. Supreme Court ruled in *Aérospatiale* that use of letters rogatory under the Hague Convention is not obligatory. It is the blocking of discovery that potentially most threatens the extraterritorial application of U.S. laws, especially antitrust. Since U.S. courts may sanction parties who in bad faith fail to respond to discovery requests, foreign defendants requesting help from their home governments under blocking statutes are especially at risk. On the other hand, good faith efforts to modify or work around discovery blockades may favor foreign defendants. Such defendants are often caught in a "no win" situation. Either way they will be penalized.

International Antitrust Cooperation

Some evidence of international antitrust cooperation is contained in a 1967 recommendation of the OECD which provides for notification of antitrust actions, exchanges of information to the extent that the disclosure is domestically permissible, and where practical, coordination of antitrust enforcement. The OECD resolution served as a model for the 1972 "Antitrust Notification and Consultation Procedure" between Canada and the United States. Following the "Uranium Cartel" litigation, Australia and the United States reached an Agreement on Cooperation in Antitrust Matters (1982) to minimize jurisdictional conflicts. Australia has taken the position that U.S. courts are not a proper institution to balance interests of concerned countries within the context of private antitrust litigation.

The Agreement on Cooperation provides that when the Government of Australia is concerned with private antitrust proceedings pending in a United States court, the Government of Australia may request the Government of the United States to participate in the litigation. The United States must report to the court on the substance and outcome of consultations with Australia on the matter concerned. In this way, Australia's views and interests in the litigation and its potential outcome are made known to the court. The court is not required to defer to those views, or even to openly consider them. It merely receives the "report." Australia, in turn, has indicated a willingness to be more receptive to discovery requests in U.S. antitrust litigation and to consult before invoking its blocking statute.

Similar arrangements have been made between the United States and Canada. No such agreement has been reached with the United Kingdom, with whom the extraterritoriality issue remains contentious, a fact which has led some to wonder whether the United States ought to have its own blocking statute against extraterritorial European competition law. An antitrust cooperation agreement seems more appropriate and, indeed, late in 1991 the European Union (of which Britain is still a member) and the United States reached such an agreement. This accord commits the parties to notify each other of imminent enforcement action, to share relevant information and consult on potential policy changes. An innovative feature is the inclusion of "positive comity" principles, each side promising to take the other's interests into account when considering antitrust prosecutions. The agreement has had a significant effect on mergers of firms doing business in North America and Europe (above).

Microsoft

The U.S.-EU Antitrust Cooperation Agreement was prominently used to jointly negotiate a 1994 settlement on restrictive practices of the Microsoft Corporation, a settlement that is being revisited concerning Microsoft's web browser tactics. In the more recent round of public prosecutions focused on Windows as a monopoly, the U.S. settlement reached in 2001 is less demanding than the Commission judgment of 2004 which requires an unbundling of media playback capabilities. This example reaffirms that transatlantic antitrust "cooperation" need not necessarily result in similar outcomes. In 2007, the Court of First Instance broadly confirmed the Commission's 2004 decision. Shortly thereafter, Microsoft settled the prosecution by altering its operating systems' licensing arrangements to favor "open source" software developers (e.g., Linux). Prior to settlement, Microsoft had been fined, including daily noncompliance penalties, in excess of 2 billion Euros. By 2008, the Commission was investigating Microsoft's bundling of its web browser with Windows, and the compatibility of its Office software with rival programs. Other U.S. technology firms are also under the EU competition law microscope: Qualcomm, Intel, Google and Apple included.

CHAPTER SEVEN

RESOLUTION OF INTERNATIONAL DISPUTES: LITIGATION AND ARBITRATION

Although a leitmotif of this book has been that a transactions counsel should try to avoid litigation by means of thorough planning of the transaction, exhaustive assignment of all risks, and careful drafting of all documents, disputes can and will arise which cannot be resolved by the parties themselves. In such instances, the parties to a transaction must seek assistance from outside sources. Faced with such a dispute, parties may seek access to resolve their dispute through the courts in one or more countries, through arbitration or through mediation. This Chapter discusses some considerations associated with access to national courts before discussing the widespread and increasing preference which merchants, investors and host countries have for arbitration.

Dispute settlement should also be dealt with when drafting the initial international business agreements between the parties, so that the dispute resolution process is known and understood before any actual dispute arises. The formal process chosen in the contract is most commonly either litigation or arbitration. Many international contracts require that mediation be used before any formal process is used, and mediation is the process preferred by many parties, especially Asian businesses. Whichever process is chosen, the contract should also choose the forum or tribunal and the governing law.

DISPUTE SETTLEMENT IN NATIONAL COURTS

A dispute between a foreign investor and a person in the host country may qualify for adjudication by a court within the host country, by a court within the investor's country of nationality, or by a court within an unanticipated third country notwithstanding the existence of law in many countries similar to the doctrines of Act of State and Sovereign Immunity in the United States. See Chapter 5. For example, in the United States the Alien Tort Statute (28 U.S.C.A. § 1350) permits a noncitizen to sue another noncitizen in Federal District Court with respect to an alleged tort which has occurred outside of the United States but which has been "committed in violation of the law of nations or a treaty of the United States".

Recourse to a local court may lead to some surprises for a U.S. investor. For example, courts in some countries may not be as impermeable to political persuasion or outright judicial corruption as are courts in the United States. The highest judicial appeal tribunal may be the country's chief political personality in some countries. In some countries the appropriate tribunal to hear an international commercial dispute may be a specialized court, such as a "commercial" court, or another kind of adjudicatory tribunal, perhaps called a "foreign investment grievances board".

Aside from the time and expense expended in getting a dispute aired thoroughly within local courts, difficulties may arise in securing persons or documents that are outside the country but are required and admissible by the litigation rules of the forum. Local court recognition of certain foreign public documents may be facilitated by the 1960 Convention Abolishing the Requirement of Legalization of Foreign Public Documents, which the U.S. joined in 1981. The Convention permits certification by the designated "competent authority" in the State from which the document comes.

Party litigants in a local court may have difficulty understanding and applying the forum rules regarding notice and proof of applicable foreign law. The 1979 European Convention on Proof of and Information on Foreign Law, with additional Protocol, illustrates the "notice and proof" problem and modern efforts to deal with it.

Service of judicial documents upon a person in another country may be required and facilitated by the 1965 Convention on the Service Abroad of Judicial and Extra Judicial Documents in Civil or Commercial Matters (generally referred to as the Hague Service Convention) supplemented for the United

States by the 1977 Department of Justice Instructions for Serving Foreign Judicial Documents and for Processing Requests for Serving American Judicial Documents Abroad. It applies in all civil or commercial cases in which a judicial or extrajudicial document must be served abroad. Under it, each Contracting State designates a "Central Authority" which is available to other Contracting States to receive requests for service. While the Department of Justice initially housed the Central Authority for the United States, it has been outsourced to a private organization.

Parties who desire the taking of evidence abroad may receive some assistance from the 1970 Hague Convention on the Taking of Evidence Abroad in Civil or Commercial Matters (generally referred to as the Hague Evidence Convention), which has a framework similar to the 1965 Hague Service Convention. One court in Germany has held that the Convention on Taking of Evidence Abroad does not permit an applicant to use it for "fishing expedition" discovery purposes, a view which finds sympathy in many other nations.

Where the Hague Evidence Convention is not used to obtain evidence, U.S. law provides foreign parties with broad evidence gathering opportunities under 28 U.S.C.A. §§ 1781–1782, but a U.S. party seeking evidence abroad may be hindered. Court orders sent abroad, purporting to use compulsory process to summon a non-citizen to appear as a witness, may be ineffective. Further, civil law countries view the taking of evidence as a judicial function and generally believe that gathering evidence within their territory, but without their consent, threatens their sovereignty. If the country does consent and participate in the evidence gathering, the evidence may be supplied in a form which is unusable in U.S. courts. In addition, a U.S. court order for production of evidence held abroad may conflict with "blocking statutes" or other non-disclosure laws of the foreign country.

The Hague Evidence Convention provides three alternative methods for gathering evidence abroad. First, a party may ask the U.S. court to send a "Letter of Request" to the "Central Authority" in the foreign country where the evidence is located. That Central Authority forwards the Request to the appropriate foreign court, which then holds the evidentiary proceeding, and will hold it under procedures specified by the U.S. court, unless they contravene the law of the foreign court. Second, a party to litigation in a U.S. court may ask that a U.S. diplomatic or consular officer accredited to a foreign country take evidence in that foreign country. And third, a party may request that a specially appointed commissioner take evidence abroad. Of these three methods, the Request is the most useful, for the others are noncompulsory proceedings. However, the Convention gives foreign judicial authorities substantial latitude in determining what evidence shall be transmitted back to a U.S. court, especially in discovery of documents.

If a foreign person is a party to litigation before a U.S. court, and the U.S. court has jurisdiction over that person, the U.S. court will apply its own procedural rules to that litigation—and to the foreign party. The U.S. court therefore has the power to compel that foreign party to produce evidence which is located abroad. Further, the Hague Evidence Convention is not the exclusive, or even the primary, method of obtaining evidence from abroad, and does not preclude the use of U.S. discovery and procedural rules to obtain evidence from foreign parties which are subject to the jurisdiction of U.S. courts. *Societe Nationale Industrielle Aerospatiale v. United States*, 482 U.S. 522. U.S. courts are wise to "consider international comity" before proceeding outside the Convention. Failure to produce evidence located abroad may be excused, after good faith efforts, if local law prohibits its release.

Problems can arise in gathering evidence abroad, even under the Convention. For example, there is not even agreement as to the meaning of the terms defining the scope of the Convention, as illustrated by a report of a meeting on the Convention, reprinted in 72 Am.J.Int'l L. 633 (1978):

There exists no agreement on the scope of the Convention, i.e., on the meaning of the term "civil and commercial matters" as used in the caption and in Article 1 of the Convention. United States practice under the Convention, concurred in by the United Kingdom expert, is to consider any legal proceeding that is not criminal as "civil or commercial" (including an administrative proceeding). French practice, concurred in by the Swiss observer, excludes from "civil and commercial matters" legal proceedings that are criminal and fiscal. Japanese practice excludes all administrative matters. The German observer offered the opinion that under German practice, in addition to criminal matters, proceedings involving the enforcement of public law (as distinguished from "private law") would be excluded. Finally, Egyptian practice excludes family law from the purview of "civil and commercial matters," since disputes involving family relations belong to the religious courts of that country.

RECOGNITION AND ENFORCEMENT OF FOREIGN JUDGMENTS

Americans are used to recognition and enforcement of the judgments of one state of the United States by any other state of the United States. Sometimes they forget that this recognition and enforcement is due to the "full faith and credit" clause of the U.S. Constitution, and that the courts of most legal systems do not recognize judgments from other jurisdictions. For example, in nearly two thirds of the countries of the world, judgments of U.S. courts either are not enforceable at all or are enforceable only if certain conditions are met. As to foreign judgments brought to the United States, the "full faith and credit" clause does not apply to make them enforceable—but there is no rule prohibiting enforcement. The result is that the courts have been left to their own analyses to develop policies and rules.

The common law rule in England was that a foreign court's judgment for money was only *prima facie* evidence of the subject matter that it purported to decide—but no more than that. It was not conclusive on the merits of the dispute and did not act as either res judicata or collateral estoppel to actions in English courts by the loser in the foreign court.

The U.S. Supreme Court adopted a different approach in *Hilton v. Guyot*, 159 U.S. 113 (1895). The Court denied enforcement of a French judgment, announcing that it followed a rule of "comity," which required the opportunity for a "fair trial abroad before a court of competent jurisdiction," "regular proceedings," citation or appearance of the defendant, "a system of ... impartial administration of justice," and without "prejudice" or fraud. The Court did not fault French justice on any of the above grounds, but it found that French courts did not recognize U.S. court judgments. Thus, the French judgment was denied conclusive effect, not because "comity" was lacking, but because "mutuality and reciprocity" were lacking. *Hilton* remains the leading federal law decision on the subject.

However, *Hilton* is rarely controlling, for most attempts to enforce foreign judgments will depend upon state law, not federal law, and state courts have felt free to pursue their own policies and doctrines. For example, the New York Court of Appeals, stating that it was not bound by *Hilton*, has given conclusive effect to a French court judgment, despite the known lack of reciprocity.

A state court, in determining its own policies, has several options. It may reject the judgment of the foreign court and accord no effect to it, requiring a *de novo* trial on the merits in its own courts. Alternatively, it may accept the foreign court's judgment as its own and "enforce" it in the same manner as a domestic judgment. Or, it may "recognize" the judgment by deciding that there are issues which do not need to be relitigated, even though the court will only "enforce" domestic judgments. Where courts only "recognize" foreign judgments, the party with a foreign court judgment must use it to obtain a domestic court judgment, which may then be enforced in the jurisdiction. Direct enforcement of foreign judgments is unusual; recognition of such judgments is more common.

Finally, there are courts which grant conditional recognition to foreign judgments. The conditions may relate to reciprocity of recognition between the two judicial systems involved, or to "comity between nations." Where comity is the criterion, U.S. courts have tended to examine (1) the jurisdiction of the foreign court over both the persons and the subject matter involved, (2) the adequacy of the notice given, (3) the possibility of fraud in the decision, and (4) whether any public policy of the United States will be harmed by enforcement of the foreign judgment. Some U.S. courts seem to classify foreign legal systems as either favored or not favored, and judgments from favored systems are not investigated in detail. Common law nations' judgments appear to be more favored.

Many states have little or no caselaw on this issue, so the National Conference of Commissioners on Uniform State Laws drafted first the 1962 Uniform Foreign Money-Judgments Recognition Act, adopted by more than thirty states, and its successor 2005 Uniform Foreign-Country Money Judgments Recognition Act. Under these similar acts recognition is given only to foreign judgments which are final and enforceable where rendered. Further, only judgments for sums of money are eligible for recognition, not injunctions or specific performance decrees. The Uniform Acts do not require reciprocity for recognition of foreign judgments, but do require an examination of the criteria and issues generally associated with "comity." Several states have added non-uniform amendments to these acts requiring either reciprocity, or "negative reciprocity." The latter requires proof only that the foreign nation has not refused to enforce a state's judgment, not that it has in fact actually enforced such a judgment. The 2005 Act generally follows the 1962 Act, adding some new grounds for non-recognition, adding a burden of proof rule, imposing a 15 year statute of limitations, adding some rules of procedure, and preferring the use of "foreign country" to "foreign State."

If a foreign judgment is given in a foreign currency, how should a state court design its award? In many states, a court's judgment must be in U.S. dollars. Although this should not induce a court to refuse recognition, it does raise issues of the proper time for computing currency conversion. The Uniform Foreign Money Claims Act, enacted in more than twenty states, allows the court to issue a judgment in a foreign currency, gives three criteria for doing so, and requires any conversion to be computed on the date of payment.

Countries have tried to facilitate the enforcement of judgments by bilateral treaty (e.g., the 1980 draft United Kingdom–United States Convention on Recognition and Enforcement of Judgments). Efforts to facilitate the enforcement of foreign judgments have been also the subject of multilateral treaties, such as the 1968 [EC] Common Market Convention on Jurisdiction and the Enforcement of Judgments (replaced by the EU Regulation on Jurisdiction and the Recognition and Enforcement of Foreign Judgment in Civil and Commercial Matters) and the 1979 Inter–American [OAS] Convention on Extraterritorial Validity of Foreign Judgments and Arbitral Awards. A major effort occurred over more than a decade to conclude a international convention on jurisdiction and foreign judgments, not dissimilar to that with the European Union, the brussels regulation. But the effort failed to produce such an agreement, settling for adopting the Hague Convention on the Choice of Court Agreements that remains to be accepted by even one state.

CONTRACT PROVISIONS ABOUT DISPUTE FORUM AND GOVERNING LAW

Because of uncertainties surrounding international dispute settlement, two contract clauses to which lawyers, and increasingly nonlawyer negotiators, give close attention are the Forum Selection Clause and the Choice of Law Clause.

THE FORUM SELECTION CLAUSE

There are no universally accepted rules regarding jurisdiction of a particular court over the parties or subject matter of a dispute. Thus, when a dispute arises out of an international transaction, the parties to that dispute, if they seek litigation, are capable of bringing an action on that dispute in the courts of many different countries. Further, the substantive rules that may be used to resolve the dispute may be different in the different courts. Even the choice of law rules may be different, producing divergent results which depend only upon the court selected to hear the litigation. Attempting to obtain such a tactical advantage through court selection is international "forum shopping," and creates uncertainty in the resolution of disputes under the transaction.

The parties to an international transaction are well-advised to seek to avoid this uncertainty by resolving the issue of which forum shall have jurisdiction to hear disputes arising out of the transaction before any such disputes arise. This means that during the initial drafting of the contract the parties should decide which court shall have jurisdiction, and then specify that court in a Forum Selection Clause. That Clause should both specify the court which has jurisdiction and state that that court has exclusive jurisdiction to preclude other courts from entertaining the case.

A court which wishes to hear a case, despite a choice of forum clause which vests exclusive jurisdiction elsewhere, may construe the clause to resolve ambiguities against giving such an effect to the clause. A clause providing that "the District Court of Luanda should be considered the sole court competent to adjudicate to the exclusion of all others," has been construed to permit litigation in England on the ground that, subsequent to the clause's drafting, a revolution in the former Portuguese Angola resulted in the present District Court in Luanda not being the Court to which the contract parties had referred. Moreover, one court has disregarded a forum selection clause's effectiveness as to part of a counterclaim because of "judicial economy . . . [and] to insure that complete justice is done."

At common law, choice of forum clauses were ineffective, since they were perceived as attempts to interfere with judicial administration by depriving a competent court of jurisdiction. The attitudes of U.S. courts have changed because of the U.S. Supreme Court's decision in *M/S Bremen v. Zapata Off-Shore Co.*, 407 U.S. 1 (1972). In that case, the Court upheld a Forum Selection Clause in which the parties had chosen, not the courts of one of their own countries, but the courts of London—a neutral forum which had no other relationship to the transaction. "[I]n the light of present day commercial realities and expanding international trade we conclude that the forum clause should control absent a strong showing that it should be set aside."

Although *Bremen* involved an international transaction and a decision in admiralty, the lower federal courts have extended its "more hospitable attitude" toward Forum Selection Clauses to include non-admiralty cases and cases involving domestic transactions. These cases can arise in two different contexts. First, when the parties approach the chosen forum, there may be an issue as to whether that court will accept jurisdiction over the action. The second, and more usual, context arises when one of the parties attempts to bring the action in a court outside the chosen forum.

Although Forum Selection Clauses are presumed to be valid, they will not be enforced if they deny one party an effective remedy, cause substantial inconvenience, are the product of fraud or unconscionable conduct, or contravene U.S. public policy. Thus, where a case involved factual disputes about the performance of a casting plant built in the United States by a Pennsylvania firm, the court refused to enforce the contract's selection of West Germany as the forum. The court characterized the clause as unreasonable and the German courts as substantially inconvenient, since the witnesses— the people involved in both the construction and the operation of the plant, as well as its customers— were all in the United States. Further, all these witnesses spoke English, which would require translation "with its inherent inaccuracy."

Many of these grounds for resisting application of a Forum Selection Clause are analyzed by the courts under the rubric of "reasonableness."

"Mere inconveniences or additional expense is not the test of unreasonableness". Moreover, where contract parties have agreed upon a Forum Selection Clause, a court in that forum may be disinclined later to consider a *forum non conveniens* motion; "In short, by their own exercise of discretion in agreeing upon a forum, the parties themselves [have] obviated considerations of inconvenience."

Forum non conveniens is a doctrine which allows a court to refuse to accept permissible jurisdiction over a case, so that the case may be tried in an alternative forum. Such decisions are almost entirely at the court's discretion, except that the party seeking a *forum non conveniens* decision usually must submit to the effective jurisdiction of the alternative forum. The factors that courts generally consider in making such decisions include the law applicable to the dispute, the location of witnesses, exhibits and documents, the language of the witnesses and documents, and the citizenship of the claimants.

It had been thought that courts would refuse to enforce Forum Selection Clauses which are found in contracts of adhesion, or in the fine print boiler plate printed clauses in a contract involving parties of unequal bargaining power, especially if counsel has not been consulted. However, in *Carnival Cruise Lines, Inc. v. Shute,* 499 U.S. 585 (1991), the U.S. Supreme Court upheld a Forum Selection Clause which was not bargained for and was contained in the middle of 25 paragraphs of boiler plate on a ticket form which was received after the conclusion of the transaction. The Court found the clause "reasonable" because it saved "judicial resources" and might lead to lower ticket prices, but the court noted that a domestic, not an alien, forum had been selected.

It may, however, still be true that a Forum Selection Clause written in a language the party is known not to understand may not be enforced. But an allegation of fraud in the transaction will not necessarily void a Forum Selection Clause, unless the inclusion of the clause was a product of fraud.

In addition, there may be a doctrine of nonenforcement of Forum Selection Clauses due to "changed circumstances", developing out of cases involving Iran–U.S. transactions. At least, U.S. courts have refused to enforce clauses selecting a forum in Iran for a variety of reasons, such as, no adequate remedy or "difficult and inconvenient."

There are many pronouncements that the public policy of the United States may be violated where the selection of a foreign forum contravenes "mandatory law" of the United States. However, the caselaw does not substantiate these pronouncements. The public policy of the state of Hawaii that cases concerning the insurance of risks located in Hawaii be tried there was not sufficient to invalidate a clause selecting a foreign forum. A forum selection clause was upheld in a potential securities fraud case even where it was assumed that the chosen forum would not apply U.S. securities law.

The Carriage of Goods by Sea Act (COGSA), has long been considered the archetype of "mandatory law." The federal circuit courts have held that forum selection clauses selecting a foreign forum for litigation of disputes under COGSA were valid, because of the Supreme Court rulings in *Carnival Cruise Lines* (above), and *Vimar Seguros y Reaseguros, S.A. v. M/V Sky Reefer*, 515 U.S. 528 (1995). (See discussion under "Mandatory Rules and Law" below.) Although *M/V Sky Reefer* involved an arbitration clause, the court stated that such clauses were merely a subset of foreign Forum Selection Clauses.

In the European Union, the 2000 Regulation on Jurisdiction of Courts and the Recognition and Enforcement of Judgments in Civil and Commercial Matters (Brussels Regulation) provides in Article 23 that parties to a contract which is either a written agreement or an oral agreement evidenced in writing may confer exclusive jurisdiction upon a court. There does not need to be any objective connection between the legal relationship and the court designated. In varying degrees, Forum Selection Clauses in contracts have been treated as presumptively valid in Austria, England, France, Germany, Italy, Latin America and the Scandinavian countries. In some countries (e.g., Luxembourg) the clause must be signed specifically by the parties; the signing of the contract as a whole does not suffice.

THE CHOICE OF LAW CLAUSE

Because the validity of a contractual Forum Selection Clause may turn on its validity under the law which governs the contract, the validity of the Choice of Law Clause assumes an added importance. Broadly put, in common law and in European civil law jurisdictions, parties may choose the law which they wish to govern their contract relationship, as long as the law chosen is that of a place which has a substantial relationship to the parties and to the international business transaction, and is not contrary to a strong public policy of the place where suit is brought.

Where the validity of the Choice of Law Clauses is determined by statute, there seem to be two different approaches. The Uniform Commercial Code (§ 1–105) permits the parties to choose the law governing the contract, as long as the transaction bears "a reasonable relation" to the jurisdiction providing the governing law. Thus, "party autonomy" is permissible, but only within "reasonable" limits. That is not helpful to the merchants in a U.S.-German transaction who wish to use neither U.S. nor German law, but wish to use the law of some "neutral" country, such as England.

The Uniform Commissioners have adopted a Revised Article 1, which would allow the selection of the law of any nation in an international transaction. However, the only states to enact Revised UCC Article 1 to date have deleted that provision from the revision, and have retained the language from original UCC § 1–105. This is probably a continuing trend.

In the EU, the 1980 Convention on the Law Applicable to Contractual Obligations (Article 3) also allows unlimited party autonomy. In sum, the legislative trend may favor fewer limits on party autonomy, and none in international transactions.

However, courts can still refuse to enforce a Choice of Law Clause if it is found to violate public policy, "a vague and variable phenomenon." In countries taking their legal heritage from Roman Law, laws expressing strong public policy may be called *jus cogens*—fundamental or "mandatory" rules of law, the operation of which parties may not contract away. These mandatory rules which are used to limit party autonomy may be either statutory or judicially-created, and will vary from country to country. Thus, they can create legal problems as to whether the parties may submit different aspects of a contract to different laws (*depecage*), or whether the courts of one country should recognize and apply the mandatory rules of a different country, regardless of the contract's Choice of Law or Forum Selection Clauses.

A forum court's notions of strong public policy may be expressed by a court conceding the *prima facie* applicability of a Choice of Law Clause but deciding that the clause, as drafted, does not preclude application of the forum's law to the circumstances of the parties' dispute. A holding in favor

of application of the forum court's public policy
(rule of law) may be accomplished also by holding
that the dispute does not fall within the meaning of
a Choice of Law Clause which has a clear meaning;
or that the parties have drafted a Choice of Law
Clause which requires considerable interpretation
for its meaning to be clearly understood.

INTERNATIONAL COMMERCIAL ARBITRATION

Uncertainty about identity of the country and the
court in which a dispute may be heard, about procedural and substantive rules to be applied, about the
degree of publicity to be given the proceedings and
the judgment, about the time needed to settle a
dispute, and about the efficacy which may be given
to a resulting court judgment all have combined to
make arbitration the preferred mechanism for solv-
ing international commercial disputes.

Some Western European countries long have
been accustomed to arbitration. For example, the
London Court of Arbitration, a private arbitration
institution, has existed since 1892. The United
States has had a Federal Arbitration Act since
1947. Arbitration in international commercial contracts is favored by the Peoples Republic of China,
if mediation and conciliation fails, either through
the Chinese Foreign Economic and Trade Arbitration Commission (FETAC) or the Chinese Maritime
Arbitration Commission (MAC). Most of the nations of the former Soviet Union also favor arbitra-

tion, and have organizations similar to the Chinese FETAC and MAC. The Japan Commercial Arbitration Association has been active since 1953. Virtually all countries in Africa have arbitration statutes.

Latin America, historically disadvantaged in many arbitral awards, increasingly is accepting arbitration. For example, the 1975 Inter-American Convention on International Commercial Arbitration undertaken through the Organization of American States affirms the validity of agreements in which parties agree to submit to arbitral decision any differences with respect to commercial transactions. The 1979 Inter-American Convention on Extraterritorial Validity of Foreign Judgments and Arbitral Awards expands upon the scope of the 1975 Convention. Many of the Latin American nations are members of the U.N. Convention on the Recognition and Enforcement of Foreign Arbitral Awards (The New York Convention).

An increasingly adopted "Forum Selection Clause" is one that chooses no court at all, but selects an alternate dispute resolution mechanism, such as an arbitration tribunal. For a long period of time, the courts resisted validating such clauses, holding that they deprived the parties of due process of law (a reaction one might expect toward a competitor). However, legislatures were far more sympathetic to arbitration, and around the turn of the century began to enact statutes validating arbitration clauses. The issue now is firmly settled. Under the principle of "party autonomy," international contracts containing arbitration clauses will almost always be honored. In addition to arbitration, there are many other even less formal alternative dispute resolution mechanisms in use, such as the "mini-trial" or the use of "conciliation." The mini-trial, for example, comes in a variety of packages, each with a different impact on resolution of the dispute. It can be nonbinding if used with a "neutral advisor"; it can be semi-binding if its results are admissible in later proceedings; or it can be binding before a court appointed master.

Arbitration provisions also appear in Treaties of Friendship, Commerce and Navigation and Bilateral Investment Treaties. The purpose of such treaty provisions is to ensure the enforcement of arbitration clauses in commercial contracts between nationals of the Contracting States to the treaty. The treaty provisions will also require the courts of each Contracting State to enforce the awards of arbitral tribunals rendered under such arbitration clauses. Thus, the treaty provision may require the courts of each Contracting State to enforce such arbitration clauses and subsequent arbitration awards, even though the place of arbitration is not located within the Contracting States and the arbitrators are not nationals of the Contracting States.

WHY ARBITRATE?

The growth of international commercial arbitration (ICA) is in part a retreat from the vicissitudes and uncertainties of international business litigation. More positively, ICA offers predictability and neutrality as a forum (who knows which court you may end up in) and the potential for specialized expertise (most judges know little about international law). ICA also allows the parties to select and shape the procedures and costs of dispute resolution. That said, ICA procedures are relatively informal and not laden with legal rights. To quote Judge Learned Hand:

> Arbitration may or may not be a desirable substitute for trials in courts; as to that the parties must decide in each instance. But when they have adopted it, they must be content with its informalities; they may not hedge it about with those procedural limitations which it is precisely its purpose to avoid. They must content themselves with looser approximations to the enforcement of their rights than those that the law accords them, when they resort to its machinery. *American Almond Products Co. v. Consolidated Pecan Sales Co., Inc.*, 144 F.2d 448 (2d Cir. 1944).

One of the most attractive attributes of ICA is the enforceability in national courts of arbitral awards under the New York Convention. Approximately 140 nations participate in the New York Convention. There is no comparable convention for the enforcement of court judgments around the world, the recent attempts to conclude a Hague Convention on Jurisdiction and Enforcement of Judgments having failed. The Panama Convention renders arbitral awards enforceable in Latin America.

Another major advantage of ICA is the support of legal regimes that give arbitration agreements dispositive effects. In the United States, for example, the Federal Arbitration Act provides a level of legal security unknown to international business litigation. Many countries have similar statutes, thus avoiding issues of subject matter and personal jurisdiction, *forum non conveniens* and the like. Excepting New York, there are no statutory frameworks supporting court selection clauses at the state or federal level. In worst case scenarios, parties selecting a court to resolve their disputes may end up with a court that refuses to hear the case.

One of the least attractive attributes of ICA is the minimal availability of pre-trial provisional remedies. In addition, many arbitrators focus on splitting the differences between the parties, not the vindication of legal rights which in courts might result in "winner takes all." But such extreme results could permanently disrupt otherwise long-standing and mutually beneficial business relationships. Perhaps, therefore, "splitting the baby" through arbitration really is the optimal outcome.

TYPES OF INTERNATIONAL COMMERCIAL ARBITRATIONS

There are two basic types of international commercial arbitration: ad hoc and institutional. Ad hoc arbitrations involve selection by the parties of the arbitrators and rules governing the arbitration. The classic formula involves each side choosing one arbitrator who in turn choose a third arbitrator. The ad hoc arbitration panel selects its procedural rules (such as the UNCITRAL Arbitration Rules). Ad hoc arbitration can be agreed upon in advance or, quite literally, selected ad hoc as disputes arise.

Institutional arbitration involves selection of a specific arbitration center or "court," often accompanied by its own rules of arbitration. Institutional arbitration is in a sense pre-packaged, and the parties need only "plug in" to the arbitration system of their choice. There are numerous competing centers of arbitration, each busy marketing its desirability to the world business community. Some centers are longstanding and busy, such as the International Chamber of Commerce "Court of Arbitration" in Paris which has its own Rules of Arbitration. Other centers are more recent in time and still struggling for clientele, such as the Commercial Arbitration and Mediation Center for the Americas (CAMCA).

Ad hoc arbitration presupposes a certain amount of goodwill and flexibility between the parties. It can be speedy and less costly than institutional arbitration. The latter, on the other hand, offers ease of incorporation in an international business agreement, supervisory services, a stable of experienced arbitrators and a fixed fee schedule. The institutional environment is professional, a quality that sometimes can get lost in ad hoc arbitrations. Awards from well established arbitration centers (including default awards) are more likely to be favorably recognized in the courts if enforcement is needed. Many institutional arbitration centers now also offer "fast track" or "mini" services to the international business community.

MODEL ARBITRATION CLAUSES

Parties who wish to refer any dispute to the London Court of Arbitration may use the following model clause:

The validity, construction and performance of this contract (agreement) shall be governed by the laws of England and any dispute that may arise out of or in connection with this contract (agreement), including its validity, construction and performance, shall be determined by arbitration under the Rules of the London Court of Arbitration at the date hereof, which Rules with respect to matters not regulated by them, incorporate the UNCITRAL Arbitration Rules. The parties agree that service of any notices in reference to such arbitration at their addresses as given in this contract (agreement)(or as subsequently varied in writing by them) shall be valid and sufficient.

The Court of Arbitration of the ICC in Paris recommends use of the following model clause to engage its rules:

All disputes arising in connection with the present contract shall be finally settled under the Rules of Conciliation and Arbitration of the International Chamber of Commerce by one or more arbitrators appointed in accordance with the said Rules.

The variations in length and in specificity between the London model clause and the Paris model clause reflect typical differences in successful contract drafting in the Common Law and Civil Law traditions. Many parties use the Rules of the Court of Arbitration of the International Chamber of Commerce at Paris or of one of its national committees, such as the international commercial panel of the American Arbitration Association. The ICC rules are modern and often used in international arbitration. More than 12,000 arbitrations have been administered by the ICC.

INTERNATIONAL ARBITRAL RULES: UNCITRAL AND ICSID

Model International Commercial Arbitration Rules were issued in 1976 by the United Nations Commission on International Trade Law (UNCITRAL) following ten years of study. The UNCITRAL Rules are intended to be acceptable in all legal systems and in all parts of the world. Rapidly developing countries favor the Rules because of the care with which they have been drafted, and because UNCITRAL was one forum for developing arbitration rules in which their concerns would be heard. The Arbitral Institute of the Stockholm Chamber of Commerce has been willing to work with the UNCITRAL Rules, as has the London Court of Arbitration. The Iran-United States

Claims Tribunal has used the UNCITRAL Rules in dealing with claims arising out of the confrontation between the two countries in 1980. Such trade agreements as the NAFTA provide for the use of UNCITRAL (or ICSID) rules in investment disputes. The UNCITRAL Rules are not identified with any national or international arbitration organization, a factor supporting their use as "neutral" ICA rules.

Among other things, UNCITRAL rules provide that an "appointing authority" shall be chosen by the parties or, if they fail to agree upon that point, shall be chosen by the Secretary-General of the Permanent Court of Arbitration at the Hague (comprised of a body of persons prepared to act as arbitrators if requested). The UNCITRAL rules also cover notice requirements, representation of the parties, challenges of arbitrators, evidence, hearings, the place of arbitration, language, statements of claims and defenses, pleas to the arbitrator's jurisdiction, provisional remedies, experts, default, rule waivers, the form and effect of the award, applicable law, settlement, interpretation of the award and costs.

In addition to its 1976 Model Arbitration Rules, UNCITRAL has also promulgated a 1985 Model Law on International Commercial Arbitration (amended in 2006), a 1996 Notes on Organizing Arbitral Proceedings, and a 2002 Model Law on International Commercial Conciliation. The 1985 Model Law has been enacted in some fifty countries (and the 2006 amendment in a half-dozen). It has also been enacted as state law by California, Connecticut, Georgia, Oregon, Texas and other states. In Model Law jurisdictions, an arbitral award may be set aside by local courts on grounds that virtually track those specified as permissible for denials of recognition and enforcement of awards under the 1958 New York Convention (below). Under the UNCITRAL Model Law, submission to arbitration may be *ad hoc* for a particular dispute, but is accomplished most often in advance of the dispute by a general submission clause within a contract. Under Article 8 of the Model Law, an agreement to arbitrate is specifically enforceable. Although no specific language will guarantee the success of an arbitral submission, UNCITRAL recommends the following model submission clause:

> Any dispute, controversy or claim arising out of or relating to this contract, or the breach, termination or invalidity thereof, shall be settled by arbitration in accordance with the UNCITRAL Arbitration Rules as at present in force.

Over 100 countries have signed the 1966 Convention on the Settlement of Investment Disputes Between States and Nationals of Other States. The Convention is implemented in the United States. An arbitral money award, rendered pursuant to the Convention, is entitled to the same full faith and credit in the United States as is a final judgment of a court of general jurisdiction in a State of the United States. The Convention provided for the establishment of an International Center for the Settlement of Investment Disputes (ICSID), as a non-financial organ of the World Bank. ICSID is designed to serve as a forum for conciliation and for arbitration of disputes between private investors and host governments. It provides an institutional framework within which arbitrators, selected by the disputing parties from an ICSID Panel of Arbitrators or from elsewhere, conduct an arbitration in accordance with ICSID Rules of Procedure for Arbitration Proceedings. Arbitrations are held in Washington D.C. unless agreed otherwise.

Under the Convention, ICSID's jurisdiction extends only to legal disputes arising directly out of an investment, between a Contracting State or ... any subdivision ... and a national of another Contracting State, which the parties to the dispute consent in writing to submit to the Center. No party may withdraw its consent unilaterally. Thus, ICSID is an attempt to institutionalize dispute resolution between States and non-State investors. It therefore always presents a "mixed" arbitration. If one party questions such jurisdiction the issue of "arbitrability" may be decided by the arbitration tribunal. A party may seek annulment of any arbitral award by an appeal to an ad hoc committee of persons drawn by the Administrative Council of ICSID from the Panel of Arbitrators under the Convention. Annulment is available only if the Tribunal was not properly constituted, exceeded its powers, seriously departed from a fundamental procedural rule, failed to state the reasons for its award, or included a member who practiced corruption. ICSID awards may not be reviewed in national courts.

The Convention's jurisdictional limitations prompted the ICSID Administrative Counsel to establish an Additional Facility for conducting conciliations and arbitrations for disputes which do not arise directly out of an investment and for investment disputes in which one party is not a Contracting State to the Convention or the national of a Contracting State. The Additional Facility is intended for use by parties having long-term relationships of special economic importance to the State party to the dispute and which involve the commitment of substantial resources on the part of either party. The Facility is not designed to service disputes which fall within the Convention or which are "ordinary commercial transaction" disputes. ICSID's Secretary General must give advance approval of an agreement contemplating use of the Additional Facility. Because the Additional Facility operates outside the scope of the Convention, the Facility has its own Arbitration Rules and its awards can be reviewed by national courts. Numerous NAFTA investor-state arbitrations have operated under the Additional Facility.

ENFORCEMENT OF ARBITRAL AWARDS: THE NEW YORK CONVENTION

In over 140 countries, the enforcement of arbitral awards is facilitated by the 1958 United Nations Convention on the Recognition and Enforcement of

Foreign Arbitral Awards (the "New York Convention") implemented in the United States in conjunction with the Federal Arbitration Act. As the U.S. Supreme Court observed in *Scherk v. Alberto-Culver Co.*, 417 U.S. 506 (1974): "[T]he principal purpose underlying American ... implementation ... was to encourage the recognition and enforcement of commercial arbitration agreements in international contracts and to unify the standards by which agreements to arbitrate are observed and arbitral awards are enforced in the signatory countries." In an abbreviated procedure, federal district courts entertain motions to confirm or to challenge a foreign arbitral award.

The New York Convention commits the courts in each Contracting State to recognize and enforce arbitration clauses and separate arbitration agreements for the resolution of international commercial disputes. Where the court finds an arbitral clause or agreement, it "*shall* ... refer the parties to arbitration, unless it finds that the said agreement is null and void, inoperative, or incapable of being performed" (emphasis added). The Convention also commits the courts in each Contracting State to recognize and enforce the awards of arbitral tribunals under such clauses or agreements, and also sets forth the limited grounds under which recognition and enforcement may be refused. Grounds for refusal to enforce include: (1) incapacity or invalidity of the agreement containing the arbitration clause "under the law applicable to" a party to the agreement, (2) lack of proper notice of the arbitration proceedings or the appointment of the arbitrator, (3) failure of the arbitral award to restrict itself to the terms of the submission to arbitration, or decision of matters not within the scope of that subdivision, (4) composition of the arbitral tribunal not according to the arbitration agreement or applicable law, and (5) non-finality of the arbitral award under applicable law.

In addition to these grounds for refusal, recognition or enforcement may also be refused if it would be contrary to the public policy of the country in which enforcement is sought; or if the subject matter of the dispute cannot be settled by arbitration under the law of that country. Courts in the United States have taken the position that the public policy limitation on the Convention is to be construed narrowly and to be applied only where enforcement would violate the forum state's most basic notions of morality and justice. Recourse to other limitations of the Convention, in order to defeat its applicability, has been greeted with judicial caution.

Whether the New York Convention applies generally turns upon where the award was or will be made, not the citizenship of the parties. A growing number of courts in developing nations are issuing injunctions against arbitral proceedings before they commence. Many of these injunctions seem deliberately intended to protect local companies. Parties who proceed to arbitrate after such an injunction has been issued do so at their peril. Subsequent enforcement of the award under the New York

Convention in the enjoining nation will almost certainly be voided on grounds of public policy. Hence enforcement can only proceed in non-enjoining jurisdictions, assuming that their public policy permits this.

MANDATORY RULES AND LAW

Majors centers for international arbitration include, among others, Geneva, London, Hong Kong, Singapore, New York, Paris, and Stockholm. Arbitration associations at such places have adopted fairly settled procedural rules for conducting arbitrations. In almost all countries, domestic law provides limitations upon the power of persons to specify for themselves what rules should govern their contractual relationship (including aspects of dispute settlement). As between two contracting parties, many provisions of local law may be excluded (called "jus dispositivum"), but the applicability of certain legal rules may not be excluded (called "jus cogens"). Jus cogens is mandatory; it is public law that private parties cannot avoid by contract.

The "jus cogens"/"jus dispositivum" dichotomy is found in the law of many European countries. It is also found in the Uniform Commercial Code and linked to the "mandatory law" rationales of U.S. cases (below). Any arbitration rules chosen by parties to govern their dispute may not be honored if such rules contravene a "non-excludable" mandatory provision of the local law. For example, notwithstanding that parties may desire otherwise, it has been a "non-excludable" rule that when there are several arbitrators, one of them shall be chairman of the tribunal.

Many lower U.S. federal courts had held that "mandatory laws" could not be the subject matter of arbitration, because of both the public interest indicated by the legislative intent underlying the enactment of mandatory law and the public policy favoring judicial enforcement of such law. However, the Supreme Court has now rejected that doctrine. In *Scherk v. Alberto-Culver Co.*, 417 U.S. 506 (1974) the Court held that Securities and Exchange Commission law issues arising out of an international contract are subject to arbitration under the Federal Arbitration Act despite the public interest in protecting the United States investment climate. In *Mitsubishi Motors Corp. v. Soler Chrysler-Plymouth, Inc.*, 473 U.S. 614 (1985), the Court held that antitrust claims arising out of an international transaction were arbitrable, despite the public interest in a competitive national economy, and the legislative pronouncements favoring enforcement by private parties. In *Vimar Seguros y Reaseguros, S.A. v. M/V Sky Reefer*, 515 U.S. 528 (1995) claims that the foreign arbitrators would not apply the U.S. mandatory Carriage of Goods by Sea Act Act (COGSA) were similarly rejected.

In both *Mitsubishi Motors* and *M/V Sky Reefer*, the Court determined that issues arising out of international transactions involving U.S. mandatory law were arbitrable. However, in *dictum* at the end of the *Mitsubishi* opinion, the Court stated that

U.S. courts would have a second chance at the enforcement stage to examine whether the arbitral tribunal "took cognizance of the antitrust claims and actually decided them." Similar language can be found in *M/V Sky Reefer* regarding COGSA claims. It would seem to be difficult to fit any such examination by the U.S. courts properly into the structure of the New York Convention. It is not clear whether *Mitsubishi* invites the U.S. courts merely to examine whether the arbitrators state that they considered the antitrust issues, or also invites them to examine whether the arbitrators considered these issues *correctly* (review on the merits). The former can be evaded by a mechanical phrase; the latter can harm the arbitral process, especially if the parties have chosen non-U.S. law to govern their agreement.

In either case, arbitrators' enforcement of U.S. antitrust laws may not be to the standards of U.S. courts, and the status of recognition and enforcement of arbitral awards involving antitrust issues is not yet clear. Under the New York Convention, a mere "misunderstanding," or error in interpretation, of a mandatory law by an arbitral tribunal has generally not been held to "contravene public policy." The cases are split as to whether even a "manifest disregard" of U.S. law constitutes such a violation of public policy. Awards have been upheld which violate the U.S. Vessel Owner's Limitation of Liability Act, previously considered mandatory law. Thus, it is not certain, under the New York Convention, that U.S. courts retain the review powers assumed by the *Mitsubishi* and *M/V Sky Reefer* Courts to be available at the "award-enforcement stage" of the proceedings.

ARBITRATION AGREEMENTS, ARBITRATORS AND AWARDS UNDER U.S. LAW

Arbitration agreements, traditionally called *compromis*, come in a variety of forms. Many arbitration centers sponsor model clauses that can be incorporated into business agreements. The New York Convention obliges courts of participating nations to refer upon request disputes to arbitration unless the agreement is "null and void, inoperative or incapable of being performed." The existence and validity of an arbitration agreement must be proved, and can be litigated before the arbitration takes place.

Article II(2) of the New York Convention requires states to recognize written arbitration agreements *signed* by the parties "or contained in an exchange of letters or telegrams." In most jurisdictions exchanges of fax, e-mail and the like embracing arbitration will also be recognized. However, arbitration clauses in unsigned purchase orders do not amount to a written agreement to arbitrate. Pre-arbitration litigation often revolves around motions to compel arbitration. If no such motion is made, and a court judgment is rendered (even by default), the right to arbitrate may be waived.

Whether a valid agreement to arbitrate exists depends on the specifics of the arbitration clause, not the entire business agreement. The arbitration clause is severable, and issues of validity (such as fraud in the inducement of the arbitration clause and unconscionability) directed to it. Many courts will stretch the limits of the New York Convention in order to uphold an arbitration clause When there is a battle of forms, the same judicial bias towards arbitration is often found. But, in most cases, the disputes must "arise under" the business transaction to be arbitrable and legal claims falling outside the transaction remain in court. The Supreme Court has held that a claim that a contract containing an arbitration provision is void for illegality should be decided by an arbitrator rather than a court (*Buckeye Check Cashing, Inc. v. Cardegna*, 546 U.S. 440 (2006)).

The closure or misdescription of an arbitration center designated in the agreement (e.g., the New York Chamber of Commerce) is no barrier to arbitration. A substitute arbitrator will be appointed by the court if the parties cannot agree. The U.S. Supreme Court held in *Commonwealth Coatings*, 393 U.S. 145 (1968) that arbitrators are subject to "requirements of impartiality" and must "disclose to the parties any dealings that might create an impression of possible bias." That said, most U.S. courts are loathe to intrude in proceedings or vacate an arbitration award on disclosure grounds.

There is a split of opinion as to whether the implied ground of "manifest disregard of the law" bars enforcement of an arbitral award in U.S. courts under the New York Convention. Article V of the New York Convention does not recognize manifest disregard of the law as a basis for denial of enforcement. Another issue concerning the New York Convention is whether to adjourn U.S. enforcement proceedings if parallel proceedings to vacate the award have been commenced in the country of arbitration. Despite the risks of forum shopping and delay, adjournment can be appropriate, depending upon the circumstances. Obtaining compulsory non-party discovery in private commercial arbitrations has been denied.

Cases in the United States have pointed out that parties cannot refer a dispute to a court while an arbitration is in progress or block enforcement of an award in the United States in reliance upon the fact that the award, although binding in the country where rendered, is under appeal there. Interim orders of arbitrators, such as records disclosures, may be enforceable "awards" under the New York Convention. After the arbitration is concluded, a party may not be able to block enforcement of the award in reliance upon the U.S. Foreign Sovereign Immunities Act, but a court may decline to enforce in reliance upon the Act of State Doctrine. One court granted enforcement, under the Convention, of a New York award rendered in favor of a noncitizen claimant against a non-citizen defendant.

When arbitral awards are annulled at their situs, courts in enforcing jurisdictions have taken different positions on the enforceability of the award.

French courts enforced an improperly vacated award to the detriment of the claimant who had prevailed in a second arbitration. One U.S. court refused to honor the clearly legitimate annulment of an arbitral award by an Egyptian court because the parties had agreed not to appeal the award. The Second Circuit, on the other hand, recognized the annulment of two arbitral awards vacated by a Nigerian court and refused enforcement. The New York Convention does not address the treatment of annulled arbitral awards.

The U.S. Supreme Court indicated in *First Options of Chicago, Inc. v. Kaplan*, 514 U.S. 938 (1995) that questions of the arbitrability of disputes may be arbitrated, but only if the parties have manifested a *clear* willingness to be bound by arbitration on such issues. Silence or ambiguity should favor judicial review of arbitrability issues. Arbitration clauses that adopt the UNITRAL Rules meet the requirement of clarity to arbitrate arbitrability because Article 21 conveys jurisdictional issues to the tribunal.

INDEX

References are to Pages

-A-

-B-

-C-

343

-D-

-I-

-L-

-T-

-U-

†